Democracy, Lifelong Learning and the Learning Society

This is a book with a difference: it produces a completely new perspective on lifelong learning and the learning society and locates them within humanity itself. Five themes run through this book:

- Humankind has always been aware of the imperfections of human society: as a consequence, it has looked back to a mythological past and forward to a utopian future that might be religious, political, economic or even educational to find something better.
- Lifelong learning as we currently see it is like two sides of the same coin – we both learn in order to be workers so that we can produce and then we learn that we have needs to consume so that we devour the commodities that we have produced – while others take the profits!
- One of the greatest paradoxes of the human condition has been the place of the individual in the group/community, or conversely how the groups allow the individual to exist rather than stifle individuality.
- Modernity is flawed and the type of society that we currently have, which we in the West call a learning society, is in need of an ethical overhaul in this late modern age.
- There is a need to bring a different perspective – both political and ethical – on lifelong learning and the learning society in order to try to understand what the good society and the good life might become.

In *Democracy, Lifelong Learning and the Learning Society*, the third volume of his trilogy on lifelong learning, Professor Jarvis expertly addresses the issues that arise from the vision of the learning society. The book concludes that since human beings continue to learn, so the learning society must be a process within the incomplete project of humanity.

All three books in the trilogy will be essential reading for students in education, HRD and teaching and learning generally, in addition to academics and informed practitioners.

The *Lifelong Learning and the Learning Society* Trilogy

> Volume 1: *Towards a Comprehensive Theory of Human Learning*
> Volume 2: *Globalisation, Lifelong Learning and the Learning Society*
> Volume 3: *Democracy, Lifelong Learning and the Learning Society*

Peter Jarvis is an internationally renowned expert in the fields of lifelong learning, adult and continuing education and is founding editor of *The International Journal of Lifelong Education* – published by Taylor & Francis. He is Professor of Continuing Education at the University of Surrey, UK, honorary Visiting Professor at City University and Professor (honoris causa) at the University of Pecs in Hungary.

Democracy, Lifelong Learning and the Learning Society

Active citizenship in a late modern age

Lifelong Learning and the Learning Society, Volume 3

Peter Jarvis

Routledge
Taylor & Francis Group

LONDON AND NEW YORK

First published 2008
by Routledge
2 Park Square, Milton Park, Abingdon, Oxon OX14 4RN

Simultaneously published in the USA and Canada
by Routledge
270 Madison Ave, New York, NY 10016

Routledge is an imprint of the Taylor & Francis Group, an informa business

© 2008 Peter Jarvis

Typeset in Goudy by Wearset Ltd, Boldon, Tyne and Wear
Printed and bound in Great Britain by CPI Antony Rowe, Chippenham, Wiltshire

British Library Cataloguing in Publication Data
A catalogue record for this book is available from the British
Library

Library of Congress Cataloging in Publication Data
A catalog record for this book has been requested

ISBN10: 0-415-35544-3 (hbk)
ISBN10: 0-415-35545-2 (pbk)
ISBN10: 0-203-00170-2 (ebk)

ISBN13: 978-0-415-35544-5 (hbk)
ISBN13: 978-0-415-35545-2 (pbk)
ISBN13: 978-0-203-00170-7 (ebk)

Contents

Figures and tables

Figures

Introduction

At the end of the first volume of this trilogy, *Towards a Comprehensive Theory of Human Learning*, I concluded that although we can discover a reasonably comprehensive theory of human learning, we cannot construct a complete picture: if we could we would actually understand the human being totally, and this we cannot. This book is about individual, personal, human learning: as such it is both psychological and philosophical. At the same time, we suggested that since human beings continue to learn, the human project is an unfinished one. It could be argued that we are continuing to evolve. We will briefly review that book at the start of the first chapter of this book, developing the social arguments of the second volume, is an interplay between the individual and the social.

In the second volume, which is fundamentally sociological although it highlights the significance of economics, *Globalisation, Lifelong Learning and the Learning Society: Sociological Perspectives*, I produced a new model of globalisation and located the information society, the knowledge society and the learning society within it. I showed that the driving forces for social change come from a global sub-structure comprising the economic and information technology institutions and supported by the political and military might of the USA. This latter support, I suggested, can be located in the global sub-structure at this specific time in human history, although in the not too far distant future other nations might become so powerful that the USA might become but one of a number of very powerful nations, not all sharing the same politic-economic ideology. However, I began to point out that the study of the learning society could not omit the recognition that power and power-holders are major players in this form of society, as they are in all societies, and in that volume the explicit values of this global society are at least questionable. I also included an Appendix, *Infinite Dreams*, in that second volume which was a utopian vision of what the learning society might be like and it is this vision that is a guiding force in this study.

This third volume begins to address some of these issues but must conclude that, like human learning, the human project is unfinished, so any visions of future society are no more than mirages that retreat as we approach them.

However, a major function of utopian thought is that it shows us the imperfections in the present and gives us a goal for the future – however misty that future might appear. Consequently, *Democracy, Lifelong Learning and the Learning Society* is both ethical and political, although it might be argued that utopian thought does tend towards the religious and that would not be denied here, although the religious is grounded in a very secular analysis of society. While the starting place of this book lies in the previous two volumes, the book has its origins in two books that I wrote a number of years ago: *Adult Education and the State* and *Ethics and the Education of Adults in Late Modern Society*. This volume certainly could not have been written without these earlier works. Its opening chapter outlines the arguments of the previous two books of this trilogy and thereafter, we will begin to explore a theory of value that can be utilised as we look at various factors of learning and the learning society that were discussed in the previous volumes.

If I may repeat just a little of what I wrote in the Preface to the second volume I want to point out that I have been working on this subject for two decades now and have published many books and papers about it, although less about the focus of this volume than the previous two. In a sense, this book gathers together much of my understanding from my previous writings, but I would not claim that they are my final thoughts. Over that period and around the world, I have given many lectures and classes on these topics and those who have listened to the lectures and others have been unstinting in giving me feedback. In addition, many colleagues who have heard my lectures and read my papers have also been generous in their criticism of my work. Naturally, they have all enriched my thinking and I am enormously grateful to them. Many other colleagues have helped me but I want to mention one in particular, Dr Pauline Jeffree, who has encouraged me to work, both by her friendship and her example. I am also immensely grateful to Philip Mudd of Routledge who encouraged me to write the trilogy and trusted me to complete it. I hope that as this third volume appears I have repaid that trust. Having said this, I must take sole responsibility for this work.

However, the person who has been most supportive of my work has been my wife, Maureen, who puts up with two rather disordered studies at home, books everywhere and a writing regime that is unsystematic.

Peter Jarvis
Thatcham

Chapter I

Lifelong learning and the learning society

This trilogy endeavours to analyse a wide variety of aspects of lifelong learning and the learning society. In the first volume we showed how learning underlies our humanity: humans learn because we are consciously alive and that our learning is not only cognitive but all that makes us human beings which is added to our bare animal existence is learned. In this sense, learning must be life long. In the second volume, we explored elements of the learning society and noted how the current social conditions of globalisation have given rise to the knowledge economy, which might be regarded as a learning society. We also questioned the moral basis of this society. While the first volume primarily utilised ideas from both psychology and philosophy, the second was sociological but since it is about a society, it could also have been political. If the society that we call a learning society is not a just society, then it is incumbent upon us to explore how it can become one, even if it is not a utopian one. Justice is a legal concept that can also be judged by its morality and, consequently, it is important that we examine human learning and the learning society from both a political and moral perspective. This takes us into different realms of thought and we will touch on ideas in our investigation about which vast amounts of literature has been written but this volume will not be able to explore all of it, even if I had the ability. But we should not talk about a just learning society without exploring these concepts, even without asking even more fundamental questions about learning and the learning society.

Among the aims of this volume, therefore, is one which begins to open up some of the political questions that underlay the learning society; another is to critically examine the processes that occur against ethical criteria; a third aim is to examine the interplay of politics, economics and ethics in the learning society; finally, it aims to look to ask what type of society is possible as a result of learning. Since a great deal of the argument has already been constructed in the previous two volumes, it is necessary to understand the argument thus far. Consequently this opening chapter briefly revisits the previous two volumes and, in the process, develops the ideas just a little further. The first part of the chapter returns to the first volume and briefly re-examines the theory of lifelong learning that was discussed in it and in so doing a few additions are introduced to the argument, although the fundamental position remains unchanged. Likewise, the second part returns to the sociological arguments of the second volume in which it was argued that the learning society has been generated by global capitalism: it revisits the model of globalisation and examines the interplay between these forces and the responses of international, national and regional governments and organisations. There was a brief discussion of power in the second volume, but this chapter will conclude with a more extended discussion.

It is also important to explore global capitalism even more thoroughly in order to understand the political and moral issues with which we are confronted and this we will undertake in the next four chapters of this book; thereafter, we will develop our notion of social relations and the moral good and how this is, itself a learned and learning phenomenon. Underlying the whole of the trilogy is the recognition that since humanity continues to learn, the human project is not complete; therefore, realising the learning society is a complex phenomenon which may never be finalised since the only time when it might be regarded as complete is when human beings cease to learn which, while a fascinating concept, is never likely to occur and so we are never dealing with a 'finished product' or even a finishable one.

Lifelong learning

In this section we will examine the processes of learning, recognising that they are both existential and experiential and so we will briefly look at the nature of experience and, finally, in this section we will examine the fact that learning and experience always occur within the life-world and so we will look briefly at the nature of socialisation and culture. This is necessary because the society in which we live is also an information society and since we are exposed to a tremendous amount of information we are presented with many opportunities to learn. In the second part, we will then examine the way that the social context of human learning is constructed by looking at globalisation and the forces that influence the nature of culture.

The learning processes

Learning is an existential process that might well begin just before we are born, and probably ends when we lose consciousness for the last time. We defined lifelong learning in the first volume as:

> the combination of processes throughout a lifetime whereby the whole person – body (genetic, physical and biological) and mind (knowledge, skills, attitudes, values, emotions, beliefs and senses) – experiences social situations, the perceived content of which is then transformed cognitively, emotively or practically (or through any combination) and integrated into

the individual person's biography resulting in a continually changing (or more experienced) person.

(Jarvis, 2006, p. 134)

It is life long but dependent upon our experiences of the world in which we live so that it is more than just a psychological process – it is a human process and may, therefore, be studied from a wide variety of academic disciplines (Jarvis and Parker, 2005). This approach differs from many studies of learning in that it starts from the person of the learner – both body and mind – and recognises that it is from the learners' experiences that learning actually occurs, but that those experiences are not all cognitive and that the different elements of any experience are transformed cognitively, emotively or through active engagement with the world and the ensuing learning integrated into the person's biography. It is as a result of learning that the person is changed, becomes more experienced and grows and develops. A diagram of the learning processes was produced (Jarvis, 2006, p. 23) and the diagram below is a slight adaptation of it, made only to emphasise the learning that occurs.

Box 1₁ depicts the situation of people in their life-worlds and we shall look at this in greater detail below but we would argue that learning stems from social experience but that experience is determined to some extent by the nature of both the body and the mind in relation to each other and the external world. However, we continue to live in a taken-for-granted situation until such time as a situation causes us to question this taken-for-grantedness. Hence the arrow from box 1 pointing forwards in time that merely depicts the unquestioning process of much daily living. It is in the social situation that people are most likely to experience disjuncture (box 1), although this state can occur when people are alone, reflect on previous events, or even when they have an experience in interacting with the natural world, so that not all disjunctural experiences occur as a result of language and interaction as some social constructivists hold (see Archer, 2000, pp. 86–117). The state of disjuncture occurs when we can no longer presume upon our world and act upon it in an almost unthinking manner; it is at this point that we have an experience (box 2) and it need not be contained within the bounds of language. Indeed, it can and does precede language in small children and in inexplicable situations (Jarvis, 1987, 1997). Experience can be transformed by thought, emotion or action (boxes 3–5), or any combination of them: the precise mechanisms of these transformations constitute considerable studies in their own right and these have not been undertaken here. Box 6 is a new addition to the diagram and it is included to underline the fact that the outcome of the transformation is that people actually learn or fail to resolve their disjuncture, but this process itself always results in a changed person, even when there is apparently no learning since the experience still affects the self of the learner (box 7). When people fail to resolve their disjuncture they can either learn to live in ignorance or with an awareness that they need to learn in order to resolve their disjuncture, or they

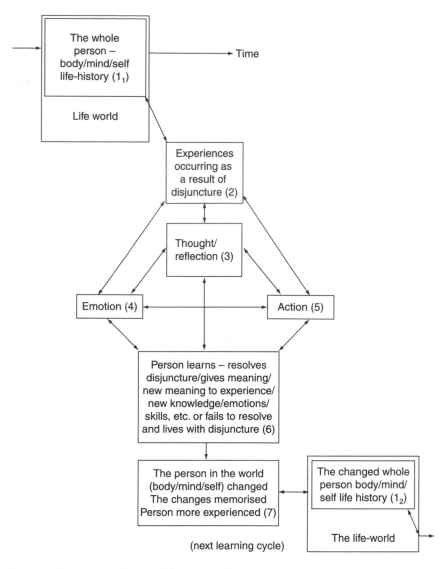

Figure1.1 The transformation of the person through learning.

can start the whole process off again. But even when they have learned the process of living is on-going and so, then, is the process of learning as box 1_2 indicates.

Since the person is at the heart of the learning processes, it is necessary to recognise that persons are both mind and body, and that experiences do not occur only in the cognitive dimension but also in the physical and the emotional ones. Experience, itself occurs at the intersection of the person and the natural or social world and it occurs when individuals cannot take their life-world for granted and need to ask questions about their situation, such as – What does it mean? What do I do? What is that smell? – and so on. Experience, then, occurs in two dimensions: the dimension of the physical senses (body) and that of the mind, and in many instances these experiences occur simultan-eously although for heuristic purposes we separate them here.

In all experiencing and learning, the process begins with the bodily processes of sight, smell, sound, taste and touch. In itself each sense experience is mean-ingless but we need to give it meaning and name it. When we can do this, and recall it then we can begin to take our sense experiences for granted and yet still have cognitive disjunctures, but in many instances our disjuncture begins with these sensations. We will all, no doubt, recall that game where we have to guess the nature of an object from a picture taken from an unusual angle, or when we are asked to feel something that we cannot see, and say what it is. These games build on the idea of disjuncture – we cannot take the taste, touch, sight, and so on for granted. Children probably have more disjunctural experiences that stem from sense experience than adults since they do not have the cognitive appar-atus to give meaning to them in the first instance. It is only as we grow that we gain that knowledge to cope with them. Initially children have sense experi-ences that they cannot explain and so they live in ignorance of which they may be unaware in the first instance. However, as they mature so they begin to give meaning to those initial sensations of sight, smell, sound, taste, touch, and their learning moves from the senses to the cognitions and the knowledge they learn from the sensations is conveyed in language and so later learning occurs primar-ily in the cognitive domain and the sense experiences relegated to a secondary position. Consequently, as we mature the more our learning assumes a cognitive dimension but there are still times when we have a sense experience that we cannot explain in language – a disjunctural experience – and so we are forced to revert to the senses until we can give it meaning. In a way this was the problem that Knowles (1970, 1980) tried to deal with when he wrote his book on *The Modern Practice of Adult Education* – the first edition he sub-titled *Andragogy versus Pedagogy*, but as a result on the ensuing academic debate the revised edition was sub-titled *From Pedagogy to Andragogy*. Yet he never really resolved his problem and the reason was probably because he did not distinguish learning from the senses and the emotions from learning from the cognitions, and so he was unable to clarify any relationship between children's learning and adult learning (Jarvis, 2007b). Adults continue to learn through the senses and both emotions and skills may be included here although in both cases there is also a cognitive dimension, so that they may also be placed within the diagram (Figure 1.3) as well.

All learning begins with the sensations and so we may depict this form of learning (see Figure 1.2).

In Figure 1.2, we see that the disjuncture is caused by an inability to take the

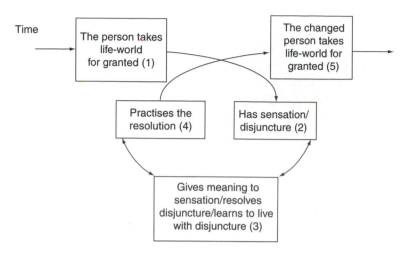

Figure 1.2 The transformation of the senses: initial and non-reflective learning.

sensation for granted: we cannot give it meaning or we are unsure about the meaning we give it, and so we need to resolve the dilemma caused by the experience (box 2). Having got an answer to our problem, i.e. we can give meaning to the sensation – as a result of self-directed learning, teaching, and so on (box 3) – we are able to practise it in a social situation. If our answer is acceptable in as much as the people upon whom we practise our answer do not contradict us in some way, then we can assume it to be socially correct even though it may not be technically correct. As we continue to practise it, so we are able to universalise it and take it for granted, until the next time that a disjunctural situation occurs. Kolb (1984) actually includes generalisation in his learning cycle, but my research does not suggest that generalisation occurs immediately following a new learning experience but only after we have tried out the resolution to our disjuncture on several occasions. If we do not resolve the dilemma, then we revert to box 2 and try again, so that the arrows between boxes 2 and 3, and between 3 and 4, are not uni-directional illustrating that there is a process of trial and error learning at both stages. At the point of taking our sensations for granted, we move to the next phase – when we discuss meaning itself rather than the sensation. Adults and older children are more likely than young children to experience disjuncture in the cognitive domain and so we can depict this learning experience (see Figure 1.3).

The process is the same as that of learning from sense experience, although in this situation the experience from which the learning began is fundamentally different, being cognitive, and depends on the fact that learning from sense experience has already occurred and is taken for granted. It is significant that primarily this is still a sense experience since we hear the sound of the words but the sounds have been relegated and the meanings take precedence. The

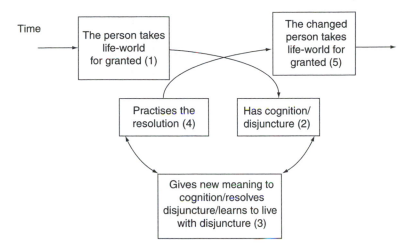

Figure 1.3 Learning from cognitive experience.

cognition, however, can be knowledge, attitudes, beliefs, values and even the knowledge associated with skills.

Naturally, there is also a third loop in which we have an emotional disjuncture and emotional learning, but it is unnecessary to do this here since it is a mere repetition of the same diagrams with the word 'cognition' being replaced by 'emotion' in both boxes 2 and 3. Alternatively, it would be possible to combine them into one diagram since the actual process combines all three dimensions but for the sake of clarity it was decided to depict the processes separately here.

The outcome of every learning situation is that the person is changed (box 5) and if persons are changed then they may have to continue learning until they can take the new situation for granted. However, the new situation is still a social one and, as changed persons, the learners do not experience the same situation, nor do those with whom they interact, and so the new situation has to be re-negotiated before it can become taken-for-granted. The outcome of almost all learning is the creation of new situations. The same water does not flow under the same bridge a second time. Social living is frequently a process of negotiation with those with whom we interact in order to create new acceptable patterns of behaviour that can gradually become taken-for-granted – until a new learning situation creates a new disjuncture. In this sense, social living always entails a process of human learning and negotiated interaction – relationship lies at the heart of social living. From the outset, therefore, we see that we learn by internalising external phenomena through the senses and the sense experience is transformed into bodily and mind languages that enable us to process them in meaningful ways.

The nature of experience

Learning always occurs as a result of experience but all living is conscious experience; it is for this reason that we regard learning as an existential phenomenon. Michael Oakeshott (1933) suggested that the concept of experience is one of the most difficult in the philosophical vocabulary (see also Capps and Capps, 2005, pp. 144–161), but it has also become predominant in the vocabulary of learning. Oakeshott is clearly right and one of the problems with a great deal of the writing on experiential learning is that it does not seek to explore the nature of experience. But we do have experiences when we as persons interact with the world in which we live – both the natural and the social – and the sum total of these episodic experiences might be regarded as the life-time experience. Experience occurs in space and time – space can be any place but time is a more problematic concept. We take time for granted. The philosopher Bergson (1999 [1965]) describes this as *durée*, a 'being at home' in the world as others would put it, the sociologists Schutz and Luckmann (1974, p. 7) write about it in the following way:

> I trust that the world as it has been known by me up until now will continue further and that consequently the stock of knowledge obtained from my fellow-men and formed from my own experiences will continue to preserve its fundamental validity ... From this assumption follows the further one: that I can repeat my past successful acts. So long as the structure of the world can be taken as constant, as long as my previous experience is valid, my ability to act upon the world in this and that manner remains in principle preserved.

The point about learning is that it begins when this taken-for-granted is interrupted and disjuncture occurs[1]: we are no longer in a harmonious relationship with our world – we now no longer fit into our world – a disjuncture has occurred and we experience dissonance. We no longer can take our life-world for granted and *durée* becomes a consciousness of time and place. We are aware of our world, we experience it, and we ask questions like – Why? How? What does it mean? We have to think about it: we have to learn about it. Now these situations are usually, but not always, social and they can be either self-initiated or other-initiated to which we respond. But we as persons are both physical body, which includes physical ability, the genetic and biological, and mind, which incorporates knowledge, attitudes, emotions, values, beliefs, senses and identity.[2] When we experience the 'now', we have to recognise that it is all of these dimensions of the person that are involved in the experience and which respond to the situation. Most learning theorists tend to restrict their analysis of the experience to knowledge and skills, although a few have more recently ventured into the emotions and attitudes, but there are few who have tried to examine the whole person in this situation. Significantly, we can see that once we discuss the whole person, disjuncture can occur and cause dissonance in any aspect – knowledge, skills, senses, emotions, beliefs, and so on. Disjuncture itself is a complex phenomenon for it seeks to relate learning to a broken relationship between being and the social world[3]:

- it can occur as a slight gap between our biography and our perception of the situation to which we can respond by slight adjustments in our daily living which we hardly notice since it occurs within the flow of time;
- it can also occur with larger gaps that demand considerable learning – this can be over a short period of time or over a longer period;
- in the meeting of the stranger, the disjuncture might not only occur in the discourse between them, it might actually occur between them as persons and their cultures and it takes time for the stranger to be received and a relationship, or harmony, to be established;
- in addition, some disjunctural situations – often emotive in category – just cause us to wonder at the beauty, pleasure and so forth that we are experiencing. In these situations, it is sometimes impossible to incorporate our learning from them into our biography and our taken-for-granted. These are what we might call 'magic moments' for which we look forward in hope to repeat in some way or other but upon which we might often reflect;
- finally, there are situations where we experience disjuncture but from which we do not learn – we block off opportunities for new learning and live in acknowledged ignorance. In this advanced technological age, this is becoming a taken for granted feature of everyday living – but it tends to make us passive actors.

Disjuncture, then, is a varied and complex experience but it is from within the disjunctural that we have experiences that, among other things, start our learning processes. There is a sense in which learning occurs whenever the harmony between our world and us has been ruptured, so that the relationship between our present understanding and our experience of the 'now' needs to be established, or re-established. The rather interesting speculation is about when there is no disjuncture and if there was ever, or ever will be, a time when human kind exists in perfect harmony with the world.

While there are a wide variety of ways in which we can discuss experience, I want to focus on two forms here – primary and secondary.

Primary experience

In this situation our major, or primary, experience of the world is through our senses, since we are embodied beings, although our cognitions and emotions also play a part. It would be false to say that in the ordinary course of events we experience phenomena through one mode only. For instance, when we hear something we might also respond emotionally; when we smell something we might well have a cognitive response as well, and so on. However, experiences through our senses are predominantly primary ones; they are, as it were, us 'touching' the world directly and the world touching us. In itself each sensation is meaningless although we might discover that it has a natural location, such as the position of the fingers in playing a piece of music on the piano, and so on. But primary experiences are more than just the sensations, since through reflection and interaction with others, we give them meaning, so that we know that a certain odour comes from a flower in the garden or the factory in the town, or tastes from a certain food, etc. But there are other primary experiences to which science cannot give meaning – for instance, what is the meaning to the cosmos? Our daily lives consist of primary experiences to which we respond in a wide variety of ways but through which we seek meaning.

Living, and therefore doing, is a primary experience! I live through my acts. Consequently, in the course of daily doing (and living) we acquire many skills and the exercise of skill is always a primary experience in the first instance. It is not surprising therefore that in preparing people to enter a new occupation practical placements have become an increasing necessity and we are rediscovering the need for apprenticeship and mentoring since the apprentice cannot learn the skills in the classroom. Learning the skills must be undertaken through the act of doing and, therefore, experiencing. But, doing something is not just an act, it has cognitive and affective dimensions as well and the interrelationship between knowledge, feeling and skill emerges.

Secondary experience

However, there is another form of experience – secondary or mediated experience – this comes through interaction and sharing. This is precisely the way that culture is shared. Indeed, it can be argued that social constructivism is grounded in secondary experience and one of its errors is in neglecting primary experience. It is through interaction that we experience other people and while the interaction is a primary experience, the discourse is secondary. But it is not just the person whom we experience, in the interaction we share our narratives and even listen to each other's discourses. The content of the narrative or discourse is also experienced, but this is a secondary experience. Indeed, the meaning that we give to primary experiences is our own but once we try to tell it to others we provide them with a secondary experience – or a mediated one. Most of what we learn about the world comes from secondary experience and much of what we are taught in college or university, often called theory, is also secondary experience, although we can also have facts mediated to us through teaching. But often it is the interpreted experiences of ourselves and others that are transmitted by us or to us and about which, therefore, we always need to be critical. Many educators have endeavoured to provide primary experiences, through role play, simulation, and so on, in order that learners experience cognitively, physically and emotionally so that they relate the theories that they learn (secondary experiences) to the world of reality. It is this provision of primary experiences that has come to be known as experiential teaching and learning. Experiential learning, in this limited sense, is also existential but all existential learning would not be considered by all experiential learning practitioners as experiential, although I would maintain that it is. It is from these experiences that we learn – but our experiences are to a considerable extent bound by our life-worlds – we learn within a cultural context.

Learning, then, is the process of transforming these experiences in a variety of ways through thought, action or emotion or any combination, and integrating the outcomes into our personal biographies. This always occurs within a social and cultural context.

Learning within a cultural context

We are all born into a social group and we learn to become members of that family/group/community. We are socialised into that group, internalise its culture and acquire an initial personal identity but at the same time, as we mature so we externalise our internalised processes and we become the carriers of culture to the next generation of learners. However, since we have not internalised the initial experience without some form of learning (transformation) we are not externalising precisely the same content as we internalised – change takes place through our learning and cultural transmission.

Culture, itself, is a word with a multitude of different meanings but from an anthropological perspective culture may be contrasted with nature. Gehlen (1988, p. 29) writes:

> In order to survive, he (humankind) must master and recreate nature, and for this reason man must *experience* the world. He acts because he is unspecialized and deprived of a natural environment to which he is adapted. The epitome of nature restructured to serve his needs is called *culture* and the culture world is the human world ... Culture, therefore, is 'second nature' – man's restructured nature.
>
> (My parenthesis – *italics in original*)

But unlike the animals, humans have minimal instincts and so they have to learn this second nature and pass it on from generation to generation, so that children's education is often seen as transmitting the most worthwhile knowledge from one generation to the succeeding one. Culture is all the knowledge, skills, attitudes, beliefs, values and emotions that we, as human beings, have added to our biological base and to the natural world. Culture is a social phenomenon; it is what we as a society, or a people, share and which enables us to live as society and the society in which we live at present is one which manifests the values of global capitalism. In order for humanity to survive, it is necessary that we should learn our culture. Learning, then, becomes necessary for the survival of societies and in the process we, as human beings, learn to be. This learning occurs through personal interaction (I–Thou) with significant others (Strauss, 1964) in the first instance, and then within the wider life-world or the generalised other. The significant others are carriers of the culture of the locality for us and objectified culture is that common culture that members of the group/community share. It is, however, never precisely the same in different people, since their difference is only in part cultural but also bodily and social, but there are often predominant cultural characteristics that are common, such as shared values, ethnic customs, and so on. At the same time, there are some who have more power to determine what is transmitted from one generation to the next, and so we have to recognise that even primary socialisation is always a political process. But culture itself has not only undergone change in an ethnic sense, for instance, but, if our model of global society is correct, culture will also change with changes in the global sub-structure – and we will explore this a little more below.

This process can be depicted in Figure 1.4.

Ego represents a single person (child, in the first instance) who is the recipient of social pressures which in contemporary Western society are generated by global capitalism culture among others and responds to its disjunctural questions; the ego is the one who internalises both the questions and the answers, and the arrows represent interaction with significant others who are the carriers of culture. While this process might appear to be unidirectional, it is clearly not long before children start to externalise, and so they begin to live in a potential tension situation with those who are their significant others, and the two sets of arrows depict the processes of internalisation and externalisation. The situation of tension is, therefore, one of disjuncture which children try to minimalise through learning. Herein lies the beginning of negotiation. Through their initial learning, children are socialised into their social world, they internalise (learn) that world so that social reality is now built into their biography, although very rarely to such an extent that they just become mirrors of that reality although the blurred reflections can usually be recognised.[4] Consequently

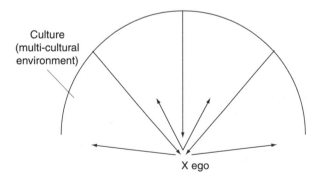

Culture
(multi-cultural
environment)

X ego

Figure 1.4 Socialisation – the internalisation of culture.

two realities exist, as Bourdieu (1992) has argued, but the internal subjective one is not a perfect reproduction of the external one.

It was Mead (Strauss, 1964) who described this process in terms of ego's interaction with the significant others within the children's life-world who carry that social reality within themselves and manifest it in their interaction with others, so that these arrows reflect inter-personal relations that occur within the life-world. Indeed, there are at least three forms of relationship within the life-world that need to be considered, and these relate to the present and the future. In the present, there are two ways in which people act with the external world – through immediate relationships with other individuals in the 'now' (I–Thou) and through an awareness of phenomena (past memories, things, events, and so on – I–It (Buber, 1959)). There is also a relationship with the internalised world (Me) which might be described as I–Me; this might also be seen as the reflective process – this is the process in which we 'talk to ourselves' as we carry on an internal conversation about the ongoing events, as we stop and reflect, and so on. This is a process that learning theorists have perhaps not examined sufficiently. In a sense, it is the process of thinking itself. Even so, there is also an envisaged relationship with the world, which occurs when individuals think about the future while they are still in the present; they have desires, intentions, the will to act, and so on. In a similar manner, we can think about the past, or about an idea – we can contemplate, muse, and so on, and thus relate to ourselves and even rewrite our own biography in our own minds. This reflecting upon our past results in our own awareness of our life history and educational biography (Dominice, 2000).

However, it is not now only significant others who transmit that dominant culture to young people: it is the media, especially television, as we shall discuss later. The most intrusive form of this transmission is advertising directly to young people, not just informing them but trying to titivate their desires to want/need or to acquire certain things. Hence there is an early learning of the emotions, something to which we will return later in this study. Fundamentally, they learn the consumer culture before they have any understanding of the cost of the things that they desire and also before they learn self-control.

In the Figure 1.4, the arc represents the all-encompassing culture of the society into which we are born. In primitive society it was possible to describe this as a single culture, but now this all-encompassing culture is what might also be described as multi-cultural. Culture is a problematic concept and merely by describing it as all-encompassing does not obviate the problem since it is not entirely the same phenomenon for all people in the same area – for instance, young people still grow up in the UK, for instance, with their ethnic cultures, even though they also acquire a sense of 'Britishness' and others a sense of being a Muslim, and so on. At the same time, as we will argue below, globalisation means that not only everybody in one society but those in many societies are socialised into the same culture of global capitalism, so that forms of standardisation are occurring and we can talk about the global village. Furthermore, the world and culture into which older citizens were socialised was entirely different to that which younger people are socialised, even though we use the same words and talk about the same nation. We all have our own life-worlds. Culture is also a difficult term to define, since it has many accepted meanings. Even so, at the risk of simplifying the concept, we will define it as the totality of knowledge, beliefs, values, attitudes and norms and mores of a social grouping, so that we can see that learning is inextricably intertwined with culture and learning is always a social and cultural phenomenon. Indeed, culture is all that is learned by every individual. Each group and sub-group has its own distinctive culture and individuals may be members of many social groups and, therefore, reflect a number of recognisably different cultures in their actions, attitudes, beliefs, and so on.

We all live in multi-cultural life-worlds that are gradually reflecting the locality in which we live. Consequently, we learn a diversity of interpretations of reality from the outset, especially through the mass media – but, at the same time, we learn dominant cultural values and attitudes. But the learning is not just embedded in the present, it is always future-orientated in order that humankind should master the world and survive:

> The acts through which man meets the challenge of survival should always be considered from two angles: They are productive acts of overcoming the deficiencies and obtaining relief, on the one hand, and they are a completely new means for conducting life drawn from within man himself.
> (Gehlen, 1988, pp. 28–29)

These actions are communicative and manipulative. But for Gehlen, the common root of knowledge and action lies at the heart of the human response to the world or, in other words, experiential and situated learning, as opposed to the instinctive behaviour of animals. Instinctive behaviour is repetitious and reproductive, as indeed is patterned behaviour in social living but in the latter forms of behaviour we know that we could have done things differently. Learning, then, is both a human and a social necessity and through it human beings learn to be and to be members of the wider society: this is a process of socialisation and we will briefly look at both primary and secondary socialisation here.

Primary socialisation

Culture is an ambiguous concept that functions both externally and internally. When we are born into the world we have no cultural awareness although we have learned a number of phenomena pre-consciously in the womb. At birth then, culture is external to us but internal to our significant others and through interaction with them we internalise (learn, often non-reflectively and unintentionally in the first instance) it. Once they have shared and we have learned the relevant knowledge, values, beliefs, etc. the culture becomes our own subjective reality and as such helps determine the way that we perceive and experience the world, and consequently we learn in it and from it. This is the process of socialisation which Berger and Luckmann (1966, p. 150) sub-divide thus:

> Primary socialization is the first socialization an individual goes in childhood, through which he (sic) becomes a member of society. Secondary socialization is any subsequent process which inducts an already socialized individual into new sectors of the objective world of his society.

Crucial to this process is learning the language of the people since it is through language that meaning, knowledge, and so on, are conveyed. Language is at the heart of the greater part of our conscious learning and it will always reflect the culture of our life-world, as many childhood educators have demonstrated; at the same time it is not the sole repository of cultural knowledge. Language, as such, is arbitrary and symbolic; no word, thing or event has intrinsic meaning, and it only assumes meaning when meaning is given to it and this occurs through narrative that unites the disparate episodic events in our lives. Consequently, young children grow up to learn the meaning of words, often as a result of their sense experiences. For instance, let us assume that my young grandson is looking at the computer on which I am writing this chapter but he does not know that it is a computer, nor does he yet know the word computer, although he can see the object/instrument that I am using. In fact the computer has no meaning for him, except as a plaything. As he looks at it, the sensations on his retina are transmitted to his brain and so he is aware of the image of the computer and he still has to learn the word. At the same time he has to learn to associate the word 'computer', a sound which is transmitted to his brain as sensations generated by the sounds he has heard. Eventually, the visual and the sound sensations are linked in his mind and the object becomes a computer. He can then take the meaning of the word for granted – he has learnt it non-reflectively, and it is almost as if there is no longer a separation between the word and the instrument. Even this non-reflective learning process is complex, associational and takes time before it becomes a subjective reality as we showed above. Once we have accomplished it, we shortcut our language by saying that the instrument is a computer and take the sound itself for granted. Naturally, in other languages the word denoting 'computer' may be very different. But once learned, the word 'computer' has two realities – an objective reality and a subjective one – but we still recognise the object through our senses. This is true of all the language that we learn in early childhood and without that language we would find it almost impossible to give meaning to phenomena in our life-world. Once we have language, it helps to organise our experience and give it meaning. But the meaning we give anything is a social construction since it reflects our culture that we have learned from others during our primary socialisation. Traditionally, as Mead demonstrated, this socialisation was affected by interaction with significant others but in more recent times the media, especially television, have also become very significant and they assume a more dominant role in the lives of most people, especially the young which we will return to in a later chapter.

However, once we have language, we can express ourselves, share our thoughts and become functioning members of our social group. We can also expand the breadth of our thinking, develop our own meanings of things and interpretations of events within our own purview and we can become creative and innovative and, as a result, we do not always find that we can accept all of our cultural interpretations of reality. This ability to think independently gives a second strand to our individuality, the first coming from our biological and genetic inheritance, so that we can see how our conception of our selves, as persons, is enabled by the development of language and meaning. With it, we develop self-confidence and this is another unintended and incidental facet of our learning. As we develop this sense of individuality, self-identity and self-hood, so we have a growing store of memories upon which we can assess new experiences and new learning and so we can engage in negotiation of meanings and interpretations with others within our life-world. In other words, we can develop our critical and creative faculties and these are relatively independent of our biological base. Consequently, the ability to learn reflectively develops with our growing ability to use language and, perhaps, our preferences for the way that we learn are also developed at this time.

Secondary socialisation

As we grow and develop so we join other groups having their own sub-cultures, such as schools, leisure clubs and work, and in each of these we go through a process of secondary socialisation. We learn to be a student, a club member and a worker; in other words, we learn specific behaviour associated with our position. However, as Turner (1962) showed, the process of secondary socialisation is not merely a process of imitating the behaviour of other role players: that is behaviourist learning. He (1962, p. 38) showed that 'role behavior in formal organizations becomes a working compromise between the formalized role pre-scriptions and the more flexible operation of the role-taking process'. It is inter-active rather than merely imitative, as has been often assumed, pointing to a more complex interaction between 'ego' and the generalised or selected other in learning to perform organisational roles. Moreover, the fact that 'alter' validates the role behaviour indicates that the role player is an accepted member of the organisation and that the role behaviour is likely to conform to certain norms and social expectations. In each status change and personal development there is social identity transformation, although our personal identity remains a con-tinuous and a less frequently changing phenomenon.

None of us remain in the same social position and play the same role throughout the whole of our life span (see, for instance, Erikson, 1963), so that we change both roles and statuses – and with it social identities, and so on.

When the change is gradual it is possible for both the individual and society to cope with it in the normal course of things, but when it is sudden or dramatic then both the individual being changed and the immediate social group have to be prepared for it. Consequently, status change is often ritualised by the social group through rites of passage, initiation rituals, and so on. From the work of van Gennap (1908), these in-between periods in status change have been regarded as liminal periods. Victor Turner (1969, p. 81) described the ritual process whereby young people were initiated into adulthood among the Ndembu people in central Africa.

> Liminal entities, such as neophytes in initiation or puberty rites, may be represented as having nothing. They may be disguised as monsters, wear only a strip of clothing, or even go naked to demonstrate that, as liminal beings, they have no status, property, insignia, secular clothing indicating rank or role, position in the kinship system – in short, nothing that may distinguish them from their fellow neophytes or initiands. Their behaviour is normally passive or humble; they must obey their instructors implicitly, and accept arbitrary punishment without complaint. It is as though they are being reduced or ground down to a uniform condition to be fashioned anew and endowed with additional powers to enable them to cope with their new situation in life.

Here then we see that the initiands were treated as non-persons – they have their old culture removed and a new 'second nature' provided for them, so that they could fit into society in their new position. Their new learning had to be free from the influences of previous learning. These teaching methods might be regarded as immoral but they were totally symbolic of 'unlearning'[5] a previously learned culture. This might be seen as a form of brainwashing; an endeavour to remove the effects of a culture upon a person through physical and psychological techniques. Our status rituals are by no means so harsh or as clearly structured since we live in a more open society, but they likewise symbolise the new position and therefore the new learning that has to occur in such social change. We shall return to Turner's concept of liminality later in this study. At the same time, such writers as Lave and Wenger (1991) borrow the language of anthropology when they discuss situated learning, which in their study is basically a description and analysis of secondary socialisation as a learning process.

Once we have internalised the external culture and made it our 'second nature' it becomes a basis for our own interpretation of our experiences and for our giving them meaning. In other words, this is the psychological consciousness. This consciousness is both learned and validated within the culture and points us to the way that our own interpretation of our own experiences is socially constructed. Thus we can begin to see the significance in understanding the culture into which the learners are born and within which they live if we are to understand their learning processes, but we have already pointed to the significance of space in this process since we have indicated how globalisation affects local cultures.

However, socialised individuals also continue to learn, albeit within a more restricted framework. The Club of Rome Report *No Limits to Learning* (Botkin *et al.*, 1979) illustrates this by dividing learning into two types: maintenance learning which is 'the acquisition of fixed outlooks, methods and rules for dealing with known and recurring situations ... and is indispensable for the functioning and stability of every society' and innovative learning which is 'the type of learning that can bring change, renewal, restructuring, and problem reformulation' (Botkin *et al.*, 1979, p. 10). In other words, innovative learning results in changes in the way individuals act and ultimately change in culture. We are continually doing both in our own learning and the more that we seek to maintain the patterns of behaviour with which we are familiar the more we will tend to resist learning. But the potential for innovative learning remains and, therefore, we can see that while this is so, learning is life long and humanity remains an unfinished project.

Having briefly looked at the learning processes discussed much more fully in the first volume of this trilogy, it is now time to try to understand how the content of that culture is generated, and this takes us to the second volume (Jarvis, 2007b).

Towards the learning society?

In order to understand the content of contemporary culture it is necessary to understand something of the processes of globalisation. The argument in the second volume is that the dominant forces in the global economy stem from those who control the economic and technology (especially information technology) institutions. This sub-structure is actually supported by the political and military might of the United States of America, being the only super-power in the world at the present time. This support might be weakened in the future as America loses some of its world domination. However, the significant thing about this sub-structure is that it is common for all societies, although there are many forces that seek to resist it, and this we see, for example, in many of the Muslim movements which are called by the West 'terrorist movements' – a point to which we will return at a later stage. In addition, we have to recognise that the political forces are still extremely powerful and that those countries, like Zimbabwe and Burma, having dictatorships which have ignored the rest of the world have become even more impoverished because the exercise of political power has placed them to a considerable extent outside the global economic world. This is the nature of neo-liberalism.

However the need for each institution in the sub-structure to survive in a competitive market means that each corporation in the core, and those smaller ones seeking to develop into larger corporations, need to produce new commodities or older ones at more competitive prices that can be sold in the market, and so make financial gain. This means that certain scientific and other forms of knowledge change with great rapidity and societies are flooded with new commodities. Through advertising, and so on, the general population is socialised into accepting the need to purchase these new commodities – advertising functions to stimulate desire as much as it does to sell new products – which will be discussed in the next chapter. Hence a consumer society is created and maintained through the advertising media. People have to learn to live with change. But it was also pointed out that not all knowledge changes with such great regularity and that 'cultural knowledge' (Scheler, 1980 [1926]) changes less rapidly than do those forms of knowledge necessary for the efficient production of new commodities, and so on. Individuals, however, have to learn to live in a culture where many aspects, but by no means all, change with great rapidity. This is now a global phenomenon.

Globalisation has at least two main elements: the first is the way that those who have control of the sub-structure in the countries of the dominant West, especially America, have been enabled to extend their control over the sub-structures of nearly all the other countries in the world and consequently over their structures and resources; the second is the effects that these sub-structural changes are having on the superstructure of each society since the common sub-structure means that similar forces are being exerted on each people and society despite each having different histories, cultures, languages, and so on, but these forces do not exist unopposed since different cultural groups seek to retain their own ways of life. In addition, individual states and national governments still exist and that they also seek to oppose or modify the forces of globalisation.

Perhaps the most significant of those forces opposing globalisation are the fundamentalist Muslim countries of the Middle East. While some of these countries tolerate the situation because they are powerless to do anything about it – or even because some countries, like India for instance, are benefiting from it; others have declared war on consumer capitalism, and we see the growth of what we, in the West, define to be terrorist activities. This 'war on terror' is actually being conducted against those countries that also oppose global economic competition – which they actually see as global market domination. It is important to note here that economic competition – the market – is at the heart of the global sub-structure. It is the market competition that is a major factor in creating a fast moving world since every competitor, i.e. transnational corporations and those many innovatory small- and medium-sized companies, has to produce and sell its products in order to survive – a consumer society is inevitable in this situation. Consequently, we can see how the world has individualised and has become fluid as people and societies respond to the rapid demands of the sub-structure and to the artificial needs created by the market. Nevertheless, a variety of peoples and societies are resisting this process by endeavouring, to differing extents, to retain their uniqueness and independence that has given rise to a different understanding of the phenomenon of globalisation (Robertson, 1995). The global–local relationship is one of tension, even resistance, since those who control the sub-structure seek to dominate the national and local cultures whereas some societies and cultures endeavour to retain their uniqueness. The global superstructure is now more like a lattice work in which the various parts are fluid and changing as some lose their distinctiveness within the sea of change, while others fight to retain their difference. Hence the local cultures are 'liquid' in many ways but there is a stable sub-structure that, in its own way, is a major cause of the liquidity of contemporary society.

Globalisation can thus be depicted in Figures 1.5 and 1.6.

The significance of this model is that there is a global sub-structure represented here by the core running through all the different countries – it exercises a centralised power in each of the countries and, in this sense, it is a force for convergence between the different countries of the world. It consists, first, of the economic system but also of the technological one, especially information technology. Those who control it exercise global power and that control rests with large transnational corporations whose directors are un-elected and very powerful throughout the world. But these forces are supported by the one superpower, the USA, and so it would be possible to place the USA at the top of the hierarchy of countries, represented by the hierarchical multi-coloured discs or as part of the sub-structure. My decision to place USA as part of the global substructure has been reinforced many times since I first made the decision but one example published (Monbiot, 2007) before the 2007 G8 summit in Germany illustrated the point nicely: the issues were breastfeeding or bottle-milk feeding of children in the Philippines. By using contaminated water, which much water

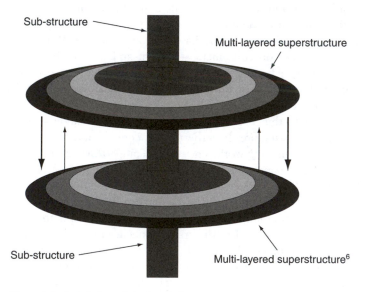

Sub-structure

Multi-layered superstructure

Sub-structure

Multi-layered superstructure[6]

Figure 1.5 A global model of societies.

in the Philippines is, bottle-milk feeding is dangerous and 16,000 children a year die as a result of inappropriate feeding practices, but the powdered milk is produced in the rich Western nations and the incidence in children's disease has increased dramatically – both the Philippine government and United Nations blame this on the decline in breastfeeding. In order to try to stem the incidence of this the Philippine government drew up a series of rules designed to prevent the advertising of powdered milk since there had been a misleading advertising campaign by industry trying to persuade more women to give bottle-milk to their children. Immediately, these rules were contested in court by the industry representatives, but their contestation was defeated. Then, as Monbiot (2007, p. 33) puts it:

> [T]he big guns arrived.
>   The US embassy and the US regional trade representative started lobbying the Philippines government. Then the chief executive of the US Chamber of Commerce – which represents 3m businesses – wrote a letter to the Philippines president ... (claiming that) the new rules would have unintended consequences for investors' confidence.

Four days later the court decision was reversed and the government could not prevent companies from breaking an international code. The US government had acted as a part of the global sub-structure giving it the political power that the corporations otherwise would not have. At this time in history the USA is part of the global sub-structure (Americanisation) and power, political as well as socio-economic, resides in the global sub-structure but it can also be exercised between countries through political, trade, aid and other international mechanisms.

One other point that needs to be made here in relation to the globalisation process is that this is very much a project of modernity with American (neo-) liberalism being at the forefront, but it will be argued in this book that there is a sense in which the modernity project is flawed and so this will affect much of the ensuing argument.

The large downward pointing arrows in Figure 1.5 illustrate that there is a relationship of power between the 203 countries of the world (this is the number recorded by UNESCO, 2006), while the two small black upward pointing arrows depict the resistance to the forces of globalisation. However, it would be true to say that there are probably blocks of countries at different levels of the global power structure, with the G8 countries being the most powerful stratum. In Figure 1.5, each layer represents a country that is penetrated through the centre by the sub-structure, and each country can now be represented in the following manner.

It would have been quite possible to add other layers to illustrate the complexity of the whole but for the sake of clarity, however, a simpler model is retained. At the same time, the layers are depicted hierarchically in order to

Economic/technological/Americal political sub-structure

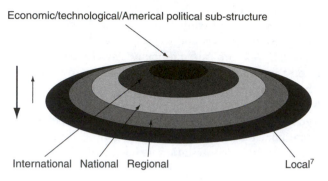

International National Regional   Local[7]

Figure 1.6 A multi-layered model of society.

illustrate that it is not merely a geographical matter but that it is also one of power stemming from the core to the periphery, although it has to be recognised that power is not a one-way process since, by the nature of democracy the 'lower orders' can and should be proactive as well, so that there is also passivity at the lower levels to the pressures coming from the hierarchy. Individuals and organisations can find their place at any level where they play their role, some at a number of different levels. Significantly, the national level for each country is not located at the core of the society: it is argued here – especially in the second chapter, that greater power and influence stem from the sub-structure and that the international organisations, such as the World Bank and the European Union exercise more influence, in many ways, that do national governments. It is, therefore, no wonder that many people are frustrated by government's inability to act since the nature of sovereignty has undergone considerable change and territorial sovereignty is a phenomenon of the past. This, in its turn, raises fundamental questions about the nature of democracy in contemporary society since major corporations with their unelected directors and transnational organisations with interests far removed from the level of daily and private life exercise as much and maybe even more power over the people than do elected governments. It could be argued that this is little different from previous times when, as Marx argued, the wealthy used the state apparatus for their own ends, but it was the apparatus of state that was used – rather than the fact that the state apparatus can now be by-passed or utilised for corporate ends. As a result of these processes, most governments now have both less power and less money to spend on traditional welfare projects and they are having to find new ways of offering welfare support – one of these is from welfare to work through lifelong learning, which might be viewed as a part of 'third way' politics. Naturally, individuals can exercise more power in an organisational context in one of the other layers of society, so that by joining trades unions,[8] churches and other non-governmental organisations, they can exercise considerably more power. However, we can see that individuals' social position and the power that they can exercise within society as a result depends to some extent on their relation to the sub-structure. This is neither a determinist position nor is it a simple class one as society has changed considerably since the time when Marx wrote and power is much more diffuse.

The first thing to note in Figures 1.5 and 1.6 is that the sub-structure is united and runs through all the different countries. Now this core is united in a manner that the individual countries are not – it runs through each making similar demands on each – as Beck (2000) puts it, it criss-crosses national boundaries. This apparent unity of the core means that its constituent members agree on the aims and functions of the centre, although there is also internal competition since each constituent company is competing with many others in order to produce products that can be marketed throughout the world. The fact that there is internal competition means that the speed of change within the core is fast, driven by the demands of the market which it is both creating and to which it is also seeking to respond. It is, therefore, changing faster than those aspects of the global system that are not so market-driven and so it produces a driving force for change in each country. Additionally, it is necessary to recognise that change is neither gradual nor even, since new discoveries and huge advertising campaigns tend to generate change in fits and starts. It is not surprising therefore, that one argument for world government is to ensure that the political process operates on similar terms to corporate management.

The second fact to recognise is that these companies, and this technological-economic core, are protected by the political and military might of America and the institutions over which it exercises hegemonic control – such as the World Bank and the International Monetary Fund. There is considerable confusion within America itself between the core and the political – this confusion has been exacerbated during the presidency of George W. Bush whose government is certainly not always entirely divorced from the corporate sector and which seems always to act in favour of the economic system of the core. The third factor to note is that because the core controls information technology, as well as technology for production, and so on, it has the power to advertise its products globally and generate both a huge market for its products but also to produce a considerable degree of standardisation across the globe. Fourth, each society is a separate entity and consequently, cooperation between countries/states is a matter of political negotiation and agreement, something that takes time – as the workings of the United Nations and the European Union show. However, the international layer is shown separately since it is not only governments that act internationally but also non-governmental organisations. Nevertheless, it is clear that countries are less able to change as rapidly as the global core and so there is almost an international global situation of 'divide and rule', with the global core exercising a degree of dominance. This means that law, democracy and civil society are all exposed to a source of power, other than the State – that of the global market; a transnational civil society is still a long way from a reality, although there are a few signs to suggest that it is occurring, even though we live in a world society (Beck, 2000). Habermas (2001, p. 61) suggests that: 'There is a crippling sense that national politics have dwindled to more or less intelligent management of a process of forced adaptation to the pressure to shore up purely local positional advantages.' The fifth factor to recognise is that while there are four layers depicted here for each society, they represent only a few of the possible ones, but they all have to negotiate between themselves in order to cooperate. Sixth, some societies are more accessible to this process than others, so that social change does not spread completely evenly across the globe, with countries like those of sub-Saharan Africa and Nepal not able to respond to the changes at the same speed as does the United Kingdom, and so on. These poorer countries get poorer while the richer ones prosper – indeed, enticing the poor into the World Trade Organisation may not be altogether beneficial to them in the long run since they forfeit some of their own protection against the might of the global powers in order to enter. However, it should also be noted that even in the first world, the poor continue to be excluded and get poorer. In the USA, for instance, 16.5 per cent live in poverty, 20 per cent of the adult population are illiterate and 13 per cent have a life expectancy of shorter than 60 years, according to Bauman (1999) citing a United Nations development report. In the UK, 17 per cent of the population live below the low income threshold (National Statistics, 2006, pp. 79–80) and the most deprived 10 per cent of the population have a life expectancy six years lower than those of the least deprived 10 per cent (National Statistics, 2006, p. 100).

In a sense, then, the core is the driving force of nearly all societies to some degree or other, but within the national and local cultures there are both wider interests and concerns than those to be found in the core and also some instances a degree of resistance to the changes that are occurring and these are to be found at every level, including the international. Since each country relates to others and although Figure 1.6 has depicted only two countries we could have put in over 200 different ones in relation to each other, the external arrows represent the unequal relationships between each country. For instance, the dominant downwardly pointing arrow represents trade, aid, consultations, and so on. The development of information technology, rapid travel, and so on means that people throughout the world are much more aware of what occurs elsewhere and are much more able to affect it. It is possible, therefore, for people at different levels in the hierarchy to communicate across national boundaries electronically and to travel rapidly and cheaply between different countries, so that there is inter-cultural sharing. There is certainly more giving by the more powerful to the less powerful countries, so that the arrows still depict a hegemonic relationship in which the dominant cultures of the West still export their culture and commodities but through a different mechanism.

At the same time, the less dominant cultures appear to have more opportunity to resist the process and have more chances of retaining their independence, unless they get into debt to the World Bank. The relationships that exist at this level are more diplomatic and interactive, and open, on occasions, for the less powerful cultures to export aspects of their culture to more dominant cultures – much of this comes through international migration of people in search of employment and the better life – although others flee from political persecution, and so on. Hence the second, smaller arrow upwards in the diagram illustrates this process. That there can be some cultural exchange is important and through this political mechanism there is greater respect for cultural diversity than there is through the change that is introduced through the global technical-economic sub-structure. Respect for individual cultures still plays a significant role in the political trade and aid relationship. Such a relationship calls for informed dialogue (Crossley, 2006) between countries enabling the bridging of cultures and a greater exercise in relationship, but we cannot escape from the fact that in every society in the world and at every level of each society, power in a wide variety of forms plays a significant role, and we will discuss the nature of power in the final section of this chapter below.

The learning society

It was argued in the second volume that society does not learn, although contemporary society is a rapidly changing one, so that the idea of a learning society's existence is a slightly misleading one. Only people can learn but they can exercise the power to create change, so that the society is not a learning one but a changing one. The pressures for change come from those who control the sub-structure that is at the heart of the competition in the global capitalist market. The forces of change are fundamentally economic and technological although these forces are generating change in management and production in order to ensure both efficient and cheap production. Hence, those forms of knowledge which Scheler (1980 [1926]) called artificial, science, technology and positive knowledge, are incorporated and used by those who exercise power in global society and who are the initiators of social change in all societies – even though the change itself may not be their immediate intention in running a global capitalist corporation. Other knowledge that is embedded in culture[9] changes less rapidly and tends to be regarded as old-fashioned and out-of-date. Hence, there is a great deal of learning in society: individuals are generating new knowledge; others are forced to learn to work with new knowledge; the general population has to learn to cope with new procedures and use new products; and so on. This has also meant that workers have to learn new knowledge and skills at work, so that there has been a massive increase in continuing and recurrent education and there has also been growth in the amount of research that is taking place.

Since the globe is united by a common core there is a form of standardisation throughout the world, which is resisted mainly by those countries that reject the values that stem from the core, and these are mainly the Muslim countries of the Middle East but they could also be Russia and China. Yet in another sense, nearly every country and region fights to retain its own cultures and identities, so that while there is a great deal that is common in different countries, e.g. shops and commodities, there is also a sense of difference between them that comes from their cultural heritage. Consequently, we are seeing the growth of tourism as countries seek to preserve their cultural heritage to show to the rest of the world.

Lifelong learning has emerged in this context and many societies in the world have introduced policies and legislation for lifelong learning. But it is not possible to legislate for people's learning, only for their education. Consequently, lifelong learning, in national policy terms, is regarded in the second volume both as individual learning throughout the lifespan and a form of recurrent education that can lead both to academic qualifications or nonformal learning that occurs on the job. It was defined in the second volume as *every opportunity made available by any social institution for, and every process by which, an individual can acquire knowledge, skills, attitudes, values, emotions, beliefs and senses within global society.* In the same way, the learning society was depicted as a society in which all these opportunities are made available for individuals to learn. The rapid changes make this type of provision of learning opportunities and continuing learning throughout the life span a necessity. One of the other outcomes of this focus upon work and those forms of knowledge essential for the present form of society is the undervaluing nonvocational education and learning.

What is clear, however, is that since all individuals continue to learn the human project is not and never can be complete while people continue to learn and so society is not a static phenomenon but a rapidly changing one. Consequently, the learning society might not actually be a state but a process in time – an open process the end (destination) of which is impossible to determine although its direction can be affected by those who exercise power in it. It was also clear from the arguments produced in the second volume that contemporary society is neither moral nor ideal so that the direction that society is taking is one that we would argue needs to be changed. Therefore our learning, seen by many as being necessary for the present society to function may also be necessary to re-direct it along a more moral path. Exploring this change in direction is part of the objective of this current study.

The nature of power

Implicit in the diagrams about globalisation and the multi-layered state is the role of power, the study of which is a major undertaking that is beyond the scope of this book. Nevertheless it is important to clarify this discussion in order to highlight some of the different forms of power and the ways in which it operates.

From the outset, it is clear that power is an inter-personal phenomenon and also a societal one. In the 'good society' it might be argued that interrelationship is something that exists with a degree of equality for the common good but then we recognise that the common good is a rather mythical concept in an individualistic world. Thomas Paine (1995, p. 5 [1776]) made the delightful observation that:

> Society is produced by our wants and government by our wickedness; the former promotes our happiness *positively* by uniting our affections, the latter *negatively* by restraining our vices. The one encourages intercourse, the other creates distinctions. The first is the patron, the last the punisher.
> Society in every state is a blessing, but government a necessary evil; . . .

And so it is with every new development, including the learning society, we hope for a better society but are confronted by government and restriction and we do not get it – even though there may well be some improvement we still feel that the better society still lies around the corner. Thomas Paine's hope was for a utopian society but his recognition of our imperfections and with it manifestations of our own individuality hides a mass of assumptions, some of which we will touch upon as this study proceeds. But the other problem with Paine's statement is the assumption that government is actually evil, something with which Marxists have always agreed. Foucault (1979, p. 25) made a very similar observation, which he applied to governments when he suggested that 'population' emerged 'as an economic and political problem' and that the exercise of power is not merely an act of repression but one of controlling desires. Yet, with Paine, we have always hoped in vain for the utopian society to appear – a new Jerusalem – but realistically recognised that power is not just used to restrain our vices, but its use is most frequently a vice in itself.

Throughout this study we shall frequently return to this theme but we shall do so in the light of an ethical debate since we cannot escape from the fact that teaching and learning is most frequently a social interaction and that education, as Freire (1972a *inter alia*) reminded us is always political and utopian: the learning society, therefore, must have both political and ethical implications.

Power is exercised at both an individual and a societal level and discussion about it tends to fuse the two together, which is realistic. From the outset we can see how power is linked to freedom – freedom to do what one wishes. Indeed, this is a fundamental Weberian approach to it and power is defined here as 'the ability to act in pursuit of one's aims and interests, the ability to intervene in the course of events and affect their outcome' (Thompson, 1995, p. 13). Power:

- is exercised by individuals;
- involves the notion of agency;
- is exercised over other individuals;
- differentiates between the powerful and powerless;
- is negative in as much as it restricts.

(Abercrombie *et al.*, 2000, p. 275)

Power is also built into the structures of every society, including the learning society, as Marxist sociology has highlighted. However, Lukes (2005, p. 29) suggests that there are three dimensions – the first being behaviourist and the other two being critiques of the behaviourist position. His three dimensions are:

- behaviour, decision making, key issues, observable conflict, interests that are translated into policies;
- decision making and non-decision making, issues and potential issues, observable conflict – both covert and overt, interests translated into policy issues or grievances;
- decision making and control over the political agenda, issues and potential issues, observable and latent conflict, subjective and real interests.

In a similar manner, Newman (2006, p. 122), following Habermas (1972), suggests that power has three dimensions: objective, social and subjective. In a sense, his objective power relates to Lukes' first dimension; the social relates to Lukes' second and part of his third dimension; the subjective relates to the other aspects of Lukes' third dimension. It is a combination of political, economic and persuasive power.

Luke's analysis suggests that power is extremely widespread in society. It is clear that the ability to make decisions and enforce their outcome is an exercise in power, but in our study of learning we may not want to say that power is only exercised through controlling the political agenda – it is also through the way that the learning materials are delivered through advertising and by the design of the educational syllabus/curriculum (agenda), and so on; consequently, it is control over the social and cultural agenda, as well. Issues and potential issues refer those areas about which decisions are, or may not be, made – such as the resources of power and authority. Conflict, or potential conflict, can be resolved through coercion, force, manipulation, influence, persuasion, and so on. Lukes maintains that interests are themselves a product of the system through which we learn what we would like, and so on, and this is precisely what we have argued in this chapter. Consequently, we can see the power of advertising moulds our desires, but it is also culturally and socially reproductive without being over-deterministic. As we have shown, we are all influenced to a considerable extent by the intrinsic power in both the media and in interpersonal relationships, even to the extent of having our own interests socially constructed. The exercise of power is not always direct or political; indeed the third dimension of power Lukes (2005, p. 109) sees as something indirect and much more insidious – it is the ability to secure a compliance of the people to be dominated. He goes on to argue that the control of techniques can result in adaptive preferences being controlled even to the extent that people 'accept their lot' in society. Indeed, there is a sense in which symbolic violence (Bourdieu and Passeron, 1977) occurs all the time since people's own humanity is violated by the techniques of persuasion used. It means that people are not free to think and learn in an unimpeded manner – in a sense their minds are closed down and their learning is non-reflective, inclined to accept the information that is transmitted without being reflective or asking, what the information actually means, why and how it is transmitted, how valid are its claims, and so on. Finally, Lukes (2005, p. 150) makes the point that:

> Power's third dimension is always focused on particular domains of experience and is never, except in fictional dystopias, more than partially effective. It would be simplistic to suppose that 'willing' and 'unwilling' compliance to domination are mutually exclusive.

Indeed, we can always resist power if we are alert to its exercise, if we are so concerned about our own psychological and bodily drives and desires, if we are prepared to face the consequences, and so on. The third dimension of power is the one in which society's sub-structure operates for a great deal of the time since it uses the incidentality of learning as its main technique, although we have also pointed out how employers utilise other dimensions when necessary. While we do not see contemporary global society in terms of a political totalitarian state, it does have many of the conditions of totalism which in some ways threatens human nature itself through its subversive techniques.

Foucault (1980, p. 217) also suggests that power is 'the total structure of actions brought to bear in possible actions' and he gives the impression that power is monolithic. Again, his emphasis is on the fact that power is exercised over people so that power is domination and yet people act in apparent freedom because they have learned to conform to the power situation. The relationship between power and freedom is something to which we will return in this study. He also employed the image of the Panopticon to illustrate this. However, it may be that the universalism of Foucault's position is one of his weaknesses, as Merquior (1985, p. 115) suggests. Indeed, Thompson (1995, p. 134) also criticises Foucault for not having examined sufficiently closely the relationship between power and visibility and Lukes (2005, pp. 95–96) thinks that Foucault does not actually offer any new analysis of power. However, Foucault's emphasis on the individuals accepting the power situation and conforming to the power networks that exist is important, as is his recognition that we do so in a state of apparent freedom. In addition, his image of the Panopticon does suggest the surveillance society and in this his work might be becoming even more realistic as surveillance becomes even more common and visible as a method of restraining people's freedom.

Following Mann (1986), Thompson (1995, pp. 13–18) distinguishes four types of power:

- Economic: material and financial resources;
- Political: authority;
- Coercive: physical and armed force;
- Symbolic: means of information and communication.

In comparing Thompson's and Lukes' approach we can see many similarities and, for instance, we note that those who have the economic resources and political authority are in a position to control agendas, and so on, which is Luke's third dimension. However, Thompson's final form of symbolic power is quite significant for our discussion and yet, his concern is much more with information and communication rather than with the exercise of persuasion – the power that seeks to persuade individuals to learn and conform to what they are informed, reflecting Foucault's position noted above; this seems to bridge the coercive and the symbolic. Certain forms of indoctrination may fall into this category and it is an important feature of the information society, to which we will return in the fourth chapter. Consequently, I want to suggest a fifth form of power: persuasive power. Power, then is a complex phenomenon and for the purpose of this study these five forms of power form the basis of our analysis.

It is significant that once we discuss power, we cannot escape from issues of values and ethics: indeed, once we examine human relationships we are confronted with ethical problems so that no political analysis of lifelong learning and the learning society would be complete without recognising its ethical dimension. Indeed, the exercise of power is not always ethical; indeed, there are many occasions when it is not so as we will argue. Nevertheless, Cohen (1985, p. 13), in his introduction to Levinas' *Ethics and Infinity* makes the point:

> Ethics is forceful not because it opposes power with power, on the same plane, with a bigger army, more guns, a finer microscope or a grander space program, but rather because it opposes power with what appears to be weakness and vulnerability but is responsibility and sincerity. To the calculations of power, ethics opposes *less* than power can conquer.
>
> (*italics* in original)

We will develop our understanding of ethics in a later chapter but it is within this context that the learning society in globalised capitalist society, if such a phenomenon exists, has to be studied.

Conclusion

Having summarised, albeit very briefly, the arguments from the previous two volumes, we are now in a position to move into the final volume. This volume is based on the idea that we do continue to learn and that learning needs to be more reflective and critical so that we can endeavour to change the direction that society appears to take. At the same time, the processes of that learning do need to be grounded in a moral debate about the 'ideal' nature of society and then the outcomes of the learning need to be seen to be political and action orientated. However, in order to understand the political and moral climate within which the learning society has emerged, it is first necessary to explore the nature of Modernity and, in the third chapter we will discuss the societal context within which this takes place and in the following one we will look at this within a more individual context.

Since we indicated in the second volume that there are the forces of global capitalism that have certainly affected the nature of lifelong learning and the learning society, we need to adopt a critical perspective upon contemporary society and to suggest that these dominant forces need to be resisted or modified and so the outcome of this study may be regarded as idealistic – or utopian, but then we can well recall Freire's (1972a, p. 40) clear understanding about the nature of education:

> This is why the utopian character of our educational theory and practice is as permanent as education itself which, for us is cultural action. Its thrust toward denunciation and annunciation cannot be exhausted when the reality of the denounced today cedes its place tomorrow to the reality previously announced as denunciation. When education is no longer utopian, that is when it no longer embodies the dramatic unity of denunciation and annunciation, it is either because the future has no more meaning for men, or because men are afraid to risk living the future as creative overcoming of the present, which has become old.

Education is the social provision of learning opportunities and so it is not just education that is utopian – it captures something quite deep in the human psyche which is the desire for a better/perfect world. And learning, both in and beyond education, is the driving force of the human being. We are the result of our learning and so, in an over-simplified form, is our society. But while this utopianism may still exist in contemporary society – the values of global capitalism reign. In the Appendix to Volume 2 we argued that such a system cannot produce a utopian form of society. The argument here is that in order to change the direction of our society, we need a learning revolution but before we can discuss this in a meaningful manner we do need to understand both the processes underlying the type of society in which we live and the values that have led to this type of society, so that in the next chapters we will look back at the emergence of capitalism, individualism and instrumental rationality and the way in which capitalism through the media in the information society undermines some of the freedoms which would allow us to construct a more just society but before we do this we will examine just how the power of global capitalism operates at the various levels in society.

Chapter 2

Global and local lifelong learning policies in the knowledge economy

From the outset of this study we have noted that the state is no longer the most powerful force within any country, although it retains the potential to be so, as dictatorships like Zimbabwe and Burma demonstrate: in Figures 1.5 and 1.6 the state is the third layer in a society, the first two being the sub-structure and the international, both of which exercise a considerable but differing amount of different forms of power in every society. This clearly has major implications, not only for politics but for all other aspects of the superstructure, including the learning society. The complexity of power structures and the negotiation between the various parties reflects some of the issues of contemporary politics.

However, the differing effects of these major global institutions have not been thoroughly researched yet, although a general picture can be constructed. What we do know, however, is that while the core generates pressures for change, it cannot produce policies and laws; these come only from international, national and regional governments. In many cases these agencies actually produce policies and laws that support the demands of the sub-structure although there are occasions when these policies and laws either seek to modify, amend or even resist these pressures. This is what Habermas (2006, p. 81) calls 'cushioning' and the provision of certain forms of lifelong learning may be seen to be one of the techniques used in this process. Previously liberalism was regarded as the freedom of liberty against the repressive powers of the state but now that the state is no longer sovereign, its function in respect to liberty has undergone change. However, the growth of these global agencies can also be interpreted as political and civil society trying to catch up with the global economic sub-structure. The aim of this chapter, therefore, is to outline the effects of these transnational institutions, to discuss some of them specifically and to produce a working model of the effects of international, national and regional institutions on lifelong learning and the learning society.

Towards a general model of social pressures to produce lifelong learning policies

It is clear that the forces of economic sub-structure exercise considerable pressure on the remaining layers of each society, and it must be recognised that the more powerful layers of society exert pressure not just on the next layer but on all the layers below it: in this sense the image of the Panopticon is very valid. The core exercises economic power. But there are other layers: the second layer – the international one; these organisations are never free from the force of economic power but, at the same time, they exercise their own pressures in each country and this is political power – but it is combined with both symbolic and persuasive power. Not all of these organisations exercise the same pressure on each national government and each society has its own obligations in relation to the international agencies. In precisely the same way the third and fourth national and regional levels also have certain forms of political, symbolic and persuasive power that are exercised at local level. It is not only at the state level that coercive power is used, although the right to use military power has generally been regarded as one of the bases of national government, occasionally international organisations, such as the United Nations, utilises military force but this is usually restricted to a peace keeping role. It is in the nature of democracy, however, for certain pressures from below to be exerted upon the higher layers of society although the upward pressures tend to be exercises in political and symbolic power. In the same way, there are forces that oppose globalisation, from some of the Islamic organisations, to non-governmental organisations and social movements. Some of these institutions have little power and so they resort to other tactics, such as terrorism, to make people aware of their situation. While these processes are quite general and apply to many different social institutions, our concern is with lifelong learning and the learning society, and throughout the following discussion these will be used to illustrate the argument.

This is a dynamic process, which can be depicted in the following manner:

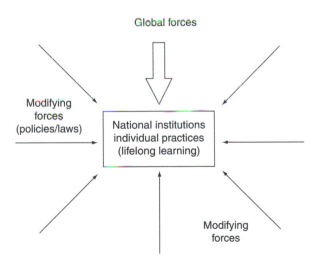

Figure 2.1 National institutions in the social context in a globalising world.

The downward arrows depict support for the global forces in varying degrees while some seek to modify the forces of advanced capitalism more than others. Since this change is not universally welcomed and there is resistance to it, the upward arrows depict that forces in varying degrees oppose the global forces, even to the extent of direct action – even terrorist action – as the ultimate form of resistance to the global forces. Among those that resist this change are religious institutions (such as Islam) but also in varying degrees many institutions and even societies resist the amorality, even immorality, of global capitalist practices. There are also popular action groups who protest against globalisation and there is a sense in which anti-globalisation movements are themselves becoming institutionalised. In addition, a variety of laws and policies in many societies, such as trades union legislation and environmental policies, also function to resist the onward spread of global capitalism in their different ways while not being totally opposed to global capitalism. It is within this framework that we find the place for politics and also for social action seeking to inhibit the influence of global capitalism through national laws and policies.

From the argument of the previous chapter we can see that the social pressures exerted by the sub-structure of global society are extremely powerful and often insidious and in a subsequent chapter we will argue that some of them are indoctrinational. These, it will be recalled from Figure 1.7, are the forces that act upon the education system and also, ultimately, upon individuals' practices. Consequently, we can see that lifelong learning opportunities emanating from different parts of the global social structures will result in different forms of lifelong learning. It is, therefore, perhaps over-simple to regard lifelong learning as a single entity within the educational context: the social forces generate different aims and objectives and these reflect the direction of these forces and will, of necessity, be both moral and political. Since each government is the recipient of the forces from above and below, the policies and practices it introduces must relate to its exposure to all of these social forces. Consequently, we will examine some of the institutions in each of the layers of society and demonstrate how they relate to, and affect, the social pressures that emanate from the sub-structures of society. We will look first at some international agencies, then some national reports and, thereafter, look at more local aspects of lifelong learning, although we will be constantly aware of the opposing social pressures.

International political agencies

Of the international agencies whose policies and practice affect lifelong learning there are four that we will briefly examine here: the World Bank (WB), United Nations Educational, Scientific and Cultural Organisation (UNESCO), Organisation for Economic Cooperation and Development (OECD) and the European Union (EU). The first two have a more specifically economic concern than the latter two, although the latter two do not neglect it, and so we would expect them to exercise social pressures that tend to reinforce the pressures coming from the global sub-structure, whereas UNESCO being an agency devoted to world cooperation is more likely to seek to modify or at least voice concerns about these pressures. At the same time, the EU seeks to influence national governments that have a wider spectrum of concern than either the WB or OECD.

The WB

While the WB has a broad but still restricted definition of lifelong learning, as something that occurs from early childhood through retirement and it recognises the hidden benefits of learning, such as enabling people to participate in their communities, increasing social cohesion, reducing crime and improving income distribution (WB, 2003, p. 1), its own report starts with the assumption of its president James D. Wolfensohn (WB, 2003, p. 1): 'All agree that the single most important key to development and to poverty alleviation is education.' The report then argues that there is a return for the country on the increase in the average number of years of schooling of children. While it is accepted here that there may well be an association between the length of schooling and the size of a country's gross national product, the report reads as if this is a cause and an effective argument for change, and in this it is limited since there are many causes to most global and local effects, and education may actually be an effect as well as a cause. In the model of globalisation depicted in the opening chapter of this study, it is the control of the wealth producing institutions that holds the power of change, and lifelong learning and education become contributory factors thereafter – but we have already argued how even schooling and lifelong education are controlled by the sub-structural forces, so that a certain form of schooling and lifelong learning are built into the key assumption of the WB. These assumptions need much more discussion, and later in this book we will argue for a revolution in learning if we are to change the social conditions and this demands a different approach to both education and lifelong learning.

Nevertheless, the WB is commonly accepted as a neo-liberal economic institution, as Hyslop-Margison and Sears (2006, p. 74) write:

> The World Bank openly operates under neo-liberal policies and principles that assume only the unrestricted market and competition can bring prosperity to developing nations. However, these neo-liberal reforms are clearly ineffective in many African nations experiencing political conflicts such as ethnic wars and border disputes, in those countries politically oppressed by dictatorships or colonization, and in countries lacking stable, democratic political systems.

The implications of this are that individualism and freedom have to be introduced into the system and it is often done in a rather crude manner through structural adjustment policies. At the same time, as we will show, education itself can act as an agency of social engineering in this way. However, not all the support offered by the WB actually reaches the people for whom it is intended. As Hyslop-Margison and Sears point out that in a corrupt system any wealth generated by the WB never really benefits the greater proportion of the population. However, they restrict their discussion to countries of the African continent, and so, it is rather limited, but Laksamba (2005) demonstrated in his study of lifelong learning policies in Nepal that similar practices obtain there also. These policies are clearly discussed in WB's own study of lifelong learning in a global knowledge economy (WB, 2003) and in Palacios' (2003) working paper on financing lifelong learning. However, when the state has received help, how should that portion of the financial support that is to be distributed to individuals reach them? Palacios reaches the conclusion that such financing should ultimately not come from the state although he accepts that the state could issue some vouchers to learners as its contribution, but that the learners should contribute both through income-contingent loans and human capital contracts.[1] In this way, we see a clear expression of neo-liberalism and an assumption that people can afford to get into debt in order to learn – but there is still a place for aid to the very poor.

Within the framework of Figure 1.6, therefore, we can see that the WB, as a neo-liberal economic institution, exerts social pressures on governments that reinforce the pressures of the sub-structure and, therefore, serves to reproduce the social and cultural conditions of global society. This economic power is even greater in those countries to which the WB has loaned or supported the loan of money, since it can place conditions on the developing countries to conform to its own understanding of global economics, even if such economics do not appear beneficial to the countries concerned: they are certainly beneficial to the developed world, and the large corporations that invest in the poorer countries to their own profit. Indeed, Joseph Stiglitz (2002) the WB's former chief economist and Nobel Laureate in Economics has recently claimed that the time has come for major changes in the WB's economic policy and the values that it reflects – he (2002, p. 252) writes that 'development is not about helping a few rich people get richer ... it is about transforming societies, improving the lives of the poor, enabling everyone to have a chance at success and access to health care and education' (cited from Bawden, 2006, p. 113). He makes the same criticism of the International Monetary Fund. At the same time, it has to be acknowledged that in many instances loans are a way of kick-starting an initiative for some of those who are individual, autonomous, strong-willed and entrepreneurial and, as we will later argue, this economic position finds support from other powerful groups, such as the Christian fundamentalists in the USA – the country which we have suggested in the first chapter functions within the sub-structures of the world.

UNESCO

In many ways we find in UNESCO a completely different picture to that presented by the WB: a champion of lifelong education having adopted the term long before it gained popularity.[2] It has both led the way in developing the concept but, at the same time, always presenting it within a humanistic perspective. From its first major report, Faure Report (Faure, 1972) and the publication of the background papers (OISE-UNESCO, 1973) to the present day we see the same concerns.

Produced before global capitalism became such a dominant force, the Faure Report is the outcome of a UNESCO Commission on the Development of Education, and yet its conclusions are still relevant today. In order to give a flavour of this report, I am summarising the conclusions provided by Edgar Faure in his Preamble: *Education and Man's Destiny* (1972, pp. xix–xxxix):

- Strong support must be given to democracy, as the only way for man to avoid becoming enslaved to machines, and the only condition compatible with the dignity which the intellectual achievements of the human race require.
- The concept of democracy itself must be developed, for it can no longer be limited to a minimum of juridical guarantees protecting citizens from the arbitrary exercise of power in a subsistence economy; furthermore, and in conjunction with this, more support must be given to educational requirements.
- The main aim of education must be re-created, to allow both for the new features of society and the new features of democracy.
- Education must be regarded as a domain where political action is of especially decisive importance.
- Science and technology must be fundamental elements in any educational enterprise so that man can control natural and productive forces, social forces and gain mastery over himself.
- The aim of education is to enable man to be himself, to 'become himself'.
- The aim of education should not be to prepare young people for employment and economic progress but to help them to give them a permanent stimulus to the desire to learn and to train oneself.
- The Commission emphasised two fundamental ideas: lifelong education and the learning society – the former is both about time-span and diversity across the whole of society.
- The 'age of change' has provided us with the instruments needed to meet the quantitative and qualitative demands for education.
- Lifelong education can only be met if the instruments derived from modern technology are put to use.
- If education is to be re-created then international solidarity and world co-operation become more clearly necessary than ever before.
- Current international and multi-national aid is insufficient.

- Uniting *Homo sapiens* and *Homo faber* is not enough; such a man must also feel in harmony with himself and with others: *Homo concors*.
- This age can only be the age of total *man*: that is to say, man entire and all of man.

Throughout the report the whole of the person is constantly emphasised: '*The physical, intellectual, emotional and ethical integration of the individual into the complete man is a broad definition of the fundamental aim of education*' (italics in original, p. 156). This is a report full of far-sighted and radical recommendations and principles which has left its mark on the world of education but the extent to which its concerns have been taken on board is another matter. But UNESCO has been consistent and before we move on to other agencies, it is necessary to look at some of its later publications.

A similar report was published in 1996: the Delors Report, *Learning: the Treasure Within*. With the growth in the globalisation of neo-liberal economic policies, we find that this report both recognises the changes but repeats similar messages. Once again, quoting from the 'Introduction: education, the necessary utopia' (Delors, 1996, pp. 13–35), we read that they wish to stress:

> the ideas on which UNESCO was founded, based upon the hope for a world that is a better place to live in, where people will have learned to respect the rights of women and men, to show mutual understanding, and to use the advances in knowledge to foster human development rather than create further distinctions between people.
>
> (p. 14)

The report's introduction recognises that 'all-out economic growth can no longer be viewed as the ideal way of reconciling material progress with equity, respect for the human condition and respect for the natural assets that we have to hand on in good condition to future generations' (p. 15) – a direct criticism of the prevailing neo-liberal economics. In order to do this we need to broaden our understanding of lifelong education at all levels – both formal and non-formal education. Once again, the significance of values is recognised and their implementation is the responsibility of policy makers. Significantly, an idea that was prevalent when recurrent education was an ideal in the 1970s (see below in the discussion of OECD), Delors suggests that there should be a study entitlement of a certain number of years for every young person.

At the heart of the Delors Report lies the significance of education in which learning has four pillars (pp. 86–97):

- Learning to know – broad general knowledge with in-depth knowledge of a small number of subjects;
- Learning to do – to acquire the competence to live and work in teams;

- Learning to live together – to develop an understanding of inter-dependence;
- Learning to be – in order to develop one's own personality and autonomy, judgment and responsibility.

This is a consistent picture with the Faure Report produced nearly a quarter of a century earlier and before neo-liberal economics contributed greatly to the development of the current global world. Obviously, this report reflects the period of its own publication and, as such, it perhaps under-emphasises the emotions, ethics and ecology and so we could add a further two pillars:

- Learning to love and care for others – this one might be seen as no more than an extension of learning to live together;
- Learning to respect and sustain the environment.

At the same time, this report once again presents us with another way of looking at lifelong learning. Between these two reports, not only have there been world conferences on adult education, there was a world conference on Education for All in Jomtiem, Thailand, in March 1990 that was based upon the UN Declaration of Human Rights. The World Declaration (1990 – downloaded 2006) claimed that all human beings have a right to educational opportunities to enable them to survive and to develop their capacities to live with dignity. It recognises that people should:

- build upon their cultural, linguistic and spiritual heritage;
- promote the education of others;
- further the cause of social justice;
- achieve environmental protection;
- be tolerant of social, political and religious systems which differ from their own;
- ensure that commonly accepted values and human rights are upheld;
- work for international peace and solidarity.

Fundamentally, this conference also presented the vision of the better world upon which both the United Nations and UNESCO were founded. Additionally, UNESCO organised a conference of non-governmental organisations at Dakar in 2000 to examine this issue and its declaration will be considered later in this chapter.

More recently UNESCO has returned to these issues in *Towards a Knowledge Society* (UNESCO, 2005), its first world report. In this report governments are urged to expand quality education. Echoing the Delors Report, this report concludes with three pillars of knowledge societies:

- A better enhancement of the value of existing forms of knowledge to narrow the knowledge divide;

- More participatory knowledge societies;
- A better integration of knowledge politics.

Throughout this report, there is a concern about the inequality of knowledge throughout the world, so that there should be knowledge sharing. Knowledge, then, like other forms of wealth needs to be equally distributed for the good of humanity. There is also a major concern that the value if indigenous knowledge is underplayed and that the knowledge itself is threatened.

UNESCO has pioneered environmental education and as early as 1977 in Tbilisi, it organised the first international environmental conference – others have followed it. But from the outset it emphasised its concern over the complex relationship between socio-economic development and the environment. Its concern was that environmental education should be available to people of all ages and every walk of life.

Unlike the WB reports, these UNESCO documents are much more utopian, full of the significance of humankind and how humankind as a whole need to enjoy the fruits of the world in which we live. It is ethical but also political. It offers a different picture of the world from that offered by the WB, and in this sense, it is a major force seeking to modify and redirect the forces of social change emanating from the sub-structure of global society. But there are many other important organisations offering their own solutions to these problems and we need to examine some of these. We will now examine the OECD.

The OECD

The OECD was established in December 1960 to achieve the highest possible economic growth and employment and increase the standard of living in member countries, to contribute to economic expansion in both member and non-member countries and to increase world trade. While the reference to non-member countries occurs here, it is perhaps notable throughout the OECD literature, naturally enough, that the focus is upon OECD member countries so that many of the major issues of globalisation are not addressed as most of the member countries are wealthy, industrialised societies, but there is a major concern for equality of opportunity within these societies running through all the documents, although many of the wider social and ethical issues do not feature quite so prominently.

The formation of the OECD preceded the widespread acceptance of neo-liberal economics that occurred a few years later, although its establishment was perhaps an early sign of the more recent form of economic globalisation. From its earliest days it was concerned with the place of education and it pioneered the concept of recurrent education as a strategy for lifelong learning (OECD, 1973) which it claimed to be a different approach to education since it argued that 'education opportunities should be spread over the individual's lifetime, as an alternative to the ever-lengthening period of continuing education for youth' (OECD 1973, p. 5 – underlining in the original). It is significant that from the outset OECD did not propose a system of formal education that was parallel to adult education since that would create another binary system. There was a genuine concern for equality of opportunity behind the OECD proposals since it focused from the outset on lower-skilled people having the right to paid educational leave, as well as those who were more highly skilled.

By 1977, however, the term 'recurrent education' had disappeared: this maybe because there was a growing sense that it would be very costly to both the sub-structure and national governments to implement systems of paid educational leave as an entitlement, or even to see post-school education as an educational system. Indeed, it was much more in line with the ideals of neo-liberalism to place the responsibility of self-improvement through education on individuals and their learning; one reason why lifelong education (a social institution) had to become lifelong learning (an individualistic concept). From the time when the term 'recurrent education' was dropped, the term 'education of adults' assumed more prominence (OECD, 1977, p. 5) until lifelong learning gradually came to the fore. Moreover, when the key concept became learning and it was suggested that there are five sets of learning needs:

- Remedial;
- Vocational, Technical and Professional Competences;
- Health, Welfare and Family Life;
- Civic, Political and Community Competence;
- Self-fulfilment.

(OECD, 1977, pp. 23–24)

Thereafter there was a further four volumes examining: new structures, programmes and methods; non-participation; participation; widening access for the disadvantaged (OECD, 1977–1981). Consequently, it can be seen that while the early publications of OECD on lifelong learning were work-orientated, they were genuinely engaged in all the issues of general adult education and many of the authors of specific chapters in these volumes were well-known adult educators.

As globalisation became more significant, so the concerns of OECD were more focused on the knowledge economy and yet there was recognition that globalisation itself brought vulnerability (OECD, 1996, p. 30). However, lifelong learning for all was the theme of an OECD Ministers' Conference at this time and while the broader adult education issues are still apparent in the discussion documents, it is clear that learning and work is the prevalent issue. Indeed, the first argument for lifelong learning provided is the learning economy. Both in placing this as the prime reason for lifelong learning and the introduction of the language of global capitalism indicates how OECD has been affected by, and has in turn affected, the dominant economic policies of the period. Thereafter, the speed of change due to technology is considered as the second reason for lifelong learning, followed by discussion about education throughout the life-cycle; the formation of human capital and social well-being of individuals is the fourth reason given and, finally, the issues of social cohesion are addressed as it is recognised that the wealth gap is widening (OECD, 1996, pp. 90–92).

The same concerns are addressed in *Promoting Adult Learning* (OECD, 2005) where the focus is on adult learning rather than lifelong learning, since it is broadly recognised that despite the benefits learning can bring, participation in learning opportunities remains low among adults and a great deal of effort is being put into seeking to get adults to return to learning so that they can improve their life conditions. At the same time, learning for the OECD has traditionally been about rational knowledge and technology since it views the world in a rational manner and it expects the same response from learners, but as we will argue throughout this volume rationality, technology and other scientific approaches to knowledge and behaviour do not emphasise the ethics necessary for people to live together in peace, harmony and in some form of equality of opportunity.

While the OECD has been a major force in promoting adult and lifelong learning policies within its member countries, it has rarely looked beyond them to the rest of the world. Perhaps this is natural, but this is a wealthy nations' organisation and while it has been concerned with such things as social cohesion within these countries, it has not really began to address the gap between its members and the poorer countries of the world. It does, however, promote policies that seek to modify or ameliorate slightly the social conditions that the forces of globalisation would create within its member countries and its arguments are relevant for much of the remainder of the world. Nevertheless, its ethics are 'insider' ethics and, as such, it does not respond to the implications of globalisation globally. We will now examine one further international organisation that is confronted with the same issues of insider and outsider relations – the EU.

The EU

Throughout the European policies documents there are two aims – they are both major ones and both demand considerable investment in time, personnel and capital. The first is to create a united Europe – a real experiment in creating a society for the future and for this to be achieved the focus needs to be on active citizenship, among other things. The expansion of the EU can be viewed as a political exercise in catching up with economic globalisation but it is certainly a major social and political project: the original intention for the EU was to bring about peace and harmony in what was a divided Europe after the Second World War. In order to achieve this union and retain its high standard of living, Europe needs to provide employment for all its workers and to advance the knowledge and technological level of its work-force. These two very demanding aims were seen to fall within the ambit of lifelong learning.

In 1995 the EU published its *White Paper on Education and Training* in which the Commission made public its concerns about the need to have lifelong learning within the whole of Europe so that it can assume its place as a global leader in the knowledge economy. In a sense, the paper locates employability, citizenship and education agenda within its view of a better society which is itself a statement having ethical overtones – a united Europe that could be a global leader in the knowledge economy, as the Lisbon conference, in 2000, had set out as its aim to be the leading area in the knowledge economy by 2010 – but recognised by 2004 as being very unlikely. But much earlier, the more social and ethical aim of creating a united Europe was spelt out:

> The future of European culture depends on its capacity to equip young people to question constantly and seek new answers without prejudicing human values.[3] This is the very foundation of citizenship and is essential if European society is to be open, multicultural and democratic.
>
> (EC 1995, p. 10)

Within two years, however, the Commission had coupled lifelong learning and citizenship much more explicitly, while still emphasising the need to promote policies to restore the employment situation.

> This educational area (Europe) will facilitate an **enhancement of citizenship** through the sharing of common values, and the development of a sense of belonging to a common social and cultural area. It must encourage a broader-based understanding of citizenship, founded on active solidarity and on mutual understanding of the cultural diversities that constitute Europe's originality and richness.
>
> (**bold** in the original, EC, 1997, p. 4)

The emphasis here is still on education for citizenship per se rather than for active citizenship, but this emphasis was to change the following year.

> The Commission acknowledged citizenship could not be taught, since it had cognitive, affective and practical dimensions – it could be learned, however, and learning for active citizenship became an aim of lifelong learning. Here, the teaching of citizenship is not enough – it is the learning of citizenship which is essential.... Learning for active citizenship includes access to the skills and competencies that young people will need for effective economic participation under conditions of technological modernisation, economic globalisation, and, very concretely, transnational European labour markets.
>
> (EC, 1998, p. 6)

Learning for active citizenship was still something for young people but it was not an optional extra – perhaps the ideal is 'the rise of the public man' in the future. But even this reading is a little misleading because we learn through our activities, so that in being an active citizen we are actually involved in lifelong learning. It is still quite significant that employability (skills) is a key to active citizenship within the EU. Indeed, as Arendt (1958, p. 70) has suggested that we already live under conditions where our only reliable property is our skill and our labour power and, as with the ancient Greeks it was the ownership of property that enabled the citizens of the city-state to play their public role, now it is skills that enable them to be active citizens and contribute to society through employment and through employment their individuality and freedom are channelled into socially acceptable paths. The conditions of *viva activa* are spelt out – learning, work and citizenship and these were further elaborated upon as a result of consultation following the *Memorandum on Lifelong Learning* (EC, 2000). By 2001, the Commission had espoused four aims for lifelong learning: *employability*; *active citizenship*; *social inclusion*; *personal fulfilment* (EC, 2001a). These aims form the bases for a social policy about lifelong learning but since they are formulated within a totalising framework, not only because the Commission has been trying to create a united Europe but also because it is ensnared within the dominant ideologies of neo-liberal economics and instrumentalism, the human condition it postulates is one in which the human potentiality is either unacknowledged or unachievable.

Employability

In the modern world, the classical concept of work (the worker as producer and creator) has begun to disappear although there are still some crafts and professions that are based on work but work has been transformed to labour. Work and the production of our own efforts underlay the rise of capitalism, since the end-product of work is the market, since a product only has value if it has either exchange value or use value. A significant outcome of work is the self-fulfilment and self-achievement of the worker, the creator, but now, the need of European society, indeed any late modern society, is labour. People have to be labourers – even flexible ones as the system's demands change – but, unlike work, labour has little intrinsic satisfaction or opportunity of self-fulfilment. In order to be active citizens people have to be labourers contributing to the common good. Employability is now the key to active citizenship and what we do is how society judges us, values us and identifies us.

In this knowledge economy, consequently, citizens have to be employable and so they have to keep on learning (both in work and in the educational system) that necessary information to provide them with the knowledge and skills (and the necessary certificates) to achieve this end. Lifelong learning is valuable because it provides opportunity for people to be employable and to be active citizens. But labourers can never transcend the system because their labour is not creative work and so their employability does no more than keep the system going and the human condition so conceptualised is not one that can encourage citizens to achieve their potential; self-fulfilment cannot be achieved through employability alone.

Active citizenship

Citizenship is a central feature in these documents, but so also is the recognition that fewer people have the desire to play that role than they did in the past. Indeed, the *White Paper on Governance* (EC, 2001b, p. 7) recognises the fact that not only do people feel alienated from the Union's work but that they have disappointed expectations. Indeed, it could have gone on to say that people no longer trust the politicians who seek to govern for the reasons we pointed out earlier in this study. While the White Paper defends the European Union and its achievements (rightly, in many ways), its only solutions are system solutions: the Union must conduct its business openly, in a participative manner, be accountable, be effective and be coherent. And so active citizens should be informed, knowledgeable, and able to participate in public debate and they should also understand the way that the European system functions. In order to be informed, there are opportunities through lifelong learning, both to teach the young but also to enable them to be engaged in practical projects so that they can learn something about active citizenship. Lifelong learning is once again an instrument of social policy. Significantly, the idea that we learn through doing, so that we need to get more people involved, maybe before they would claim to be knowledgeable, so that they can learn in the process of doing – this is what learning from conscious living is all about.

More recently, however, the Commission (2001a) published *Making a European Area of Lifelong Learning a Reality* in which it was more specifically recognised that the Europe of Knowledge threatens to bring about 'greater inequalities and social exclusion' (p. 6) so that it is claimed that lifelong learning

> is much more than economics. It also promotes the goals and ambitions of the European countries to become more inclusive, tolerant and democratic. And it promises a Europe in which citizens have the opportunity and ability to realise their ambitions and to participate in building a better society.
>
> (p. 7)

Significantly, the emphasis on the relationship between lifelong learning and employability is explicitly downplayed (p. 9): now the aims of lifelong learning have become: personal fulfilment, active citizenship, social inclusion and employability/adaptability. At the same time, building a 'better society' has become an aim of citizenship and this might be an ethical statement unless the good society is only materialistic, and the EC documents do not really read this way, then space is implicitly being made for political action in the public sphere.

Active citizens then should be involved in the process of governance and through democratic means, as civil society, the voices of the citizens should be heard expressing citizens' needs and warning those in government if its direction is wrong. This is hardly the public service role of active citizens in the city-states of Greece when they ruled their cities and through their involvement they achieved both esteem and a sense of personal achievement and fulfilment. But then the citizens were free to play that role since they owned sufficient property to give them security. Now most of today's citizens' only property is their skill which can keep them in a job for a period of time. In this sense, life-long learning is an investment through which citizens acquire the necessary skill to remain employable for the next few years. Few jobs are lifelong and unchanging and even fewer people have tenure in their occupation that enables them to be secure if they speak out for the common good against those who exercise economic power. Indeed, just look at the negative connotations of the word 'whistle blower' and look how often whistle blowers are forced to leave their employment: this is one of the 'rewards' for active citizenship!

We live in an apparently open society having a form of representative democracy, but there are opportunities for the few to engage in the process of governing and even for the few, the powers of the economic sub-system of the knowledge economy means that even the power of the state, even the multi-state, is circumscribed to some considerable degree. It is clear that political power is still to some extent dependent on economic power and that the two do not always coincide, so that these first two aims of lifelong learning in the EU policy documents reflect the tensions being explored in this study. It may be that human potentiality might be achieved through being actively involved in trying to bring about that better future through public service although the type of citizenship described here fails to recognise the human condition since it is framed within a totalising system. The opportunity to achieve and the honour and esteem that comes from this form of active citizenship might best be captured with the phrase 'public service' – but this is not the way that active citizenship is presented within these documents.

Social inclusion

In a sense the third aim is but one example of the previous discussion since one of the outcomes of governance should be a better society – in this case, one which acknowledges our diversity and seeks to include everybody within the system. The fact that inclusion is within a system signifies the fact that individuals are included in organisations, which are part of an organised system, even though the organisation is fairly loose since it is, to some extent, controlled by the market and through this they learn to conform – they are governed through their freedom within an organisational setting. In another sense, it is reflected in Levinas' (1991 [1969]) concern that we should welcome the Stranger who inhibits our freedom because when we learn from the stranger we are enriched. The more we are concerned about the stranger the richer our lives and the more we can strive for infinity – but, paradoxically, seeking infinity takes us outside of the system. Active citizens should work to insure that everybody is included within the system and so lifelong learning opportunities should be offered to all people, whatever their gender, class, age, position in society, and so on. Indeed, those who are excluded from the system are actually resources (human and social capital) lost to it. But this aim, laudable as it is, hardly recognises the human condition of being inhibited by a social system that constrains through making us free to conform, although it does recognise that people need to strive to transcend the present bonds of the system within which they live; it remains totalising rather than pointing towards the infinite.

Personal fulfilment

This aim is expressed but hardly elaborated upon in these reports, which is not surprising since that fulfilment and sense of pleasure only emerges when we, as human beings, are enabled to achieve through our actions (*viva activa*) or in the depths of our contemplation. Each of the aims of lifelong learning in the paper reflect the requirements of the system and do not recognise the human condition or call upon the human potential which can offer the opportunities of achieving personal fulfilment: work has been transformed into employability; active citizenship into democratic participation; social inclusion recognises that there are bonds but does not look towards the infinite possibilities that exist when we welcome the stranger and learn together – this is the idea of potentiality rather than merely fulfilment. And so, instead of living with the vision of a better social world in which we can explore the potentiality of humanity we are confronted with the demands of the system in which we can labour in order to consume rather than fulfil and ignore the idea of public esteem through service while celebrating the social esteem of others through the celebrity culture and hero worship of our current culture.

More recently the European Community (EC, 2006) has published another policy document on adult learning, which it now recognises as a part of lifelong learning. It provides five messages to the Member States:

- increasing participation in adult learning and making it more equitable is crucial;
- in order to foster a culture of quality in adult learning, Member States should invest in improved teaching methods and materials adapted to adult learners and put in place initial and continuing professional development measures to qualify and up-skill people working in adult learning;

- within the next five years Member States should implement systems of validation and recognition of non-formal and informal learning;
- Member States should ensure sufficient investment in the education and training of older people and migrants;
- the quality and quantity of data on adult learning must continue to improve.

While still recognising the rightful places of employability and active citizenship, this document is more concerned with the equity and quality of the educational processes themselves.

Like the OECD documents, the EC policy papers are still insider papers, as one would expect, but it is very clear from the 2001 document on lifelong learning that there has been a deliberate attempt to downplay the place of employability in lifelong learning, or put it the other way – there has been a deliberate attempt to emphasise some of the other major aims of lifelong learning so that it emphasises exercise modifying forces on the pressures that stem from the global sub-structure.

Having examined four major agencies involved in lifelong learning policies, we can see that it is the World Bank that is the strongest supporter of the forces that stem from the global sub-structure and UNESCO provides the strongest alternative picture. The agencies having membership offer modifying forces for their own Member States although they both underplay the place of the global and also the values and ethics that stem from the practices of the sub-structure. Politics might well be seen as the art of the possible – even that of compromise, or as some politicians now recognise that it is a partnership in which politicians do not always have the stronger hand to play! Indeed, Habermas (2006, p. 6) wryly asks whether politicians 'should continue with the politics of deregulation that will end up making them redundant'. It is now, therefore, important to turn our attention to the next layer – that of the nation state – and to look at some national policies.

National policies

It would be quite impossible to examine the policies of every society and that is not the intention here. The purpose of this section is to show how different countries actually respond to these global pressures and in order to do this it is necessary to consider how different societies responded to the neo-liberal economics dominant in the Regan–Thatcher era, when the minimalist state was advocated. At that time, there was a maxim: 'Leave it to the market!' It was as if the 'invisible hand' of the market would work everything out in a satisfactory manner – it was almost as if God was seen as being active through market forces. But the market has never been free or really humanistic and even if it were, reciprocity may not always be the manner of human conduct that reflects the highest forms of ethics. The market has been part of the forces generating or reinforcing the inequalities of the world. Some societies, however, adopted the neo-liberal economic policies more than others and the reasons for this can be found in a number of theorists of the period.

Indeed, the existence of the welfare state asks the fundamental question about who is responsible for the welfare of others? As Wolfe (1989, p. 108) asks: 'if everyone is free to act as he or she chooses, what exists to insure that people will recognize their obligations to one another?' Wolfe makes the point that while society was conservative, this question did not need to be confronted, but as society has segmented, then the question has to be confronted, or at least discussed and Wolfe suggests that government has that responsibility, but as we see here, government does not always have the will to undertake this role – even if it has the power and, indeed, it may be doing little more than trying to protect the weakest members of society and in some cases it has never assumed that role.

Nozick (1974) argued that when the state intervened and taxed the wealthy progressively according to their income it was equivalent to the state robbing those citizens who had justly and legally earned their wealth. This is an assumption that great wealth is always earned legitimately and morally which is an assumption that needs considerably more discussion. For him, the just society was one that protected the rights and property of all its citizens. The state's role is not to intervene but to enable those who wish to undertake entrepreneurial activity to do so and certainly much entrepreneurial activity is both legal and moral but we cannot necessarily equate entrepreneurship with wealth. Hayek (1986 [1944]) had also adopted this approach, arguing that the state's role was to enable its citizens to be free: the more society is planned and centralised, the less freedom individuals have and so state intervention is *The Road to Serfdom*.

Both of these studies and others similar to them emphasise the place of the individual and individual rights rather than either relationships or responsibilities – both of which, it will be argued below have a more sustainable moral basis than egocentricism. At the same time, countries like the USA and the UK adopted this neo-liberal economic position and the UK, in particular, placed considerable emphasis on these policies, even to the extent of dismantling some of the main elements of the welfare state. Other countries, like the Scandinavian ones, resisted these pressures and retained a stronger state apparatus – although as globalisation gathered pace even these countries have been exposed to the global forces and have begun to dismantle aspects of their welfare state provision.

Towards the end of the twentieth century, however, the UK adopted a 'third way' initiative (Giddens, 1998). Giddens (1998, pp. 23–24) summarised the different political positions: the neo-liberal wanted market freedom but strong control over moral issues; libertarians wanted individualism and low state involvement; socialists were distrustful of markets and wanted more state involvement while they were still wary of government on moral issues. While Giddens' work certainly influenced 'New Labour' it can be seen that the UK was neo-liberal within this conceptual framework and had a positive attitude towards globalisation while other countries, such as the Scandinavians were socialist. Habermas (2006, p. 81), as we have noted, suggests that there have been two general responses to globalisation at national level: 'cushioned' and 'catch-up'. The latter is the vague hope that politics will eventually catch up with the runaway markets and be able to regulate them while the former assumes that the forces of global capitalism have been unleashed and cannot be tamed, so that governments have to introduce policies that can cushion the effects. Certainly it is the latter that many national governments and international agencies have adopted and lifelong learning policies are seen as one of the cushioning effects – or welfare to work. Habermas' two types may be a little too sweeping, since some governments and other agencies, while accepting the globalisation position, have tried to introduce some aspects of the ethical and moral debate into the learning processes, as has Habermas himself in many places. In addition, it might be true to claim that elements of both of Habermas' types are prevalent simultaneously in some policy statements. The UK government has certainly adopted this latter approach and has invested considerable financial support in lifelong learning activities, even though it had, for many years, adopted a minimal state policy.

In the United Kingdom there was considerable activity in the 1990s that led to the formulation of policies for lifelong learning. In response to both the economic global pressures of the neo-liberal core and the socio-economic and political pressures from the EU, countries within the Community have introduced national policies for lifelong learning. In the UK, for instance, a National Advisory Group for Continuing Education and Lifelong Learning was established making its first report in 1997 (Fryer, 1997). This Report argued for a culture of lifelong learning for all and suggested a ten point agenda in order to create this change:

- A strategic framework;
- A revolution in attitudes;
- Widening participation and achievement;
- Home community and workplace;
- Simplification and integration;
- Partnership, planning and collaboration;
- Information, advice and guidance;
- New data, targets and standards;
- New technologies of broadcasting and communication;
- Funding and finance.

(Fryer, 1997, pp. 3–10)

While it is clear that the impetus for this report is economic and work-oriented, it does also make considerable reference to the social needs of the nation, which is in accord with the European reference to social inclusion and some reference to citizenship although there is little in the report about personal fulfilment.

This report led to a government policy document. *The Learning Age* (DfEE, 1998a) which was even more but by no means exclusively orientated to the economic needs of the nation and proposed such innovations as the University for Industry and Learn Direct – a national information service. This report certainly reflected the neo-liberal principles of the New Labour government and with it its desire to introduce lifelong learning, although in the first instance it made little reference to those other specified aims of lifelong learning, although there is the one reference in the Minister's Foreword that says 'learning offers excitement and the opportunity for discovery. It stimulates enquiring minds and nourishes our souls' (DfEE, 1998a, p. 10). A neo-liberal agenda had been set and the UK became a leading country in Europe in implementing an agenda that was much in accord with the demands of the global sub-structure. Significantly, citizenship does not play quite such a leading role in the UK as it does in Europe, but the UK has been less concerned with Europeanisation than the Commission, although British citizenship – and the learning required from it – has become an issue as a result of the problems of migration which in itself, in many cases can be traced back to the globalising forces and the wealth of the West. Economic migration is perfectly understandable in an unequal world.

Many initiatives in the UK followed this Green Paper which has led to almost continuous change within the educational system ever since. Indeed, there has been an ever increasing focus on education for employability and continuing professional development in the UK to the extent that liberal adult education funding is being successively cut and the provision of life-wide education is being restricted yet again, and non-government organisations, such as the National Institute of Adult Continuing Education distanced itself even further from the neo-liberal policies of the UK government as it continued to curtail non-vocational education and give increasing financial support for vocational training. Tuckett (2005), who was deputy chair of the Fryer Committee and has led NIACE through this difficult period, has called upon the present government to cease cutting non-vocational adult education: in other words, they reconsider the demands that neo-liberal economic policy is making upon other aspects of citizen's lives and recognise that the state has involvement not only in civil society but in fostering the conditions within which citizens would be free to play an active citizenship role.

In contrast to the emphasis of the UK government, it is interesting to look briefly at similar documents from two other industrialised societies – one inside the European Community and the other in South-East Asia[4] where there may be a broader perspective than that suggested by Habermas, since they are trying to introduce more ethical opposition to the lifelong learning processes instituted by the neo-liberal global forces. The Finnish government's socialist policy document had its own vision:

> By the year 2004 Finland will be one of the leading knowledge and inter-action societies. Success will be based on citizens' equal opportunities to

study and develop their own knowledge and extensively utilise information resources and educational opportunities. A high-quality, ethically and economically sustainable mode of operation in network-based teaching and research will have been established.

(Ministry of Education, 1999, p. 29)

As the Finnish vision is based on the citizens' opportunities, so Hong Kong's vision is based on the student's all-round development and the aims of education in the twenty-first century are three-fold: enabling students to enjoy learning; enhancing student's effectiveness in communication and developing a sense of creativity and commitment (Education Commission, 2000, p. 30). This will be achieved through following these principles: student focused; 'no-losers'; quality; life-wide learning; society-wide mobilisation (Education Commission, 2000, pp. 36–42).

While the UK vision has been driven much more by neo-liberal economic policies from both the global sub-structure and the political ideology of New Labour, we can see more humanistic approaches from both Finland, Hong Kong and, I suspect, many other countries. Yet it is the rapid changes in global society, driven by the global sub-structure, which has necessitated these educational reforms and we can see different levels of resistance to the pressures of the global sub-structure, with those countries that adopted a minimal state approach being much more open to the sub-structural forces. Whether the policies are actually put into practice in more humanistic ways or whether the policy statements are mere rhetoric is another matter – but the wording of the statements illustrate the different ways that the governments think that they can win support for their policies and this alone illustrates profound cultural differences between the countries since government policy statements rarely appear without consultation at a number of levels of society.

But some other countries, such as some Islamic countries, may oppose some, or all, of the forces of globalisation and their attitudes towards lifelong education or the Westernisation that comes from having the USA as part of the sub-structure. Countries such as China, India and Russia may be strong enough to resist the Westernisation without resisting the forces of global capitalism. Indeed, they may try to influence the direction of its forces in the same way as the USA has, and then we will see new manifestations of global but not Western capitalism. In addition, other countries might be less secular and work-orientated and the power of their religion may seek to stem the tide of global capitalism by other means. In addition, some countries might be much less individualistic, placing more of their emphases on the group – either the family or the local community affecting their policies and practices. Barber contrasts these societies with those who have adopted neo-liberal economic policies, although he has probably made too crude a division in actuality, but not for heuristic purposes. He (2003, p. xii) calls societies that have adopted the knowledge and beliefs of late modern society 'McWorld' – 'integrative modernism and aggressive economic and cultural globalization' whereas those societies that still espouse the characteristics of primitive societies he calls 'Jihadic', which he defines as 'disintegral tribalism and reactionary fundamentalism' (p. xii). In this sense Jihadic is both religious and politico-economic and this is an important division in so far as some forms of Christian fundamentalism are concerned These societies may be seen among the forces that oppose the sub-structural forces.

Clearly the Jihadic movements in Jihadic societies have opposed both the spread of globalisation and McWorld, with all its artificial forms of knowledge and innovative learning and all the economic exploitation and social inequalities that have accompanied the neglect of cultural forms of knowledge. While some of these countries tolerate the situation because they are powerless to do anything about it – or even because some countries, like India for instance, are benefiting from it; others have declared war on McWorld, and we see the growth of what we, in the West, define to be terrorist activities.

However, it is possible to describe all forms of religious fundamentalism as Jihadic and, therefore, Christian fundamentalists are also Jihadic in the religious sense but not the politico-economic sense. But they might also be a combination of McWorld and Jihadic at the same time, since individuals have the ability to act in different sectors of society and keep the implications of both positions separate in their minds and activities, conforming to both even though they have profoundly different implications.[5] In this sense, the conflict between Islamic and Western societies is politico-economic and in both cases the religious fundamentalism legitimates the two positions about the politico-economic situation and the ensuing conflict. In both social situations individuals have different experiences, and they are free to choose from which social situation they learn at any time and their priorities may differ according to the situation. In McWorld, innovative types of learning framed within the terms of artificial knowledge dominate, while in the Jihadic, maintenance learning and cultural forms of knowledge legitimated by religion and revelation are the more significant. Late modern society is now a segmented society and some people have tried to combine both McWorld and Jihadic responses to it. When the late modern societies respond in a tolerant manner it may lead to innovative learning and responses to the situation but when it responds in a Jihadic fashion – whether Christian or Islamic – because those in power choose this response, whatever the excuse they give for it, we may have a holy war, or a 'war on terror'.

We can see, therefore, that different countries' cultures and histories will act upon their attitudes to learning in different ways, from countries like the USA and the UK seeking to modify the sub-cultural forces far less than those countries that retained a stronger state apparatus earlier in the twentieth century. However, when religion also enters the debate we see other types of response.

Regional and local responses

Many of the policies that have already been mentioned have their outworking at regional level – this is the nature of globalisation – and so it is unnecessary to spend a great deal of time on them here. However, there is one initiative that we will look at briefly: that of the learning region, town or city. This is an entirely different concept from that of the local adult education centre – it is about the resources from the whole area being drawn together and being used for the development of that area. During the 1990s this initiative was promoted very strongly by many governments. The learning city:

> addresses the learning needs of its locality through partnership. It uses the strengths of social and institutional relationships to bring about cultural shifts in perceptions of the value of learning. Learning cities explicitly use learning as a way of promoting social cohesion, regeneration and economic development which involves all parts of the community.
>
> (DfEE, 1998, p. iv)

In this context we see that learning cities are structured around three strands of development: partnership, participation and performance and may be viewed as having three levels of learning: building, dialogue and reflection.

Over the past decade, learning city networks and partnerships have been built up throughout Asia, Europe and other parts of the world, supported by governmental and EU initiatives. In fact, the European Commission endeavoured to create European networks to promote learning regions (EC, 2003). There is also an international network of educating cities based upon a charter that was accepted in 1990 in which the city is regarded as a learning space in which citizenship and identity can be worked out. The OECD has also promoted local learning although the OECD initiative is much more economic and labour market orientated. On the whole, the learning region initiatives, however, have been much more orientated to local and regional development and less concerned with the pressures of the global sub-structure although economic development is certainly among the aims of many of them. However, the learning regions, towns and cities are a potential area of democratic development to which we will return towards the end of this study.

Non-governmental organisations

Having examined the national governmental organisations, it is now necessary to look briefly at the non-governmental organisations. Already we have commented on the position of NIACE in the UK, occupying a delicate position between advising the government within the normal democratic processes and opposing it when its policies have, in its opinion, aligned themselves too closely with the demands made by global capitalism. NGOs, generally, have been strongly outspoken about the educational needs of all, as the Dakar Declaration (2000) argues that there must be:

- a renewed commitment that education is a right;
- a commitment to providing quality basic education for all;
- a commitment to provide quality education to all, including the marginalised;
- a recognition that education is a state responsibility;
- a recognition that education depends upon a democratic system;
- a commitment to establish and reinforce democracy, social justice and peace;
- quality and learning at the centre of the educational process;
- gender equality in education;
- an integration of adult literacy into the process of community development.

These are but some of the bullet points made in the Declaration but they reiterate UNESCO's stance on lifelong education and globalisation. They also illustrate the type of position NGOs will adopt in their different countries, once again some being closer to their government's policies than others.

Finally, there have been mass protest and other individual and group actions seeking to divert the forces of globalisation in different ways, such as the protests in Genoa and Seattle.

Conclusion

We are now in a position to return to that diagram presented in the opening of this chapter (Figure 2.1) and to see how the different forces act upon society and produce differing approaches to lifelong learning. It will be recalled that the global forces were seen to be acting upon society but the sub-structure is not in a position to initiate global policies, only the corporations' own internal initiatives. The institutions and agencies produced policies that cushioned their citizens and members from the full forces of the sub-structure: what might be called a third way. However, in the concentric layers of society, the international ones differed from the World Bank in the one extreme to UNESCO not quite diametrically opposing it, but at least generating fundamentally different forces as a result of its policies. OECD and the EU exercised considerable force upon member states but states themselves differed not only as a result of the political hue to their governments but initially, as a result of their past responses to the neo-liberal pressures of the 1980s. These differences are to be found in national policy documents and in the laws and educational initiatives of individual countries. On the other hand, some non-governmental agencies have endeavoured to divert these sub-structural forces the most, although others are much more supportive of the current trends.

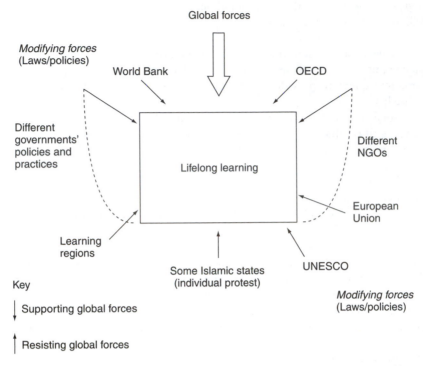

Global forces

Modifying forces
(Laws/policies)

World Bank

OECD

Different
governments'
policies and
practices

Different
NGOs

Lifelong learning

European
Union

Learning
regions

Some Islamic states
(individual protest)

UNESCO

Key

Modifying forces
(Laws/policies)

Supporting global forces

Resisting global forces

Figure 2.2 Forces national institutions in the social context in a globalising world.

It is clear from Figure 2.2 that lifelong education is never neutral and it always occurs within a socio-economic and political context. Among other things, it is clearly a moral process but acting within a world in which the morality is often downplayed.[6]

Having undertaken a brief survey of the way that different agencies and governments have responded to the socio-economic forces emanating from the global sub-structure, it is clear that any lifelong policies or recommendations must be seen at least within both an ethical and a political framework. But it is also a question of religion. Addressing the question of the greater part of the world's population living in miserable conditions, Habermas (2006, p. 167) makes the following point:

> Just imagine for a moment that the G-7 states were to assume global responsibility and agree on policies that met John Rawls' ... second principle of justice: 'social and economic inequalities are to be arranged so that it can reasonably be expected to be of the greatest benefit to the disadvantaged.' To be sure, the unjust distribution of the benefits of good fortune has always been a central preoccupation of the major world religions. But in secularized society, this problem must first be placed on the political and

economic table, not shoved in the cupboard of morality, let alone moral theory.

At the same time, it is a religious question – but it is also economic, political, moral and educational and to focus on just one dimension, as economists have tended to do, is to do a disservice to the wider debate, so that it is the hope that in the following chapters of this book we might touch upon some of the issues of the wider debate when we ask what type of learning society do we need if we are to address some of the problems that we have highlighted in the previous chapters of this trilogy. But before we do this, it is necessary to understand the values of modernity and then we can turn to the processes by which capitalism makes itself indispensable to the people.

Chapter 3

The spirit and values of modernity

Some forms of lifelong learning and the learning society are the result of new forms of commodity production and global economic systems: they are features of the so-called post-modern or late modern world which is a more reflective approach to the modern period, although education really developed during the rise of modernity. However, this globalised world is still basically a form of modernity and in order to fully understand it, this third chapter explores the spirit and values of modernity. Modernity itself is said to have begun with the disappearance of pro-modern societies and is typified by a capitalist economic system, industrial production, the rise of the democratic nation state, the emergence of rationality and a growing individualisation of social structures. Hamilton (1992, pp. 21–22) suggested that modernity has ten features: reason, empiricism, science, universalism, progress, individualism, toleration, freedom, uniformity of human nature and secularism. Such a classification is difficult because many of the categories overlap. Other scholars have made similar classifications. Nevertheless, the division between the pre-modern and the modern is not as clear cut as some commentators might have us believe and we will show in this chapter how the problems of pre-modern society prevail even today. But since we now talk of late modern, or post modern, we can begin to see that the process is not only on-going but undergoing considerable change at this time and this will be seen in the following pages.

However, in looking back to the past, if we continue to use a simple sub-structure/superstructure model of society, it might be claimed that over this period as sub-structure developed into the economic capitalist system, then the superstructures changed with it. Now, we have argued that the sub-structure is even more complex for contemporary society. The aim of this chapter is to demonstrate the changes that occurred and to show how economic and industrial capitalism emerged, and how the superstructural culture and values have developed. The chapter has three main sections: the development and utilisation of scientific knowledge; individualism and freedom; rationality and pragmatism, but we will also indicate some of their potential flaws in each section.

The development and utilisation of scientific and technological knowledge

At the heart of our diagram on globalisation and the shape of society lie the economic and technological institutions. Once humankind was free of the inhibiting effects of the power of the Church,[1] new forms of knowledge emerged – namely scientific and technological knowledge and with it the development of the Industrial Revolution. With the Industrial Revolution, mercantile capitalism was replaced by industrial capitalism and the free-market. As this developed, so it became necessary to introduce more education, not only to equip the work-force but also to control the young.[2] In this sense, mass education was part of the modernist project although this is a gross over-simplification as we will show below.

With the Industrial Revolution, new forms of knowledge began to appear and take root in society – the knowledge of the age was scientific and later technological knowledge which enabled new discoveries, new ways of production and, ultimately, new commodities for market. In this way, scientific and technological knowledge gained ascendancy over other forms of knowledge. Scheler (1980 [1926], p. 76) first addressed this problem when he postulated seven types of knowledge:

- Myth and legend – undifferentiated forms of preliminary knowledge;
- Implicit knowledge – that which is implicit in everyday language and everyday culture;
- Religious knowledge – various levels of fixation up to the fixed dogma of the established churches;
- Mystical knowledge;
- Philosophical and metaphysical;
- Positive knowledge of mathematics and the sciences;
- Technological knowledge.

We can clearly see a number of weaknesses in this typology, such as the omission of the humanities and social sciences, although the latter might be included within the sciences, and fact that some of the first four forms might easily be conflated. However, the strength in Scheler's formulation is the recognition that different forms of knowledge relate to different speeds of social and cultural change. In a world of slow movement, then it is possible for the first five forms of knowledge to survive and become embedded in the cultures of such societies, but as the speed of change increases, these forms of knowledge appear to become dated and new forms take their place: scientific and technological ones. While early forms of science and technology are to be found in ancient civilisations, the idea that they should predominate over religion and other belief systems is a much newer phenomenon. As we have already seen above, this leads to the world views embodied in these forms being displaced by new ones and established beliefs losing their potency. The age of modernity is clearly one of science and technology but we are faced with a major problem because we need to relate this knowledge to the concept of truth – how do we know that the knowledge is true? This is a problem to which we will return to below, since knowledge was traditionally legitimated by religion.

For Scheler, however, the fact that these latter forms of knowledge change rapidly suggested a form of artificiality: he (p. 76) actually suggested that they change 'hour by hour'. More slow moving forms of knowledge, however, can get embedded in society's cultures and they assume a greater sense of validity. Indeed, a great deal of early knowledge was legitimated by religious beliefs which pre-modern people attributed to an objective God. However, once that belief was questioned then the legitimation function lost its significance and such beliefs became regarded as out of date, and to some extent we can see that this is true for all of Scheler's first five forms of knowledge. One of the results of this has been that for many believers, but not all by any means, the text itself became its own legitimation in textual fundamentalism (biblical or Koranic) or in the pronouncements of the religious communities: knowledge is still regarded as revealed and this has isolated it from more scientific approaches to the legitimation of knowledge.

However, with the rapid growth of knowledge, new disciplines were born and quickly developed, many of them emphasising the values of the age, such as individuality and rationality: this new knowledge was naturally legitimated by the values of the age – rationality, empiricism and pragmatism. Knowledge is true, if:

- it can be legitimated by a rational argument built upon solid premises;
- it is based on empirical facts – demonstrated by scientific research;
- it is pragmatic, that is if it can be shown to work technologically.

But no fact has meaning and so empirical facts have to be given theoretical interpretation – meaning is not scientific but is based upon beliefs, many of which may be well-founded in an extensive body of knowledge and stand a very good chance of being valid. But there is always the chance that it may be false. However, scientific interpretations are seen to be the most legitimate way of interpreting facts in the modern world and other disciplines have to approximate to this approach.

The humanities and social sciences have had to conform to this way of legitimating knowledge. We are actually seeing this in learning theory as the following sentences indicate: one approach to learning is behaviourism which looks for empirical outcomes of the learning process – learning is seen as instrumental since the outcomes of certain actions (called learning) result in specified outcomes; another is information processing since the learner takes in information, processes it and utilises the outcomes in specified ways, and so the brain is just like a computer. Once we approach learning this way, we can scan the way that the brain works with certain forms of electrical and chemical activity occurring when we think different thoughts, and so we can reduce learning to individual bodily processes and explain it 'scientifically', but not only is the reductionism to biology over-simple, the division between the individual and the group is artificial. All that the brain functioning reveals is that certain parts of it are functioning in respect to different thoughts but it does not tell us anything about the motives of the learner. In addition, individuals are not born in isolation nor do they have their first experiences alone: individuals are always individuals in a social context and learning always occurs within a social context, so that to locate learning entirely within the bounds of psychology is to fall into a modernist trap. Learning, when it involves the functioning of the body or the brain might well be 'pure' science and even psychology but this is never the whole story of any learning event since it is always about the whole person which is much more than the body and brain. People do have a brain but they also have a mind, and children are born in relationship within a primary group, so that in this sense learning is humanistic and multi-disciplinary or better still inter-disciplinary (see Jarvis, 2006; Jarvis and Parker, 2005). This misplaced designation of learning as something that falls totally within the preserve of psychology has been to the detriment of academic studies in learning but is a reflection of the trends of modernity.

However, as we have seen this misplacement is indicative of a far greater form of reductionism – the reduction of things human to scientific facts. Buber (1947, p. 97) made the point for biology, although it is true for all 'pure' science disciplines that:

> Every attempt to interpret human action in biological terms (however much one must remember biological existence when explaining man) is a trivialization; it is a poor simplification because it means the abandoning of the proper anthropological content, of that which constitutes the category man.

Biological reductionism is a contemporary fad although it does have some significant things to teach us but we are beginning to recognise that the disciplines themselves have constrained knowledge production: what Gibbons et al. (1994) called Mode 2 knowledge production is an example of this. In a sense, the production of this book is itself a critique of some aspects of modernity while remaining embedded in some of its constraints. Mode 2 knowledge production demands: transdisciplinarity; heterogeneity and organisational diversity; social accountability and reflexivity and quality control. That these authors have never stepped beyond the constraints of modernity is reflected in their fundamental thesis (Gibbons et al., 1994, p. 13) that: 'the parallel expansion in the number of potential knowledge producers on the supply side and the expansion of specialist knowledge on the demand side are creating the conditions for a new mode of knowledge production.' In a sense, the speed of change is such that the mechanisms of modernity cannot contain the demands of the market for new forms of knowledge production. Nevertheless, modernity is the age when scientific values reign and the individual rather than the group is the starting point for most academic discussions.

Individualism and freedom

These two elements of the modern world are closely interconnected and so they are discussed together in this part, although for heuristic purposes, they are treated separately within it.

Individualism

It is often suggested that individualism – liberalism – is associated with the rise of capitalism and reference is often made back to Weber (1930). However, social change does not always occur by epochs and there is often a long history (genealogy) behind the events and so it is with individualism: it is clear that the debate is far older than modernity and so we have to look back to earlier discussions. In the seventh century before Christ,[3] for instance, we find this assertion about individual responsibility: 'The fathers have eaten sour grapes, and the children's teeth are set on edge. But every one shall die for his own sin; every man who eats sour grapes, his teeth shall be set on edge' (Jeremiah 31 vv 29–30 – Holy Bible).[4] Individuals are responsible for their own actions: this is one of the earliest references in literature to individual responsibility. People are free to act in their own self-interest despite the group, but they have to take responsibility for their actions rather than putting that responsibility on the group. By contrast, in the book of Jeremiah in the Bible, we also see the other side of individualism – Jeremiah himself had to be an individualist in order to condemn the ways of the people. All people are responsible for their own actions, be they good or bad, and morality is based on individual action in relation to the group. But Jeremiah's individualism was not one detached from the traditions of his people (Anderson, 1958, p. 352) since he wanted to call the people back to their traditions so that they could build a New Community. Confucius' teaching shows the same concern for solidarity whereas Socrates' death was a demonstration of the significance of individualism. Hence, there is a degree of ambiguity here that was to pervade a great deal of thought about individualism – like all action it can be for good or bad depending on who exercises it or assesses it and in what context. This conclusion echoes Buber's (1947, p. 103) conclusion that 'Man is not good, man is not evil; he is, in a pre-eminent sense, good and evil together.' In the exercise of individuality one or the other is usually prevalent and individuals can take the responsibility for their actions.

But the complexity is compounded by the fact that if we start any analysis of human action from the liberal/individual position, then the persons choose their own values and actions but if we start from the perspective of society, then there is a premise of relationship and the binding tie may, but need not, inhibit individual action: it is the nature of the relationship that now becomes significant.[5] Individualism is not self-evidently good or bad and it is this complexity that affects both our understanding of social values. But, as educationalists, it is also important for us to understand how individuals learn their own values and we shall have to confront this problem as the study proceeds.

Nevertheless, when individuals seek to make financial gain through interactions at the expense of others, there is a sense in which they are always individualistic, acting on their own behalf rather than for the good of the whole. Herein lie the ideas of competition and the market: individuals compete and the successful come to the fore: 'the weak go to the wall': this is true of people as well as organisations! This is about cultural values whereas we will seek to distinguish between a universal ethic and relative cultural values in this study (see Jarvis, 1997), and we will return to it in Chapter 7. However, both the universal ethic and the relative values have been used at various times in history to condemn all forms of capitalist enterprise, but it was often the money-lender who was the specific object of such attention rather than the more powerful institutions such as the Church and the organisations that the Church used. Indeed Tawney (1926 [1938], p. 57) claims that the Church's scheme of economic ethics prior to the Protestant Reformation had a straight forward objective – 'to prevent the well-to-do money-lender from exploiting the necessities of the peasant or the craftsman' which was about personal morality. At the same time, however, the Church itself continued to amass wealth often at the expense of the poor.

With the advent of the Protestant Reformation individualism found a new major form of legitimation: the belief in individual salvation for those who believed that they were pre-destined to find their place in heaven. This doctrine of salvation was elitist but it was clear that in the doctrine those who were chosen did not know that they were and so they had to look for signs, and the sign that they looked for was wealth since, in the Book of Job in the Old Testament, God would reward his own.[6] Wealth then was the sign that the wealthy were predestined to heaven and in this sense it became its own legitimation since the ideas of the powerful always dominate a people. Weber points out that, elsewhere in the Old Testament, there were other messages but they were 'interpreted away' (Weber, 1930, p. 164).[7] For Weber, it was the individualism inherent in Calvinism that had a great affinity with capitalism. However, this belief could also be understood as a legitimation of the position of the wealthy rather than that they were predestined to be rich – unless they were children of the already wealthy! Calvin, however, was careful to combine this individualism with a belief in the institution. Tawney (1926 [1938], p. 120) suggested that:

> Calvin did for the *bourgeoisie* of the sixteenth century what Marx did for the proletariat of the nineteenth ... the doctrine of predestination satisfied the same hunger for an assurance that the forces of the universe are on the side of the elect.

Tawney (p. 121) goes on to point out that: 'The two main elements in this teaching were the insistence on personal responsibility, discipline, and asceticism, and the call to fashion for the Christian character an objective embodiment in social institutions.' Both individualism and Christian Socialism can be deduced from this position, as Tawney reminds us. Indeed, in Locke and Hume we also find a similar debate between the rights of the individual and the need for social contract. Individual responsibility for one's actions found considerable support in the Protestant Reformation and so, coupled with the demands of industrial capitalism it is not surprising that there was little or no opposition to the ideas of the division of labour and the subsequent changes in the structure of society: in Durkheim (1933) the change from mechanical to organic solidarity, and from organic solidarity to contractual solidarity. It is in this latter form that individualism and the need to relate through contracts become significant. But Durkheim (1933, p. 228) makes the significant point that:

> altruism is not destined to become ... a sort of agreeable ornament to social life, but it will forever be its fundamental basis. How can we ever dispense with it? Men cannot live together without acknowledging, and consequently, making mutual sacrifices without tying themselves to one another with strong durable bonds. Every society is a moral society. In certain respects, this character is even more pronounced in organized societies. Because the individual is not sufficient unto himself, it is from society that he receives everything that is necessary to him, as it is for society that he works. Thus is formed a very strong sentiment of the state of dependence in which he finds himself. He becomes accustomed to estimating it at its just value, that is to say, in regarding himself as part of a whole, the organ of an organism.

Durkheim's position led to his functionalist sociology for which he has been criticised by those who start from a more individualistic perspective but such criticism does not negate either his emphasis on the individual nor his moral claims about individualism. In the same way that Durkheim was concerned with structural changes so was Toennies (1957) when he focused on community and association. But increasingly we find that the association is coming to mean that people are seen as individuals who associate with each other. Indeed, at the heart of Mill's (1910, pp. 115–116) writing on liberalism, we find his ideas on individualism – citing von Humboldt's *The Sphere and Duties of Government*, he wrote:

'the end of man, or that which is prescribed by the eternal or immutable dictates of reason, and not suggested by vague and transient desires, is the highest and most harmonious development of his powers to a complete and consistent whole;' that, therefore, the object 'towards which every man must ceaselessly direct his efforts, and on which especially those who design to influence their fellow-men must ever keep their eyes, is individuality of power and development:' that for this there are two requisites, 'freedom, and a variety of situations;' and that from the union of these arise 'individual vigour and manifold diversity', which combine themselves in originality.

In liberalism, we find the individual assuming priority over the group rather than the group being prior to the individual: herein lies the crux of much of the following debate both political and moral. Indeed, without freedom, claimed Mill, but not without his critics (Berlin, 1991 [1969] *inter alia*), society would be crushed by collective mediocrity; or as Hayek (1944) put it we would be on *The Road to Serfdom*. Such mediocrity is often manifest in bureaucracies! However, a holistic communitarian approach to society does not destroy the possibility of human freedom. But contemporary society is more than an individualistic society in the sense that Mill wished it to become, but it has become a neo-liberal economic society in which individualism is both praised (Hayek, 1944; Nozick, 1974) and curtailed without the apparent loss of freedom by the exercise of covert economic and political power – a point to which we will return in the following chapters. At the same time, Mill's view of individualism does reflect the long debate to which we have already referred above in which individuals seek to develop themselves in a social situation and in so doing they incur moral obligations.

But the moral obligations may actually indicate that it is impossible to argue for a totally individualistic position and Buber's (1947, pp. 60–108) analysis of Kierkegaard's 'single one' demonstrates this most clearly: perhaps even Kierkegaard recognised this when he wrote in his journal 'Had I had faith, I would have stayed with Regina' (cited in Buber, 1947, p. 79).

Individualism is an ideological position that has been legitimated by religion and by other thinkers but also opposed by religious and other thinkers. It is an ambiguous ideology, as we noted from the fact that Jeremiah had to be an individual to call the people back to their traditions. But individualism has, as Durkheim and Toennies showed, become a structural phenomenon and perhaps this ambiguity is to be found most clearly in America – the country to which the Puritans went in order to find the freedom to practise their own religion, and where it 'lies at the very core of American culture' (Bellah *et al.*, 1985, p. 142). Bellah *et al.* have noted how modern individualism 'has pursued individual rights and individual autonomy in ever new realms' (p. 143) in which it has been confronted by opposing forces of individual dignity and other biblical traditions. Indeed, they also note that the popular American hero who seeks only to serve society: the lone ranger' and the 'hard-bitten detective' – individuals standing alone for what is right. Here we see the ambiguity present in individualistic thought since the time of Jeremiah!

However, following Tocqueville, they point to another feature of individualism, one to which we will return in a future chapter of this book, that one of the central ambiguities of individualism is that it is compatible with conformity:

> Middle-class individuals are thus motivated to enter a highly autonomous and demanding quest for achievement and then left with no standards against which achievement can be measured except the income and consumption levels of their neighbours, exhibiting anew the clash between autonomy and conformity that seems to be the fate of American individualism.
>
> (p. 149)

They recognise that there are limits to individualism but it is one that underscores flaws in the modernity project. But the findings of this study are re-echoed in Robert Putnam's (2000) *Bowling Alone* in which he documents the decline in community life in the USA. This book has rung bells throughout Western civilisation – it was published at a time when the problems of individualism were just beginning to be recognised and studies on such topics as social capital were just beginning to appear. In a sense, this recognition is a sign of the failure of individualism per se: an implicit criticism of the Enlightenment.[8] But as the beginnings of individualism, like the beginnings of capitalism itself, are shrouded in the pre-history of the relationship between the individual and society it would be over-simple to blame modernity alone for it – although it would be true to say that capitalism has embraced it and that global capitalism has certainly traded on it since it has enabled money to become the standard by which individual achievement is measured and in this sense it is, as Goodchild (2002) argued and Marx claimed before him, that capitalism is the modern religion.

Yet it is at this very point that some of the social problems implicit in individualism come to the fore since an agglomeration of individuals cannot provide itself with a binding moral law and so it is recognised again that there is a need for some form of rule, for the group, the community, or the people. However, there have been relatively few scholars, Keddie (1980) being a notable exception, in adult education who have criticised this liberal position. It is significant that at this time and in lifelong learning and the learning society that the concept of social capital has come to the fore (Baron *et al.*, 2000). Much debate surrounds the term but I do not wish to go into this here; what is significant, however, is that the idea that there is no such thing as society, frequently cited by Mrs Thatcher when she was Prime Minister of the UK, merely illustrates a neo-liberal myth since society had merely changed. Social capital points us back to the fact that individuals cannot survive in splendid isolation –

we all need each other and once we have community, in whatever form, we re-engage with those forces that seek to weaken it.

That there has been recognition of the need for community has given rise to considerable re-emergence of utopian thinking (see Jarvis, 2007b, Appendix). Utopian thinking, looking to the perfect New Jerusalem – be it the City of God or the City of Man – underlies our aims for the creation of a just learning society: an end-product which may appear to be an impossible dream within the bounds of rationality, humanity and time. But recognition that utopia is impossible within the bounds of time does not prevent us from working towards a better world, nor can it inhibit our freedom of choice be it for our own or other people's benefit. If the former, then it also means that we are free to seek to enrich ourselves at the risk of other people's negative freedoms which constitutes the problem of moral choice and capitalism but if the later, it means that we voluntarily lay down our own freedom for the sake of the other. Underlying all of this discussion is the question of the ultimate ends of humanity and the belief and value systems upon which we, as individuals, decide to act.

Freedom

There are at least three issues in any discussion about individual freedom: that individuals have a right to be free, that they are free to choose and, finally, when they have freedom do they actually want it. The first is a political question, the second philosophical and the final one psychological.

That individuals have a right to be free is grounded in the idea of liberalism itself – simply by being human one has the right to be free. Liberalism is based upon the individual being free to act individually and without reference to the group – a viewpoint that neglects the rights of the group, as we will see below. In addition, such a doctrine totally downplays the idea that individuals have duties to others as well as to themselves. That individuals are free to choose, that the market is also free allowing for free-choice, free to act against the best interests of the whole group in order to achieve what they consider to be their own best interests seems to be an indisputable fact so that we have no intention here of arguing the philosophical case for free-will, although we shall be forced to recognise it in this study and argue that people are also free to act in the best interests of the whole – or at least the Other. However, this debate is, like the others we have encountered in this chapter, shrouded in pre-history. About a century before Jeremiah's recognition of the problems of individualism, we find another story in which the author tried to account for human freedom. Written in the ninth century before Christ,[9] the story of Adam and Eve (Genesis 3 – Holy Bible) is a philosophical story in which the author is trying to explain why individuals are free to contravene the will of God, and the answer appeared to be that because God gave them free will they were tempted to use it and 'fell from grace'. Archbishop William

Temple, however, suggested that if this was a fall, then it was a fall upwards (see Jarvis, 1992) since human beings had learned to learn (Jarvis, 1992). Learning is itself either a constructive and/or potentially a subversive activity and people are free to learn – it is fundamental to our humanity, as we argued in the first volume of this trilogy (Jarvis, 2006) but like our humanity itself it is a paradoxical phenomenon. Habermas (2006, p. 162) writes most insightfully about this myth:

> In order to confirm his own freedom through an alter ego, God must set limits to this very freedom. Thus he equips Adam … with the unconditional freedom of good and evil, and thereby accepts that Adam may make the wrong use of this gift by sinning and dragging the whole of ideal creation down with him into the abyss. He would thus topple God from his throne. As we know, this 'worse case scenario' is precisely what happened. The story solves the problem of theodicy, but at the cost of inaugurating a new world era, the age of world history, by this terrible act of freedom. In the second age, a humbled God must await redemption, because humanity has taken upon itself the burden of resurrecting human nature.

However, freedom has always been a problematic concept and, as Berlin (1991 [1969], p. 129) remarks, 'it was absent from the legal conceptions of Romans and Greeks; this seems to hold equally of the Jewish, Chinese, and all other ancient civilizations that have come to light'. However, as we have pointed out, the Jews were concerned about this in religious terms from very early on and they did develop a sophisticated religious philosophy about it, but the political and legal formulation has always been much weaker.

Clearly, the fact that human beings have always had the ability to act individually and in their own perceived best interests rather than in the interests of the group, indicates the fact that human beings are free. It was Kant (1997, p. 53), however, who linked this freedom with morality when he argued that 'free will and a will under moral laws are one and the same' when exercised by rational human beings. Perhaps that, in this approach to rationality, we are faced with one of the fundamental problems of our thinking about humanity since we do not always equate free will and a will under moral laws, nor are we always rational! For him, however, the determinate concept of morality can be traced back to freedom (p. 54). The moral imperative of this freedom lies in reason itself: human persons are members both of this world of reason but they are also members of the world of senses. It is in the former that Kant locates both will and freedom while desires and inclinations are to be located in the latter one. It is by the exercise of the will that individuals can overcome their desires – they are free so to do. In discussing reason in this way, Kant was pointing to human learning. Berlin (1991 [1969], p. 138), in a similar approach to this argument wrote:

Kant's free individual is a transcendent being, beyond the bounds of natural causality. But in its empirical form – in which the notion of man is that of ordinary life – this doctrine is at the heart of liberal humanism, both moral and political.... In its *a priori* version it is a form of secularized Protestant individualism, in which the place of God is taken by the conception of the rational life, and the place of the individual soul which strains for union with Him is replaced by the conception of the individual, endowed with reason, straining to be governed by reason and reason alone, and to depend upon nothing that might deflect or delude him by engaging his irrational nature.

In this argument religion is now replaced not by money but by reason and, so, now ultimately, reason is god – but the problem with this is that it provides no benchmark to measure achievement and no answer to the problems of meaning – not even penultimate ones! Consequently, not only the ends but also the means of achievement have to be set by those who have the power to do so – which, in many ways, is now a political power, but also influenced by economic power.

For Berlin, like Kant (1997), there are two types of freedom: a negative one and a positive one. The former concerns the area of a person's life that 'should be left to do or be what he is able to do without interference by other persons' (Berlin, 1991 [1969], pp. 121–122). Hence, it is possible to argue for a minimal state. This is our desire, even our right as human beings, and to be coerced is to lose our freedom. By contrast, positive freedom is about the individual wishing 'to be the instrument of ... (his or her)..., not other men's, acts of will' (p. 131). Basically, this is that individuals wish to be the masters of their own destiny – 'to be the subject, not an object; to be moved by reasons, by conscious purposes, which are my own, not by causes which affect me, as it were, from outside' (p. 131), but in order to do this, they have to have to have the power of self-control. As Berlin was aware, these two approaches to freedom are quite close to each other but, in the last resort, the difference points to differences in our conception of humanity itself: we can only fulfil our potential, so the argument would run, if we are free to do so. This, then, is the ambiguity we traced back to Jeremiah's announcement that people were to be punished for their own acts rather than the whole family, but in order to make that enunciation, he had to be positively free himself.

However, for some to exercise this positive freedom might well mean that others cannot even exercise their negative freedom! But this would not be so if that freedom were used wisely and morally within society through negotiation and other democratic approaches to social living – which is a form of a learning society, but it is in some way a voluntary loss of freedom and as we have known it does not often happen at societal level. Consequently, the exercise of positive freedom creates moral dilemmas that need to be solved or else it results in the exercise of power over others who therefore lose even their negative freedom.

This is one of the problems of modernity itself since the idea that everybody is free is non-sustainable in social living. But those who exercise their positive freedom over others can still declare that people are free and, in their hearts people do know that they can act against those powerful forces if they are prepared to take the risk – people who are enslaved within a system can still declare themselves free and feel that they are free if they want to be – but some, like Fromm (1942) have argued that people fear freedom. This led Berlin (p. 165), among others, to claim that no power can be absolute, this can only belong to rights and that there are inviolable frontiers defined in terms of rules beyond which the normal human being should be protected. But what legitimates this? That the exercise of positive freedom by everyone is impossible is perhaps one of the clearest conclusions that can be dawn from this discussion and the respect of all other persons – respecting their negative and positive freedoms where possible – lies at the heart of ethics and political justice.

Earlier, however, we pointed to the ambiguity of the free individual with reference to the prophet,[10] Jeremiah: indeed the complexity of the human problem of both the need to be free and the need to be a member of social groupings lies at the heart of human living. Inclusion is not a matter of being included in a monolithic enterprise – Durkheim's mechanical solidarity – but being involved in a contractual-type relationship – a social contract. However, there are dangers of conformity to the over-arching culture without reflective thought and these are stagnation and ineptitude, among others. In contrast, one of the features of late modernity, drawn out very clearly by Beck (1994, p. 14) is that:

> individualization means the disintegration of the certainties of industrial society as well as the compulsion to find and invent new certainties for oneself and others without them. But it also means new interdependencies, even global ones. Individualization and globalization are in fact two sides of the same process of reflexive modernization.

The obvious outcome of reflexive modernisation is the learning society. Individuals have to be free to think and to learn for themselves – to construct their own biography. Consequently individuals have to be free to break away from the dominant sub-culture and to act independently: to think and act independently, however, produces a multitude of different roles, such as innovator, leader, entrepreneur, moneylender, deviant and criminal. Significantly, to be an individual in one group does not necessarily excommunicate the individual from that group, and even where it does individuals are members of other groups in society in which they may play a more conformist role. In this sense, we see that autonomy can be exercised within the wider society while there is a sense of feeling free, acting individually and conforming to the whole. Society is much more open and individuals much more flexible.

However, in past generations deviants were condemned and very often excommunicated, or as Douglas (1970) points out, they were considered unclean and had to be located outside of the normal.[11] In this sense, those who are socially excluded are often excluded because they threaten the taking-for-granted of people's life worlds. Beck (1998, p. 125) writes:

> the *stranger breaks open from the inside the established categories and stereotypes of the local world (the world of locals)*. Strangers do not fit into any of the neat containers that they are supposed to fit into, and therein lies an extreme irritation. To put it another way, strangers are those who actually should be excluded according to the stereotypes of social order.
>
> (*Italics* in original)

In other words, we are unsure of the unfamiliar and so we ignore or exclude it – in bygone ages we labelled it unclear or made people outcastes. Levinas (1991 [1969]) focuses on the stranger as we noted in the Appendix to the second volume of this study (Jarvis, 2007b). Strangerhood is socially created: strangers are not outside of our society but they are within, part of it, but deviants to the norm – even leaders. When people are excluded they are free but they cannot be controlled, even controlled in their freedom!

Beck (1998, p. 82) suggests that it is this tradition of freedom that is the social cement that holds society together, but this is a dubious claim since the possibility of freedom must allow the freedom to destroy as well as to construct. Freedom in itself cannot be the social cement, but the way that people behave and the values that emerge in the space between people are not only those of hate and violence, as Beck suggests, but they are also being responsible for our own freedom and the mutuality of love, care, concern and respect that emerges between people in social groups.

But by the very nature of human learning (Jarvis, 2006) is an individualistic enterprise that is fundamental to our humanity. At the same time, society needs free people if it is to change or develop in any manner – mechanical society is unchanging and inept in contemporary society. Society needs people who will keep on learning and acting independently but doing so for the good of the whole group, it needs independent learners who will take the risk of following the results of their own learning. Learning and acting upon that learning is always a risk-taking business. Consequently, the modern learning society is one that is prepared to jettison the traditions in the face of new knowledge and so it is a post-traditional society, since people are learning in ever changing social situations. But there is another significant point here: even the conformist learns and chooses to be a follower, but the learning may have not been reflective or analytical or based on sufficient knowledge and expertise, and so on. Sometimes, acknowledgement of not knowing and therefore conforming might be a wise and individual decision. In this sense, this type of analysis potentially leads to an egoistical type of society – one in which the highest good is perceived to be the pursuit of self-interest and welfare. Yet a further paradox is to be discovered in the fact that even in pursuing their self-interest there are times when bonds begin to emerge between individuals who act together, work together and think together, so that social groups are inter-individualistic, although once there are bonds, there is a sense of compulsion, obligation or responsibility. Paradoxically, this gets us back to a position whereby we can see that individuals have to learn to conform.

While human beings have always fought to be free of the claustrophobic ethos of the tight community, this does not mean that they have always sought total freedom. Fromm (1942, p. 15) makes the point that '(t)o feel completely alone and isolated leads to mental disintegration just as physical starvation leads to death'. Fromm suggests that human beings need to cooperate with others and we need to feel part of creation, and so we need to relate to an understandable part of it – like the human group. Isolation and the powerlessness that accompanies it are contrary to our human being and yet in our learning and maturing, we cultivate our individuality.

Since learning is a process of individualising and freeing the individual, we are always responsible for our own learning and our own actions and in this sense we are always entering the unknown where, whether we like it or not, we are always confronted with the fact that what we are to do is not always self-evident. Indeed, it is not necessarily obvious how we choose to act in a good manner since it is not always rational or common sense, so that we are forced to ask questions about the extent to which freedom is necessarily always good or desirable.

Consequently, we are already beginning to see that these basic values of modernity do not provide answers to the problems of human living: it is impossible for all human beings to be individually free without there being the chaos that Locke envisaged, but within modernity there is nobody to lay down the rules apart from those who have or achieve power – power to curtail that individual freedom. Power, as we have already suggested has many bases, including both the economic and the political – but once we recognise this, we can see that both political and economic power can deny people their individual freedoms in a wide variety of ways which points us to flaws in the modernity project.

Rationality and pragmatism

Among the other bases of the modernity project is reason and so we will start this section with a discussion of rationality and, thereafter, briefly return to the ideas of pragmatism.

Rationality

As the above discussion illustrates, the idea of revealed knowledge began to disappear from the Enlightenment onwards as scientific knowledge was discovered, and this was accompanied by a growth in rational thinking. Indeed, among the thinkers to whom we have already referred above were those who were to become known as the rationalists and others as empiricists: they believed that it is possible by reason alone to acquire knowledge of all that exists since everything is capable of being explained. This, however, is itself a belief that has yet to be proven; indeed, the need to separate demonstrable knowledge and belief is fundamental to our understanding of contemporary society. Knowledge has now received new forms of legitimation by reason or by empirical evidence – later pragmatism was to be added to these two – but religious belief was no longer regarded as rational and religion had no power to legitimate knowledge. Basically, rationalism has come to mean, first, a rejection of religious belief because it apparently has no rational foundation although it cannot be denied that many religious philosophers of all ages have utilised rational argument; second, just a commitment to reason itself, but by utilising this meaning rationality does not actually destroy the grounds of belief systems; third, an emphasis on scientific knowledge, and it is this that also leads us into the significance of technology. At the same time, any learning society needs to be grounded in rationality but perhaps more in human experience and so we have to recognise that human learning must be grounded in experience as much as in rationality. One significant fact must be made at this point, and that is, that it is instrumental rationality that has come to dominate the rationality debate but there are other forms of rationality, one being value rationality, which stem from the writings of Max Weber. As we will show in later chapters, the adoption of values is not a mindless enterprise and that the adoption of values, especially ethical values, is a reasoned exercise. Hence one of the bases of this study is that value rationality is fundamental to human living but it has been neglected since the dominant ideology demands instrumental rationality. But, like all the other concepts referred to in this chapter there have been a multitude of books written on the topic of rationality (see, for instance, Brown, 1988; Habermas, 1971; Nozick, 1993; Wilson, 1970, *inter alia*). However, if there are at least two forms of rationality – instrumental and value rationality, there is no certainty at all that two rational people thinking about the same problem will reach the same conclusions – especially if one utilises instrumental rationality and the other value rationality. Consequently, rationality leads to pluralism rather than uniformity. However, the more instrumental rationality and power prevail in a society under the guise of rationality, the more uniformity is likely to occur.

This was recognised by Simmel, as early as 1903, since he realised the significance of the money economy on life style and even on thinking itself: he claimed that as a result of it people have become more calculative (Simmel, 1971 [1903], pp. 82–93; 1978 [1907], pp. 443–446) and act with their head rather than their heart.

> The modern metropolis ... is supplied almost entirely by production for the market, that is, for entirely unknown purchasers who never personally enter the producer's field of vision. Through this anonymity the interests of each

party acquire unmerciful matter-of-factness; and the intellectually calculating economic egoisms of both parties need not fear any deflection because of the imponderables of personal relationships. The money economy dominates the metropolis; it has displaced the last survivals of domestic production and the direct barter for goods.

(Simmel, 1971 [1903], p. 85)

We live in an impersonal society, so the claim goes, one in which we are calculating and take for granted our own economic gain: action is instrumental. We are free to make our own rational choice, as individuals became the basis of liberalism. If we find that we do make gains in this way, then we repeat our actions – we act according to the probability of success (Heller, 1984, pp. 166–172). It is both pragmatic and common sense in this world! Yet in my own early studies (Jarvis, 1980) on superstition, I failed to find anybody in a wide ranging sample of people who were not superstitious which demonstrates that the modern period had not resulted in the eradication of irrational beliefs. Indeed, Handy (1989) also pointed out that the concept was not without its problems! Indeed, human beings are not totally rational or logical – they are not computers – and herein lies another flaw in the modernity project.

However, the second meaning of the term has come to be mean, 'common sense', in this educated society. It makes sense to act according to reason, and to seek to achieve its aims appears to be common sense: in this sense it approaches both later versions of utilitarianism and pragmatism.

Utilitarianism, as formulated by Bentham (1789) in its original ethical meaning saw utility as the foundation of ethics and its object was to promote the greatest happiness for the greatest number. This was a quantitative approach to happiness, in as far as it could be, but it was developed further by Mill (1910) to include the quality of happiness. But why should happiness be an end and not wealth or health? There is no rational reason why happiness should precede health or wealth. Perhaps an objective of all our actions might be to enhance our wealth so that it will make us happy – but wealth does not automatically produce happiness so that it is not rational to make such a claim. A wide variety of forms of utilitarianism have emerged since Bentham's day, such as act utilitarianism and rule utilitarianism (Frankena, 1963) and more recently to preference utilitarianism (Sprigge, 1988, p. 23) which 'provides people with what they would prefer to have and prevents their having what they would prefer not to have'. However, why should preference be the object of all our actions? This is fundamentally ego-centric and is contrary to Bentham's idea that utility should result in the greatest happiness for the greatest number of people. In fact either utilitarianism smacks of intuitionism – something that is anathema to the rational basis of utilitarianism itself – or in this guise it is ego-centric. In precisely this manner, games theory is maximising self-interest.

It might therefore be argued that the acquisition of more wealth as the end-product of utilitarianism is ego-centric by definition: it will be recalled that we defined capitalism as 'economic action ... which rests on the expectation of profit by the utilization of opportunities for exchange that is on (formally) peaceful chances of profit'. There is no way in which we can claim that all capitalism is rationally based on good actions. Indeed, we can see that it cannot be proven that it is a rational, let alone the most rational, way of life – but we might want to argue that at least it is pragmatic. Nevertheless, we might well want to argue that it contains within it the most rational way to utilise resources and to distribute the commodities produced.

Pragmatism

We have seen above how pragmatism has been in some ways equated with utilitarian rationality – if it works it is legitimate – but pragmatism is actually a much more sophisticated philosophy than this. James, in his lectures of 1906 and 1907 on *Pragmatism* (James, 2000, p. 25) argued that pragmatism is 'primarily a method of settling metaphysical disputes that otherwise might be interminable'. It is a method that seeks to trace the practical consequences of beliefs and while pragmatism is certainly not an ethical system, in his fourth lecture he returns to the problem on which this chapter concentrates – the one and the many. Second, it is a theory of truth. James (2000, p. 32) makes the point that a new theory is 'true' 'in proportion as it gratifies the individual's desire to assimilate the novel experience to his beliefs in stock'; that is, it is true by the way that it works. However, when beliefs clash he (p. 39) says that 'the greatest enemy of any of our truths may be the rest of our truths'. Third, pragmatism is relative to whatever the prevailing beliefs and ideologies hold and, in this sense, it also relates closely to common sense. Pragmatism, then, is a means of reconciling beliefs but it does not provide us with a means, other than self-satisfaction, of deciding upon the truth of differing beliefs and ideas since it has 'no prejudices whatever, no obstructive dogmas, no rigid canons as what shall count as proof' (p. 39).

However, common sense is itself a relative concept: it is common sense because it seems to fit into our system of beliefs and practices – our taken-for-granted world. But if we live in a world where religion dominates, then it would appear common sense for our actions to conform to this system, as it would in our accepting of new ideas and ideologies. But we are socialised into the dominant culture of our capitalist society, a point to which we will return in subsequent chapters and so we take the values of this form of society for granted – as common sense – although we will want to question their validity at that point.

Conclusion

In this chapter we have briefly discussed some of the cultural values and beliefs embedded in modernity: we have seen that they are relative to society and that they have undermined traditional knowledge, beliefs and ethical values. However, the significance of this discussion for human learning is immense: learning is an individual act, even when we learn in a group or in a class. We all bring our own biographies to the learning experience and while we may be exposed to similar situations and experiences, they cannot be identical. Consequently, we may all reach different conclusions: learning is an individuating phenomenon and as we go through life so we learn to be individuals. This is even more so, if we are enabled to practise reflective learning in either a critical or a creative manner: we will grow in our individuality, and as society's structures changed from mechanistic to organic to contractual, so people's experiences were not only more individual, their individuality developed. But even their individuality had to be controlled by codes of conduct, dress, forms of behaviour, and so on. But society still needed people to be individuals and to play their part as active citizens in society – individuality and the freedom that accompanied it was necessary to the development of the society.

But that freedom had to be controlled and individuals had to learn to recognise their place in society and so education, the social institution of learning, was introduced in the nineteenth century. In a most insightful way Rose (1999, pp. 69ff.) argues that schooling was introduced not to limit freedom but to educate people in the art of being free in a socially acceptable way and to regulate it in ways that make it useful to society.

> Simultaneously, the worker has to be individualized: freed from collective bonds through laws against combinations and collective action. Once the worker has been individualized and wage labour generalized, the dull combination of the labour market would combine with the disciplinary organization of time, space and activity in the factory, mill or mine to produce the forms of life and the modes of individuality in which docile and utilizable labour would present itself at the work place 'of its own free will'.
>
> (Rose, 1999, p. 70)

Education, therefore, became the responsibility of the state. By introducing this form of education individual freedom could be cultivated in a rational way in a socially acceptable manner. But it could also be contained!

Consequently, individual freedom was a foundational principle of liberal education since it allowed for, and encouraged, individuality within the social framework, but for the many, that freedom was very highly regulated. Nevertheless, it was still possible to be an individual and step outside of the routines of society and be innovative or creative, and so on. Indeed, the neo-liberals of the latter half of the twentieth century whose position was typified by Hayek (1979, p. 152 – cited from Rose, 1999, p. 63) claimed this:

> The only moral principle which has ever made the growth of an advanced civilization possible was the principle of individual freedom ... No principles of collective conduct which binds the individual can exist in a society of free men.

While we can understand fully Hayek's position, we have to recognise that his conception of freedom needs careful examination and he is wrong, as I believe we have shown above, in his failure to recognise the human need for relationship and upon his emphasis on 'the only moral principle'. Levinas (1991 [1969]) suggests that we actually need the Other in a teaching and learning relationship in order to reach towards infinity (see Jarvis, 2007b, Appendix) – but we will return to this discussion later when we look at lifelong learning and the learning society. The major issue here, however, is the way in which learning and schooling play major roles in the development of individuality and creativity, but also necessary in the development of rationality and in late modern society we need to re-conceptualise our basis for learning and education based upon our understanding of the significance of society as a whole.

While human beings' own quest for knowledge demands that they keep on learning, we will see in the next chapter that learning is channelled in a specific direction by capitalism, which has fuelled the need to gain new scientific and technological knowledge and has also created a rapidly changing society that demands that people continue to learn to keep abreast of change.

Chapter 4

Capitalism and society

While capitalism embodies many of the values of modernity, it would be true to say that it emerged long before the modern period and we can trace at least three different types of capitalism: mercantile, industrial and global. Each has embodied many of the same values and generated similar concerns among both those who have political and religious power and those moralists, and it has done so because it is potentially a divisive system in a social world: it separates the individual from the group/community and generates individualistic rather than communitarian aims and aspirations.

Capitalism itself was described very simply by Weber (1930, p. 17) as 'the pursuit of profit, and forever *renewed* profit, by means of continuous, rational, capitalistic enterprise'. However, even this simple description is tautologous; he actually went on in the same page to define it as 'economic action … which rests on the expectation of profit by the utilization of opportunities for exchange that is on (formally) peaceful chances of profit'. The nature of peacefulness is perhaps quite fundamental to the growth of global capitalism over the last half of the twentieth century. Abercrombie *et al.* (2000, p. 37) suggest that capitalism has the following five features:

- private ownership and control of the economic instruments of production;
- economic activity geared to making profits;
- a market framework that regulates this activity;
- the appropriation of profit by the owners – subject to taxation by the state;
- the provision of labour by the workers, who are free agents.

The *Concise Oxford English Dictionary* offers three definitions:

- an economic system in which the production and distribution of goods depend on invested private capital and profit making;
- the possession of capital or wealth;
- the dominance of private owners of capital and production for profit.

In a broad sense, these approaches agree about the nature of capitalism and it is clear that the emergence of industrial production capitalism was very much dependent on the Industrial Revolution – which some scholars see as being basic to the development of modernity. Hence industrial capitalism utilises scientific knowledge but its success also depends upon a number of other values such as individualism, freedom, financial rewards for successful undertakings often of an innovative nature, competition and even a potential ethic of service. It is an ideology of pre-modernity as well as a practice of industrial modernity. Many of these other values will be discussed in the following pages, but since this is a study of learning and the learning society rather than about capitalism per se it is only undertaken so that we can see the context within which the present learning society has emerged.

In order to see the way in which it has divided society we will briefly look at each of the three phases of capitalist development and so the chapter has three parts: in the first, we will look at the relationship between mercantile capitalism and religion; in the second, we will discuss the rise of industrial capitalism and with it the decline of the significance of institutional religion and its partial replacement by the state in seeking to regulate the market; finally, we will look at the emergence of global capitalism and the decline in the power of the state to regulate it.

Mercantile capitalism and religion

From the Weberian perspective, capitalism is no new phenomenon and the gaining of excessive economic reward at the expense of others has always been open to moral criticism. For instance, from the eighth century before the Christian era traders were entering and leaving China through the port of Macao bringing their wares into Europe and the Middle East through Palestine; this trade was making immense profits for the traders and we find condemnation of their excessive wealth at this time in the Bible – wealth was to some extent a sign of individuality, of difference from the people as a whole and gained at the expense of the people.[1] In the Book of Amos[2] we find this passage:

> Woe to those who are at ease in Zion,
> and to those who feel secure in the mount of Samaria,
> the notable men of the first of the nations,
> to whom the house of Israel come!
> ...
> Woe to those who lie in beds of ivory,
> and stretch themselves upon their couches,
> and eat lambs from the flock
> and calves from the midst of the stall;
> who sing idle songs...
>
> The Lord God has sworn by himself...
> I abhor the pride of Jacob, and hate his strongholds;
> And I will deliver up his city and all that is in it...

For behold, the Lord commands,
and the great house shall be smitten into fragments.
(from Amos 6 Revised Standard Version of the Bible)

A great deal of this prophetic book is a condemnation of the rich who enjoy such a sumptuous life-style as a result of the profits of mercantile capitalism. Long before Christianity emerged, this form of trade was a problem that prophets and other moral thinkers were forced to confront. Why should some individuals get richer at the expense of others? What gives them the right to do so? This moral condemnation of capitalism in the book of Amos is as ferocious as almost anywhere in literature and it was justified in the name of the God to whom the people believed that they were accountable. Economic activity carried to its extremes has always raised major questions for morality and first religion and later governments have endeavoured to control it, for running through this study is the paradox of individual and the group which is at the heart of a great deal of social morality.

The beginnings of capitalism may be lost in pre-history of trading and the idea of the gift relationship did not necessarily precede it, as some scholars have suggested, but perhaps it occurred in other cultural settings and it is still very significant in private relationships. We have no intention of trying to discover when making profit from trade began or in what cultures or at what time in history. What we do know, however, is that the relationship between all forms of trade and profit and religion[3] and morality has frequently been very tempestuous, so that the situation today is not entirely new. Since the Enlightenment, however, it has been the state rather than the church which has endeavoured to regulate capitalism. In the modern period there has been the apparent decline in the influence of institutional religion and with it some forms of moral debate about the merits of the capitalist system.

Capitalism, that is the making of profit through rational economic action, has taken a number of forms, such as trade, usury (loaning money at high interest rates), manufacture, profiting from land ownership and selling products for profit, is then possibly as old as civilisation itself and part of the problem has always been the idea of a minority gaining wealth at the expense of the wider community. Apart from the Bible, we find this discussion going on in Aristotle's writings, in the early Christian Church and certainly among the divines of the Holy Roman Empire. Capitalism's problematic relationship with moral systems, as the above quotation shows, is also extremely old. Indeed, Tawney (1926 [1938], p. 161) wrote:

The first act which strikes the modern student of this body of teaching is its continuity with the past. In its insistence that buying and selling, letting and hiring, lending and borrowing, are to be controlled by a moral law, of which the Church is guardian, religious opinion after the Reformation did not differ from religious opinion before it.

But as Tawney shows the relationship between capitalism and religion has not always been straight forward in Western society. For instance, in Calvinism we can find the seeds of both 'intense individualism and a rigorous Christian Social-ism' (Tawney, 1926 [1938], p. 121) – a combination of the one and the many: individualism being a matter of personal responsibility, discipline and asceticism, while the Christian character was to be embodied in social institutions such as the economy – in other words, support for individualistic economic enterprise and an ecclesiastical discipline that could control its activities and still look towards the establishment of a new Jerusalem on earth. In a sense, this was trying to hold together two opposing forces: the individualistic and the social, and yet both called for discipline and hard work. However, as Tawney points out, it was only individualism that found favour with the English upper classes in the seventeenth century but the asceticism of the Puritans was also to prevail – especially in the new country of America. Social change does not happen in a simple linear pro-gression as different powerful factions of society seek to impose their interests and interpretations of social reality on the remainder of the population and through-out Tawney's study we can see that how different interpretations of Christian ethics led to different approaches to the economic system. The relationship between the two was not always harmonious, but gradually the power of the Church waned since, as Tawney (1926 [1938], p. 163) points out, at the Reforma-tion, the Church effectively became an arm of the state and the strength of reli-gious sanction was weakened. Eventually, however, as the market freed itself from the Church the people were able to propound their own laws without divine sanction: Locke (1690 [1993, p. 193]) wrote, 'That God has given a rule whereby men should govern themselves, I think there is nobody so brutish as to deny. He has the right to do it...'.[4] But the significance of this quote is that it was not too long before those who assumed the new reigns of power had to seek authority for their own exercise of power and they had to turn to the people and movements for democracy began to emerge. In other words, God[5] was left out of the reckon-ing – God was murdered – and then resurrected in a different form:

> The meaning of the murder of God, that is the emergence of the secular world-view with a corresponding affirmation of atheism, is that God is no longer required to pay a foundational role in organizing humanity's activity in relation to reality. The murder of God therefore reflects a shift in pieties. God has stopped paying us our ordered existence: or rather, there is another god who pays us, who responds more immediately, directly and tangibly to our prayers: Mammon.
>
> (Goodchild, 2002, p. 27)

Industrial capitalism, the church and the state

Puritanism, as both Tawney (1926 [1938]) and Weber (1930) point out, was the driving force behind the Industrial Revolution and the ultimate power behind the triumph of economic virtues. Consequently, the Industrial Revolution could not have happened without the Reformation; and the Enlightenment changed attitudes towards knowledge and also inspired a different approach to understanding the world. As a result of the historical processes, individuals were free to seek to understand the world more fully and scientifically but, unsurprisingly, it was out of a religious belief that many early thinkers took this path (Hooykaas, 1972) since it was a form of natural theology. This led to the growth of science and to the development of technology that resulted in the Industrial Revolution and to the extension of capitalism from mercantile to industrial production capitalism. Paradoxically, it also contributed to the decline in religious belief as science and technology gained more prominence.

While the dynamics of capitalism itself may not have changed, in some ways, methods of generating wealth changed: now industrial production has resulted in greater wealth being created. In addition, the conditions under which capitalism functioned changed immensely. With the Reformation, the economic and political power of the Church was broken but not destroyed – the exercise of power became more complex. Individuals gained greater freedom, that called for thinkers to re-conceptualise the issues in the debate, such as, if God was not the source of human activity and ideas, then humankind had to be, but since human beings have no innate ideas all ideas must ultimately stem from individuals themselves[6] (Manent, 1998, p. 117). Manent notes that the consequences of Locke's argument include the fact that 'moral ideas do not correspond to anything in nature; they are the product of the work of man, the "archetypes" created by him'. Once this position was accepted, although later in this book we will argue that this simple dichotomy is not the complete picture, then it was assumed that 'society is not natural to man' (p. 124) but created:

> The starting point of political theory can only be the 'idealess' individual, the biological individual separated from his fellows, and without relation to them. Starting with the solitary animal, we do not adopt any moral notions that might be found to be badly constructed.
>
> (p. 124)

For Locke, who started with the solitary individual who needed to relate to others, interaction had to be guided by a humanly constructed set of moral notions. Indeed, moral ideas have no legitimation other than the fact that their construction reflects the dominant ideas of the day and that they are seen as rational, logical or pragmatic. Manent (p. 134) sums up Locke's position that human beings fashion moral notions, have rights and undertake labour: 'The first will give rise to the idea of "culture" and "values", second to the idea of the "rights of man and citizen", the third to the idea of "labourer" or *home oeconomicus*.' These points are crucial to this argument, although the second is debateable. In Locke's thesis, man is ultimately defined by rights, including property rights, and so Manent is able to draw the logical conclusion that once we accept the law of man, then the outcome should be the creation of the 'City of Man' rather than the 'City of God' – created by economic rationality and activity – and so the question remains – can we create a utopian City of Man? Do we have the knowledge and moral ability to do so? This question runs through this study and we will seek to answer it later, but this must be followed by subsequent questions: Why should we want to? What are the ends of man? To seek to answer these questions takes us beyond the remit of this book! While capitalism may have overcome the restraining force of Christianity in the West, it is clear that since it is about value and wealth for individuals (as well as for states), it has not freed itself from either the religious or the ethical questions that under-lie it, as Marx himself saw very clearly. Indeed, the New Jerusalem may not descend from heaven but if it is possible to create such a utopia, it may ascend from the world and in economic society wealth is the end-product for many people. Indeed, Wolfe (1989, p. 7) makes the point that according to the eco-nomic approach to society, society works best when individuals maximise their self-interest. Goodchild (2002, p. 85) cites Marx's analysis of capitalism as the religion of money – a material religion without dogma but even then we are confronted with the inequalities of the system – the rich exploit the poor in order to produce commodities which will produce surplus value (profit) when they are marketed: indeed, the greater the technological efficiency the less important human labour becomes and wealth is concentrated into the hands of fewer and fewer people while the remainder become proportionately poorer. And so capitalism is still confronted with a moral dilemma: it needs individual difference and competition to be innovative and to grow but in order for the market to function it also needs social order, even if the laws that generate it are human constructs rather than divine ones. Indeed, 'Man defines himself by the fact of having rights' – the rights of man and they are 'human rights' (Manent, 1998, p. 138): 'Man is he who declares his rights' (p. 148) but it is hard to legitimate these claims apart from by man's own reason. However, Locke was forced to recognise that while he could start with individuals, he had to move on to relationships and once he did this, human beings are forced to recognise their inter-dependency – and this becomes a question of obligations and morals as well as rights and as Wolfe argues society becomes a gift that demands that we care for it.

However, as a result of this movement in thought, humans were free and the makers of their own laws – but who or what legitimates them? Once this question is raised it is necessary for the people to work out contractual laws and norms through which peaceful interaction can occur; and so it was Hobbes (1968 [1651]) also who recognised the need for a social contract,[7] although the idea of covenant between peoples is far older,[8] and sovereign power also lies at the heart of the debate since this was previously the preserve of God. Indeed, it is clear that many of the ideas of modernity were little more than secularised theological concepts. Rousseau, a few years later, also discussed the social contract and for him (Rousseau, 1973, p. 191) the social contract solved the problem:

The problem is to find a form of association which will defend and protect with the whole common force of the person and goods of each associate, and in which each, while uniting himself with all, may still obey himself alone, and remain as free as ever.

Hobbes (1968 [1651], p. 192) had argued that 'the mutuall transferring of Right, is that which men call CONTRACT' (upper casement in the original).

But as men, for the atteyning of peace, and conservation of themselves whereby, have made an Artificall Man, which we call a Common-wealth; so also have they made Atificiall Chains, called *civill lawes*, which they themselves, by mutual covenants, have fastned at one end, to the lips of that Man, or Assembly, to whom they have given Soveraigne Power; and at the other end to their own Ears.

(pp. 263–264)

Herein lies the power of the nation state which could control the freedom of individuals in the name of the people and in this sense the state assumed a similar but slightly different role to that previously performed by religion in relation to trade and production: to regulate the markets for the good of the people but like the Church, those states in which capitalism thrived also got rich. Now the mechanism for regulation came from the policy and law of the nation state and, indeed, active citizens needed to assume a major role in this process. Recent studies have shown, however, that the public sphere declined during this period. Habermas (1989) discussed how the public sphere was reformulated and became bourgeois: in this sense, we see the need for the educated person if democracy is ever to be a meaningful form of government and we see in some early democratic experiments how education and learning took place in such informal settings as coffee houses. However, this open democratic situation was not to last long and then Habermas claims that the public sphere was colonised by the state. While his study was tremendously insightful, Thompson (1995, pp. 69–75) offers a number of criticisms of it suggesting that Habermas' position is too narrow and that we have to examine new forms of 'publicness' in which the media play an important role. Sennett (1986) also illustrated how the public person, the active citizen, began to disappear in the nineteenth century and it is hardly surprising that with the complexities of the following century the public role had almost disappeared apart from having experts discuss the issues through the media – a form of vicarious citizenship – and that active citizenship itself became relegated to such actions as being knowledgeable about things that occur in the world even though much of this knowledge is mediated and edited through a capitalist and nationalist media system and voting in local, national and even European elections. This viewpoint is also to be found in certain European Commission policy statements (EC, 2001b) as we have seen. However, what becomes increasingly significant is that in order to play an effective and active role in complex society people need to be learned and, therefore, involved in continuing learning.

Basically, we see here how the tensions in the emerging complexity of society led to government and the economic institution exercising power in at least two different ways: first, for government to claim its own authority and ignore the people to a considerable extent and second, for the capitalist system to pursue its own ends without recourse to the people and wherever possible without reference to government as well, unless it colonised government in some way, as Marx was to suggest. Perhaps this debate is typified in the work of Marshal (1950) who recognised that tension exists between the capitalist system and certain forms of citizenship. In his *Citizenship and Social Class* he suggested that citizenship has three dimensions: civil, political and social: civil being about human freedoms and rights; political about the right to participate in political processes; social the right to live, and to be supported if necessary, in a civilised life-style according to the standards of the society in which individuals live. Marshall's three-dimensional formulation, however, has not gone uncriticised (see Heater, 1999, pp. 19–24) but the three dimensions serve as a basis for our understanding of citizenship even though citizenship itself is being redefined. Marshall regarded the civil and political dimensions as having emerged in the eighteenth century, but the social dimension perhaps emerged later – perhaps in England with the universal provision of education in 1870. But Marshall was also concerned with the relationship between citizenship and capitalism, and he actually suggested at one point that there was a war between them, although he later claimed that the phrase was too strong, although this point is one with which we will agree in this study in relation to global capitalism.

Nevertheless we find echoes of this position in some of the recent work of Bauman who also clearly illustrates Sennett's concerns, when he (Bauman, 1999, p. 156) suggests that once the state recognises the law of the market over that of the city, then the citizen is treated as no more than a passive consumer:

> Once the state recognizes the priority and superiority of the laws of the market over the laws of the *polis*, the citizen is transmuted into the consumer, and a 'consumer demands more and more protection while accepting less and less the need to participate' in the running of the state.
>
> (*italics* in original)

But then the state, like religion, has also lost its own battle to regulate capitalism and this recognition was to become even more apparent with the development of global capitalism, when the state's power position changed even more radically, as the argument in the opening chapter implies.

Global capital and the weakened state

Once capitalism had freed itself of the nation state, it gained freedom from the public domain and was enabled to operate in the private sphere – free to varying degrees of both the Church the state. All the promise that capitalism's productivity offers is a utopian 'City of Man', full of the products of humanity's creation and labour – 'a land of milk and honey'. Capitalism offers a 'city of gold' and in this sense it has replaced Christianity's New Jerusalem – as Goodchild (2002) argues, capitalism has become the new religion. However, the new religion was to gain power through the processes of globalisation and it was only with the emergence of global capitalism that it could finally begin to free itself almost totally from the bonds of the state and civil society unless the state itself assumed new forms and also unless the public sphere found new ways of operating.

Global capitalism must be regarded as the third stage in the development of capitalism – one that is in many ways different from what has gone before and, in this sense, it is the sub-structure of late modernity but it has a much more complex sub-structure as we pointed out in the first chapter. This process can be seen in the latter part of the twentieth century when, after the Second World War a number of things occurred that led to this: these were briefly referred to in the third chapter of the previous volume and so we will merely repeat them here. Global capitalism, as we know it today, began in the West (the USA followed by Western Europe) in the early 1970s which was the period of post-Fordism, when it was beginning to be claimed that the modern period in which industrial capitalism was born was, in some way being superseded by new developments which were generally referred to as late or post-modernity. There were a number of contributory factors at this time which speeded up this process, such as:

- the need for peace and stability;
- the belief that the economic market enabled people to be free;
- the nature of capitalism itself and the need to make a profit on commodities produced;
- the recognition that modernity itself was being questioned;
- the oil crisis in the 1970s, which dented the confidence of the West;
- the demise of the Bretton Woods Agreement, that eventually led to the GATT Agreement, enabled both free trade and the flow of financial capital to develop throughout the world;
- the prevalence of the idea of the minimal state and of neo-liberal economics allowed for power to pass from the state to the capitalist institution;
- the development of sophisticated information technology through the star wars programme, through which the information technology revolution took off, with one development leading to another, as Castells (1996, p. 51f.) demonstrates. He (p. 52) makes the point that 'to some extent, the availability of new technologies constituted as a system in the 1970s was a fundamental basis for the process of socio-economic restructuring in the 1980s';
- the development of the World Wide Web itself;

- the economic competition from Japan, which challenged the West;
- using scientific knowledge in the production of commodities in the global market;
- the fall of the Berlin Wall – the democratisation of the Eastern Bloc – for, from the time it occurred, there has literally been 'no alternative' (Bauman, 1992) to global capitalism or comparable political opposition to the USA and so it reinforced the process. It is this factor that is the main reason why I have included the USA in the sub-structure in my understanding of global capitalism in the opening chapter on this book.

We can see that during the immediate decades after the Second World War, especially after the demise of the Bretton Woods Agreement, corporations began to relocate manufacturing and to transfer capital around the world, seeking the cheapest places and the most efficient means to manufacture, and the best markets in which to sell their products. They were being forced to do this because of the loss of Western confidence, when the oil crisis demonstrated that the West was vulnerable to those who controlled oil production and because, as the Japanese economy took off, the West realised that it would be forced to compete with another very efficient economic enterprise. This process was exacerbated in the Thatcher–Reagan era by the belief in a minimal state (Nozick, 1974) in which the freedom and responsibility of individuals were paramount and the state was regarded as a 'nanny state' if it was too concerned for the welfare of its citizens – although this was rhetoric for the fact that the state did not wish to tax companies at a sufficiently high level to provide welfare funds for those who needed them since, if they did, the companies might quickly relocate to places that allowed them to pay less taxes. In addition, during the process of privatisation not only of companies but of public assets, such as water, as well, giving even more power to those companies that purchased these commodities. It was perhaps not recognised by many who supported this process that it was not just a transfer of economic processes 'for the sake of efficiency' but it was a building of an economic power base for those corporations who were given ownership of public assets. Corporations were able to use the functions that the state had specified to build up their own power-base and as they have expanded so they have become the transnational corporations that form the sub-structure of the global world. Privatisation was, thereafter, quite central to the economic policies of the World Bank. Global capitalism was born. With the fall of the Berlin Wall, the United States of America remained the only super-power and as its governments have been inextricably intertwined with the large multi-national corporations, it has lent it political and military might to support the capitalist system which in turn furthered its own imperialist aspirations, and global capitalism rapidly grew up.

Global capitalism, however, has developed such power that, together with the application of technological knowledge, it has become the driving force for change in society. The need to produce new commodities or to produce older ones more efficiently has resulted in the concentration of effort on certain forms of what Scheler calls 'artificial knowledge'. This form of society is based upon knowledge – it is used in production, the distribution of data and information and even in many aspects of everyday life. Consequently, it demands workers who can adjust to change, be flexible, and be prepared to learn new jobs and even new life-styles. Since the knowledge is new and does not get embedded in society's culture, it cannot always be institutionalised in educational forms and so it is the learners' responsibility to learn whatever knowledge they feel that they need or want to learn. They are also free not to learn if they so desire, but then it is their own fault if they are not successful in this new form of society – it is a learning society. But the dominance that global capitalism has means that it strongly influences what knowledge is regarded as important, relevant and is taught and other forms of knowledge are regarded as out of date and irrelevant. Part of the thesis of this book is that some of that apparently irrelevant knowledge is more important to social living than the type of knowledge that is demanded by the global capitalist system.

Despite the fact that capitalism now appears self-evident, it is also a paradoxical phenomenon – appearing to be very powerful but having a number of fundamental weaknesses: the individualism of its practices actually needs a peaceful group that accept its premises if it is to survive and so it has to continue to create situations in which the group will be peaceful, accept its premises and practices and not endeavour to demonstrate its weaknesses or its malpractices. In addition, it needs a compliant work force that will accept relatively low financial returns for their efforts and a high unemployment rate so that it can be a profitable enterprise fails. It is most healthy when it can produce goods cheaply (through cheap labour and unemployment) and sell them profitably. Another major weakness is that if it fails to get people to purchase its products the system will fail and getting people to purchase its products can best be done by providing them with what they want, or desire, and so, it must use its economic and persuasive power to do this, even by creating those wants and desires itself. In order to do this, it must undermine and control the liberty and freewill of the individuals, almost without them being aware of it, and it does this through education and even more in the control of the people's learning. This it does effectively in the information society through the use of information technology and psychological techniques in the form of advertising – which is a form of transmitting information (teaching?) through techniques that persuades the recipients that its is right and desirable, i.e. they learn that it is right and desirable, as we shall argue in the next chapter. Finally, it needs an educated but compliant and flexible work force that will work hard and efficiently for low wages and so it needs education to be vocationally orientated. In fact, it needs the type of learning society which we have in the West today.

With the development of global capitalism, the position of the state was considerably weakened and the markets became even more unregulated, but the state did not wither away as some theorists from right and left have suggested.

However, the weakening of the state was only in relation to the new global institutions – it did not denote the loss of all political power by the state. Indeed, different states have been able to react differently to the social pressures emanating from the sub-structure, such as China and Russia, depending on their own ideological orientation. Clearly, with considerable power stemming from the sub-structure, the idea of democracy and of active citizenship has been threatened even more than by the fall of the public man in the nineteenth century suggested and so while the nature of political power has altered it has not disappeared. Even if the state cannot, or does not, regulate global capitalism, Habermas (2006, p. 81) suggests that the state now has a cushioning role, shielding people from its harsh effects – perhaps a new manifestation of Marshall's social dimension of citizenship – as a new form of welfare. Habermas also makes the suggestion that the political system might be trying to catch up with global economic through the formation of transnational political organisations, such as the EU. Additionally, we see the formation of transnational voluntary organisations using new technologies to make a public voice heard. Perhaps new forms of global political power are beginning to emerge. This is implicit in the model of globalisation discussed in the first two chapters of this book and also discussed in a previous volume (Jarvis, 2007b).

Conclusion

In these two chapters we have seen how first modernity and, since the 1960s and the emergence of global capitalism, late modernity, have emerged and how the values of modernity (scientific knowledge, reason, individualism, freedom and instrumentalism) have become the dominant values which are the same as those needed to produce a successful capitalist enterprise. We have also seen that capitalism is by nature socially divisive but we have not yet examined how global capitalism became the knowledge economy. It is, however, in this context that the learning society and lifelong learning that we know in the West has come about. In addition, since the individual prevails over the group the rules and norms of social interaction have to be worked out and we will show that the values of this form of society are not conducive to the survival of society itself, or in other words, the values of modernity are self-defeating. Indeed, relationship is necessary for the individual to exist and what has been undermined in this process has been the recognition of the significance of the group and persons have replaced the people (Gray, 1995). Indeed, we are already beginning to see how the values of modernity cannot provide the type of society for which many early reformers had hoped.

Chapter 5

The information society
Learning global capitalist culture

In the previous two chapters we have explored how global capitalism emerged and also we have looked at some of its dominant values. The aim of this chapter is to continue this process and to explore the way in which global capitalism perpetuates itself through the process of teaching and learning; in other words to look at one way in which our global capitalist society is also a learning society. The chapter has three main sections: global capitalist culture, the information society and lifelong learning and the global capitalist culture.

Global capitalist culture

We will explore three elements in this section of the chapter starting with a definition of culture, we will then look at the nature of this form of culture and finally we will point to the way in which we are socialised into it.

Culture, as Arendt (1968, pp. 211–213) reminds us is a word of Roman origin, from *colere*, meaning cultivate, dwell, take care of, to tend, to preserve, and it relates human beings to nature although it gradually assumed the double meaning of 'developing nature into a dwelling place for a people as well as … taking care of the monuments of the past' that it has today. However, this former meaning has been extended even further and it has come to mean in anthropology everything that human beings have created and added to the natural world and everything that they have learned. It has also come to mean all that is added to bare life that makes us human beings: it is the sum total of our learning. In a sense, power has never been far removed from this phenomenon since it is those who exercise power who decide on the nature of the place and even on what should be learned. The content of culture, then, has always been controlled – the school curriculum, for instance, has been defined as a selection from culture (Lawton, 1973, p. 21) that one generation wished to pass on to the next and so the state controlled the content of the education – a process of secondary socialisation, in the same way as the family controlled the content of what was passed on to children during primary socialisation. Education acted *in loco parentis*. In both the public world and the private world cultural transmission was controlled. It might perhaps be argued that the family and the school are the dominating socialisation institutions and that if either of these fail, then individuals do face a problematic future in an inclusive society, as statistics about criminality show.

It is not a great step to move from this position to claim that that culture which was considered important by those who had to 'decide' on public taste might be regarded as 'high culture' while 'mass culture' became that which was valued by the remainder of the population. The concept of mass suggests that there is an agglomeration of individuals rather than a conglomeration of groups and being able to individuate the masses is an important step in the process of domination. 'Mass' is only possible because society has been progressively individualised and, as we shall show, as home entertainment, etc. continues to increase there is a continued decrease of group activities. Mass culture has itself been extended to the enjoyment of such individualising phenomena and enjoyment has moved on so that the entertainment industry has grown phenomenally over the half century. Even mass culture, however, is not random since there are those who set trends and those who follow and the trendsetters tend to come from industry and are the celebrities chosen and sponsored by it to advertise their commodities. But we can also see, therefore, that the control of mass culture has moved from the state to industry and nearly all the population are exposed to the media of mass culture. Arendt (1968, p. 205) commented many years ago: 'Mass society wants not culture but entertainment and the wares offered by the entertainment industry are consumed by society like any other consumer goods.' She was writing from a position of accepting high culture and the situation has not changed but probably continued in the same direction as we now talk about closing the minds of people and the decline of the public person. The majority of people are exposed to this form of entertainment through the media every day of their lives, which is provided by corporations in the capitalist system primarily for profit rather than human growth or human benefit.

As children grow and develop they experience other groups than school during their secondary socialisation, such as work groups, leisure groups, educational groups and associations, church groups, clubs, and so on. In each they learn to be members and in order to play one's part in society individuals need to be included in these groups and their inclusion is a major element in secondary socialisation. Through joining these groups and associations, we learn to conform to society's culture – this is a process of social inclusion and a voluntary surrender of some elements in our own freedom. Society comprises a multitude of groups, associations and organisations – it is a totality, in this sense and we begin to see that the exercise of power does not need to be overt in the face of these social structures.

From this brief discussion it is clear that the term 'culture' is used with imprecision and so a simple definition – all that the human being learns as a result of social living – means that it is almost meaningless. Only when we add prefixes, such as high culture and mass culture, do we recognise that we become who we are as a result of social processes, many of which are controlled or at least greatly influenced by the capitalist sub-structure.

This argument fits the model of society that we presented in Figure 1.6 when it was argued that the economic and technology institutions were at the core of every society and that they exercise substantial power without having the authority to make policies and laws which are still made by the state, which, while it is still a powerful institution, does not have the same degree of power or flexibility as does the sub-structure. Since this sub-structure is common to nearly all societies, it is fairly easy for the core to by-pass the state and reach the global mass of the population through the means of mass media and continue the process of the dumbing down of individual life pursuits. The state can either support or exercise only a restraining role on the sub-structure until such time as the different countries of the world reach a political agreement through diplomatic negotiation – a slower process than the rapidity with which global capitalism can move. Until the political processes are united the political layers of society will never move sufficiently rapidly to control the sub-structure. Consequently, we can now see that the external mass culture is determined to a considerable extent by the sub-structure that provides the mass entertainment, fast food, and so on, with all the values, attitudes, opinions and beliefs that are contained therein.

We depicted this process in the opening chapter (Figure 1.5) and we return to it here but we will elaborate upon it since it is not just a matter of global society, the culture of which we internalise, it is also the sub-culture of each group within it which we join. Learning always occurs in a social context: it occurs in interpersonal relations – in formal, non-formal and informal relations, which we suggested are I–Thou (Buber, 1958) ones, but we also learn from, and through, the wide variety of media. There is a sense in which personal interaction is always a two-way process but learning through the media is predominantly a one-way process. We will focus much more on the place of the media in our discussion of learning in the information society below, but the process of learning to be a member of associations and groups can be depicted in precisely the same way as we illustrated in the opening chapter (Figure 1.5) but in secondary socialisation, the self has already undergone considerable development so that the learning process might be more reflective than it was in our earliest years. Consequently, the two-way direction of the arrows is even more realistic – it is an I–Thou relationship – and Figure 5.1 depicts this process.

In this diagram Ego, the person, is both body and mind, and the arc represents the sub-culture of the organisation which envelops us – that is, all that is added to us when we become members of the group. Ego, therefore, receives not just cognitive information but all forms of sense impressions through interaction with other members of the association and with the social environment in general. It will be recalled that our definition of learning is about learning in all aspects of the person and all dimensions of the mind (see Chapter 1). The arrows pointing in the direction of Ego depict internalisation while the others

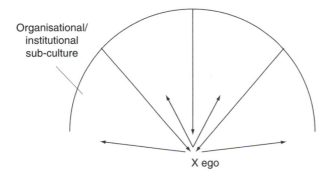

Figure 5.1 Learning and the internalisation of associational sub-culture.

signify externalisation. Interaction is with people (I–Thou) in all types of situations – from formal schooling to informal friendships, so that the arrows point in both directions and depicts the interaction with the generalised other.

However, and very significantly, we do not only learn through the reception of cognitive knowledge, we learn to conform by trial and error practices, watching experienced members of the group behave and copying them, and so on. In short we learn to conform, because we either want to or need to, or both. But the 'messages' that are transmitted by all forms of media are usually non-formal and unidirectional so that they point only to the person.

Culture is always carried by the people with whom we interact: in a real sense it is the same concept as Mead's (Mead in Strauss, 1964) generalised other, so that it is the information carried by those with whom we interact in the process of being a member of a group or an organisation. In recent years there has been much more emphasis on the cognitive than on the behavioural in the study of learning, so that terms like 'group mind' (Weick, 2001, pp. 259–284) have been utilised rather than generalised other, although there is a problem with the way that this concept is formulated, even if the agreement were only cognitive which is itself a dubious proposition. Group mind appears to suggest one mind as if the group was a mechanical solidarity (Durkheim) rather than an association of individuals. It is not like a monolithic community culture. Group mind not only omits all other aspects of the person, it also denies individuality, something fundamental to the development of modernity: however, the very usage of the term is a covert exercise in power exercised through language itself: the idea of a 'group mind' distracts people from the actual exercise of power – not only what to include but what to omit from the agenda, which is a major feature in Lukes' third dimension of power. In a sense, part of our argument is that to a great extent each of these processes not only reinforces primary socialisation but that it suggests a process of over-socialisation (Wrong, 1963), although individuals have the potentiality of freeing themselves from their imposed freedom! Nevertheless, there is a great deal of value in collective intelligence: the old adage that 'two minds are better than one' may well be true but it is still two minds! Organisational action might well occur as a result of democratic consultation and agreement – but it is collective rather than singular.

Initially, we tend to accept the sub-culture of the group although as we develop and become more familiar with it we may well reflect upon what we learn and even articulate diverse views. However, in a rapidly changing world, the organisations, of which we are members, have to change rapidly in order to keep abreast with what is going on, or else they will become irrelevant and out-dated – even large organisations, such as the churches, run this risk as we have seen in an apparently increasingly secular society. Organisations have to change in order to keep abreast with the current situation and appear relevant to its members and so the changing organisation has been called a learning organisation (Jarvis, 2007b) reflecting a behaviourist concept of learning. Most of the research on these organisations has been conducted on work organisations which are compelled by the nature of society to change at ever increasingly rapid rates in order to keep up with the demands of the market. In contrast, those voluntary organisations which oppose the spread of global capitalism still have to change in order to make their message relevant. Members of organisations that are forced to change rapidly by the rapidly changing social conditions are forced to keep on learning if they are to remain members of the group and while membership might appear voluntary, it is far from voluntary in many work organisations where there are unemployed others who would like to fill the position that we hold. Consequently, learning to conform to the expectations of the group and, therefore, to the wider society to which the organisation is responding is a function of membership. It also means that political power need only operate in very covert manner.

The covert nature of power means that people feel free and, indeed, there is a sense in which they are and this is the basis of liberalism. As Rose (1999, p. 62) points out that 'human beings are, in their nature, actually, potentially, ideally, subjects of freedom and hence ... they must be governed, and must govern themselves, as such'. As Rose notes, to be governed by our freedom seems paradoxical, and yet, we can see that this is actually happening, but this is, in many ways, a precarious process because there is always the potentiality that we might exercise our freedom in a different manner since our learning need not be non-reflective or reflective and conformist but it can also be reflective and nonconformist! We are free to engage in the solidarity of the group or we are free to isolate ourselves from it: free to be included or to be excluded.

Rose (p. 69) argues that freedom is a discipline and it is one which is learned in school, where children learn rationality and civil behaviour. School is also a place where they learn moral sentiments: it is the place where they learn to interact with others, while the peace is maintained through the discipline of the school. From as early as 1836:

David Stow's training manual for the nineteenth-century popular school, first published in 1838, emphasized the role of pedagogy in intensifying the inner life of the child. This was not an airy dream but a technical project. It required in particular, detailed and continual knowledge, not only of the general characteristics of the inner life of children, but also of the specific inner world of each child to be governed. The better the teacher knew the child, the easier it would be to guide him or her.

(pp. 77–78)

Having learned these things, freedom can be viewed as a civilised practice of daily living which Brown (1995, p. 5 – cited in Rose, 1999, p. 94) describes as 'neither a philosophical absolute no(r) a tangible entity but a relational and contextual practice that takes place in opposition to whatever is locally and ideological conceived as unfreedom...'. The point is that the practice of freedom is also a learning experience based upon our understanding of the situation in which we find ourselves. Feeling free within most organisations of which we are members means that we accept the sub-culture and conform to it in a civilised manner, or otherwise as the case may be, and learn to act accordingly. In this sense we are always free in these relationships and so this involves a moral dimension and this is the more significant since we actually control our own learning and feel that we are autonomous beings: the fact that we feel that we could have acted otherwise is 'proof' to us that we are have freedom.

At the same time, nearly all of the organisations of which we are members are carriers of the global capitalist culture and so not only are we socialised into it, our secondary socialisation process is constantly reinforcing our membership and, therefore, our conformity to it, even though we feel free!

The information society

Culture is controlled and transmitted through interaction between group members who have initially undergone socialisation in the family and in school where a selection of culture is transmitted (curriculum). But we have also raised an important distinction between high culture and mass culture: high culture being much more the preserve of the middle and upper classes while everybody is exposed to mass culture.

The concept of mass is important here because it suggests that there is an agglomeration of individuals rather than a conglomeration of groups and being able to individuate the masses is an important step in the process of domination. Mass is only possible because society has been progressively individualised and as home entertainment, etc. continues to increase there is a continued decrease in group activities, i.e. a decline in social capital. It is easier to mobilise or manipulate individuals than groups or organisations. Mass culture is a leisure time pursuit and the entertainment industry has grown phenomenally over the half century. However, mass culture is not a random phenomenon since there are those who set trends and those who follow: the trendsetters tend to come from industry and are the celebrities chosen and sponsored by it to advertise their commodities.[1] But we can also see, therefore, that the control of mass culture has moved from the state, and the upper classes, to industry, and all the population are exposed to the media of mass culture. Arendt (1968, p. 205) commented many years ago: 'Mass society wants not culture but entertainment and the wares offered by the entertainment industry are consumed by society like any other consumer goods.' This has not changed – only increased. The majority of people are exposed to entertainment through the media every day of their lives and it is through the incidental learning of mass culture that the power of global capitalism is exercised.

This argument fits the model of global society (Figure 1.6) which we discussed in the first chapter when we argued that the economic and technology institutions are at the core of every society and that they exercise substantial power without having the authority to make policies and laws. Since the substructure is common to all societies, however, it is fairly easy for it to by-pass the state and reach the mass of the population through the means of mass media, and so, the global corporations can only be restrained when governments act in order to do so within their own territories, but even then in advanced countries the mass media can by-pass the state, but even then the political and economic might of the USA can be exercised to force governments to accede to the economic power of the global core. The state's power is limited, but even more limited in developing countries that either needs capital investment or has already been a recipient of loans from the World Bank or the International Monetary Fund.[2]

Consequently, we can now see that the external mass culture is determined, to a considerable extent, by the sub-structure that provides the mass entertainment, fast food, and so on, with all the values, attitudes, opinions and beliefs that are contained therein and to which the people – including young children are exposed. In contrast, the authority of the family and the state, while still existing, is constrained by the power of the sub-structure – or to put it the other way around, the family and the state are in a weakened position to prevent the sub-structure from communicating its messages through the information technology it controls and in the entertainment and enjoyment that it provides. The incidentality of learning means that individuals will acquire the information transmitted by the mass media without always being aware of what is happening to them. Additionally, it has to be admitted that the same media provide opportunities to experience and to learn specifically chosen things which considerably broaden the recipients' experience, and so, it could be argued that this brings with it great advantages as well. The transmission of information is value neutral but how it is transmitted, and for what purpose, are much more significant questions which we will deal with in the remainder of this study. What is clear is that the ability to transmit and receive almost limitless information – an information society – is by no means always 'good'.

The information society has, according to Castells (1996, pp. 61–64), five foundational characteristics:

- information is the raw material upon which technologies act;
- these new technologies are pervasive;
- sets of technologies always have networking potential;
- the information paradigm is based on flexibility;
- there is a convergence of these technologies into a highly integrated system.

The information society, then, is based upon sophisticated technological means of transmitting information at every level, including schooling, work and leisure. These five characteristics are relevant to our study: our concern is how and what people learn in today's society. The capitalist global sub-structure forms the information society, or what Castells (pp. 66–150) calls the informational economy. It is the profit motive that drives the information provision rather than the desire to pass on to the people worthwhile knowledge or even enjoyable knowledge or the knowledge that the older generation wish the younger ones to learn. Castells (1996, p. 81) also suggests that there are four main ways in which the corporations that control productivity may increase profitability: reduce production costs, increase productivity, broaden the market and accelerate capital turnover. In order to sell commodities in the information society it is necessary to advertise the goods and for the people to learn about them, and so, amidst the mass entertainment, also a commodity, the people are provided with the necessary information to enable them to purchase other commodities that are being produced and sold. However, advertising information is not neutral data – the information being provided is sometimes false, often misleading, always presented with bias and in such a manner as to create the desire to purchase the goods through the use of psychological techniques such as association of the commodities with desirable states, and so on. In this sense, advertising performs the same functions that Althusser (1972) accused education and religion of doing: he claimed that they were state ideological apparatuses – now advertising is the ideological apparatus of global capitalism. A consumer society has been created and is maintained by constant advertising, propagating certain life-styles in the entertainment provided, and so on, which create desires in the population to emulate.

Webster (2002, p. 154) makes the same point:

> Informational developments are central to the spread of consumerism since they provide the means by which people are persuaded by corporate capitalism that it is both desirable and an inevitable way of life. Through a sustained information barrage, attests Schiller, 'all spheres of human existence are subject to the intrusion of commercial values ... the most important of which, clearly, is: CONSUME'.
>
> (upper casement in the original, Schiller, 1992, p. 3)

Webster continues this argument by suggesting that there are four ways by which consumer capitalism is encouraged by information technology:

- television is both a means of selling goods and services but it also bolsters the consumerist life-style;
- the bulk of the programmes encourage the same life-style;
- information and communications technology is exacerbating the tendency of the market place to replace self and communal organisation;
- communications technologies allow a great surveillance of the general public that enables the corporations to address their messages of persuasion to it.

It is this almost unrestricted 'selling' of a consumerist life-style through advertising that, like some political statements themselves, need to bear little relationship to the truth that comprises a great deal of the information with which we are presented. This 'selling' is undertaken by those who exercise power in the sub-structure of societies. It could be argued that it is the duty of the families, the schools and even the politicians to ensure that what is communicated is true, inoffensive, and so on. However, the superstructure of society depends to a great extent on the sub-structure, although, it is not determined by it, and the core has already infiltrated the political and educational processes[3] and influences them in a wide variety of ways, as it already influences families by their constant exposure to the media which it controls. But the other significant fact is that the power of the sub-structure depends on the superstructure: if there were no consumption, the sub-structure would have no power – consequently, the various layers of the superstructure also have power, a power by which it could possibly undermine the core. The core must create a consumer society in order to survive; sales are both its means of survival and its means of growth and power. Its aim is the accumulation of capital – profit and capital to re-invest in research to produce future commodities to sell, but its aim is not primarily addressed to the good of humanity, as such, but to those who own capital. But commodities must be sold and so people can never have enough if the capitalist system is to survive, so that we have the modern version of potlatch – planned obsolescence of all goods (Baudrillard, 1998). Advertising is the manner by which the sub-structure creates the conditions of consumption, but in examining these we will return to the techniques used to make us learn and conform to the demands of the core. Paradoxically, because the capitalism system depends on consumption, there is a sense in which the ultimate power lies with the consumers and this is why capitalism spends so much on seeking to create desire to purchase the latest commodities. There is, consequentially, a major issue about the nature of the learning that is at the heart of these processes.

Indeed, we have already pointed out that what is being transmitted is biased, seeking to create the desire to purchase goods and to continue to consume them, so that it is often difficult – almost impossible – for families who are already caught up in the consumer society to help their children to stand back and consider the processes more critically.[4] Indeed, the fact that in Western society the standard of living is so high, materially indicates the success of the system and, therefore, it can well be seen why many people will not want to be critical of it. Children are, therefore, socialised into the consumer culture by their families, aided and abetted by sophisticated advertising techniques from the core, so that the consumer culture is continually reinforced. However, as corporations have assumed an increasingly major place in school education, we find that they are providing school learning material that contains advertisements, advertising through other methods in school such as sponsoring certain activities, and so on. In this sense, schooling has become a medium for corporate advertising and since the corporations are providing finance, they are frequently welcomed into the schools by the school management and the local authorities. Hyslop-Margison and Sears (2006) have clearly demonstrated the power of the neo-liberal economic ideology within schooling in Canada, and their argument is also valid for other parts of the Western world (see below).

The creation of desire does not only lead to the purchase of the commodity, it also leads to the creation of value. As Foucault (1974, p. 194) reminds us: value is created by consumption.[5] The market value of a commodity is not dependent upon the workers' labour but on the consumers' desire to spend their money on a commodity and the more that they desire it the more that they will spend on it whether it is 'good for them' or not. In creating value, there is a sense in which the market undermines the authenticity of individuals to place their own value upon phenomena. Consequently, advertising serves not just to create desire, but to increase the market value of the commodity for those who are persuaded to purchase it and thereby to decrease the humanity of the purchaser. The producer gains a greater profit while the consumer is the poorer: it is not a system of reciprocal exchange but one of exchange that enriches the one at the expense of the other. The greater the monopoly of the seller, the higher the market price of the commodity – but higher prices mean greater profit not higher wages for the workers.

Indeed, this argument can be extended a little further here, in as much as Webster (2002, p. 133) points out that 90 per cent of the international news published by the media comes from only four sources – Western news agencies, which themselves are capitalist organisations and need to sell the information that they have gained as commodities in the market place, and so even their information is not going to be free from the same pressures as the remainder of the society in which we live.

Fundamentally, the all-encompassing culture (Figure 1.5) is one that is controlled to a considerable extent by the global sub-structure. Its power, while not totally unrestrained, as we saw in the second chapter, is still considerable and varies in different countries. There have been efforts by politicians and the general public to curb the desire to sell commodities at any cost – this is the state cushioning the people from the unrestrained forces of global capitalism. In the UK, for instance, it is generally agreed that pornographic material should not be made available to young people and now it is becoming an offence for anybody to download from the Web violent pornographic literature in the same way as it is an offence to possess child pornography; there are restrictions on television advertising before 9 pm in the evening, and so on. It is even being debated as to whether certain forms of fast food should not be advertised before 9 pm, but as children now have access to television at all hours and as advertising uses other media this will probably not have a tremendous effect on sales. There is an advertising agency in the UK that examines the public's complaints about offensive advertising but it is much more a reactive than a proactive agency. Nevertheless, the amount of restrictions that politicians and the general public have been able to place on the corporations in their endeavour to sell their commodities has been extremely limited and certainly the corporations are under no obligation to present information in a truthful or unbiased manner – despite the claims of advertising agencies. Indeed, even public service institutions, like the British Broadcasting Corporation, do not only receive information from the news agencies, but they are frequently accused of being biased when they seek to expose any capitalist agency or public figure, and it is notable that the more powerful the corporation the more it appears to be immune from such scrutiny, although this may also be because the larger global corporations are so much more complex and their dealings harder to penetrate. Nevertheless, when any employee (insider) exposes any of their activities,[6] their employment is almost inevitably terminated immediately and this generates a sense of fear and, therefore, conformity to the prevailing culture.

Lifelong learning and the global capitalist culture

Our argument here is that lifelong learning means that we are exposed to the forces of the global culture all of our lives and in the process we actually become over-socialised (Wrong, 1963) into the consumer culture. We will examine this in everyday life, school and work.

Learning in everyday life

The connotations of the concept 'information' are misleading since it tends to convey the idea of knowledge, data, factual material, and so on, whereas, as we have argued throughout these volumes, it is not just the mind that receives information in learning but the whole person is recipient of all forms of sense experience and information also contains values, attitudes and opinions, emotive statements, beliefs, false data and unproven claims, and so on. Traditionally, the transmission of information has been carefully guarded as far as children have been concerned: parents and immediate family were the main transmitters of information, followed by schooling which was the responsibility of the State in the majority of cases, although private education has enabled parents to opt out of the state system of education for religious or other reasons. Significantly, one understanding of education was that it transmitted the knowledge that one generation considered sufficiently important to pass on to succeeding ones. Hence, the curriculum was carefully selected segments of culture – academic subjects – that children were expected to learn. In a positive sense, children received that knowledge that the elders regarded as worthwhile but in a negative sense this could be regarded as restrictive and even claustrophobic. Radio and newspapers and magazines played a small part.

In recent years, however, the overall control on the type of information transmitted to children has been relaxed and the media are generally open to the same accusation; television has become the most intrusive of the media into the private lives of individuals and its messages have been far broader than that which the traditional guardians of the cultural tradition have transmitted:

> Television has traditionally played an important part in people's leisure time occupying around half of that time. According to the Broadcasters Audience Research Board (BARB) television viewing in the United Kingdom has increased slightly over the past decade from 25.6 hours per household per week in 1993 to 26.1 hours in 2003. Nearly nine in ten adults in the United Kingdom watched television every day of the week in 2003 according to Ofcom's The Public's View survey, with nearly a quarter of viewers watching it for two to three hours a day and one in ten viewing it for over seven hours. Over half the adults stated that they have one or two sets in the home, while nearly one in ten said that they had five or more.
>
> (National Statistics, 2006, p. 192)[7]

The statistics are just as stark for the USA: a recent survey published by the US Census Bureau suggests that 'Americans will spend a total of 65 days watching TV next year (2007) and 41 days listening to the radio' (*Guardian*, 15 December 2006, see Goodchild, 2002). They will also spend a week reading newspapers and another surfing the internet. Of course it could be argued that the television can always be switched off and this would be a valid argument if there were no other media for advertising, but almost every medium and every possible place is used for advertising, even to getting consumers to advertise the products they pay to wear through the prominent positioning of brand names on clothing, and so on. Consequently, it is a facile argument to say that we can switch off the television – we can do that for the many poor programmes broadcast but we cannot do it for advertising.

We can see, therefore, the significance of television in the transmission of cultural information to every household, and indeed to every person from childhood to old age, in the UK and the USA. But we are also aware that information is increasingly being transmitted via other media such as the Web, personal computer, mobile telephone, and so on. Increasingly people spend more time receiving information from the media than they do from other people in an inter-personal manner – maybe even more than they receive at school – but this information is rarely haphazard or uncontrolled even though it may seem to be so. It now emanates from the sub-structure of global society and in this sense it is still carefully created, selected and controlled although the parameters are very different. This information is what advertising is about, often it is misinformation,[8] seeking to instil in others, especially young people, a desire to purchase a given product and the techniques used are also open to question. Be as it may, desire is created and this constitutes the basis of a new form of totalitarian society since it orientates the interests and concerns of many of the recipients. Consequently, those who have do have a high standard of living but this means that people no longer feel the need to be active citizens standing up for human rights[9] as Bauman (1988, pp. 76–77) notes in his discussion of the good life:

> These pressures (of advertising), however, are not experienced as an oppression. The surrender they demand promises nothing but joy; not just the joy of submitting to something greater than myself ... but straight-forward, sensual joy of tasty eating, pleasant smelling, soothing drinking, relaxing driving, or the joy of being surrounded with smart, glistening, eye-caressing objects. With such duties, who needs rights?

For those who enjoy this life-style, the manner in which the consumer society is working must be right. This is a pragmatic attitude towards society, and it is one of the reasons for the decline in social capital (Putnam, 2000) in the Western world.

Initially, it was through interaction with significant others by which individuals gained their first understanding of society and even their own sense of identity, but now that process is much more diffuse. As Berger and Luckmann (1966) showed, there is a sense in which, through socialisation, we all internalise the external world, or as Bourdieu (1992, p. 127) suggests: 'Social reality exists, so to speak, twice, in things and in minds, in fields and in habitus, outside and inside of agents.' What we have internalised is a picture blurred at the edges, perhaps, but nevertheless recognisable because much of our learning has been unintended and/or non-reflective.[10]

It is important to recognise that while we reject a simple stimulus–response model as the basis of all human learning (Jarvis, 2006), we do see incidental learning as the basis of non-reflective learning, through which we internalise what we hear and undertake acts of conformity. Also, if we have internalised a desire to partake in the delights that the commodities on sale offer, for instance, it increases the probability of non-reflective learning – or continued conditioning – throughout our lives.

However, it is significant to note at this point that it is the whole person who is the recipient of these external stimuli – body and mind – whether they come through interpersonal interaction or via the media. The person receives these, i.e. has an experience, which may be in the form of pictures or other sense data as well as knowledge, values, beliefs or attitudes, and they may be transformed into new knowledge, beliefs, emotions, values, attitudes, identity and even desires. We then usually act – itself an exercise of will – as a result of our internalised understanding of the external world rather than as a direct response to an external stimulus. While our learning may often be unintended, it would not be true to say that the information was transmitted in a haphazard manner, rather it is carefully controlled but less carefully regulated.

Learning in formal education

But there has been a gradual acceptance of the neo-liberal economic ideology and this has permeated schooling. Wolfe (1989, p. 73) cites A *Study of High Schools* (Powell, 1985) which concluded that:

> American high schools are best compared to shopping malls; students are buyers, and fickle ones at that, where as teachers view themselves as sellers, often of commodities that the buyers would rather avoid. 'The shopping mall high school cares more about consumption than about what is consumed.'

Wolfe points out that no moral value is attached to the mastery of a subject and the consumers (pupils) have sovereignty. As he points out, this freedom is a direct response to the much more oppressive regimes of an earlier generation. Hyslop-Margison and Sears (2006, p. 15) have also argued that both through the practices of teaching and learning and through the content of the curriculum ideas of democratic citizenship are played down:

> the central aim of neo-liberal schooling is to prepare students as politically passive and compliant workers for the dynamic labour market conditions consistent (with) the global economy. This preparation is attempted through a range of policy and curricula practices that collectively indoctrinate students toward a neo-liberal worldview focused on creating consumers as opposed to citizens.

It might also be argued that as schools seek the support of local industry and commerce, so they lose some of their independence to the financing organisations. If nothing more, these organisations are seen to be valuable in supporting the children's education, and so on, because they provide essential finance. In precisely the same way, universities have become dependent on the market and the subjects that they teach and research tend to be those that are favoured by neo-liberalism. In recent studies of the university we see how corporations are seeking to present themselves within universities and Bok (2003) fears that corporations are making themselves indispensable to universities. He (p. 151) gives an example:

> In 1998 ... the Novartis Company agreed to give the Department of Plant and Microbial Biology at the University of California, Berkeley, the sum of $25 million over five years, a figure accounting for approximately 30–40 percent of the department's entire research budget. According to the agreement, Novartis gained the right to review in advance all proposed publications based on the research supported by the company (or by the federal government) and to ask the university to apply for a patent on any findings contained in the research. The company not only reserved the right to negotiate for a license on any patents resulting from the research; it also received two of the five seats on the committee to decide how to distribute research funds.

The company no doubt acted perfectly honourably in this instance, as the University maintains, but the problem arises when this situation is multiplied many times over and when not all companies act in such an honourable manner. Indeed, Bok (p. 208) warns the universities of the dangers of losing their academic integrity and that they will then lose 'essential values that are all but impossible to restore'. The financial motive is extremely powerful but once exposed to its advantages, the disadvantages are harder to fight and eventually universities lose their independence and become part of the same process of reinforcing the existing system. This danger has been recognised in a number of studies of higher education in recent years (Lucas, 1996; Readings, 1996; Shumar, 1997; Slaughter and Leslie, 1997; *inter alia*).

Learning at the work

Learning to become a worker may be regarded as a secondary or even a tertiary socialisation process: the new workers not only learn about the work and the work place, they also learn about their employing company's culture and expectations for them as workers. Indeed, transnational corporations 'are the greatest single contributor to cross cultural training and practices in recent years' (Lo Bianco, 2006, p. 218). This secondary socialisation process is summarised by Meister (2000, pp. 39–43) as the 'three C's', the initial curriculum being:

- corporate citizenship;
- contextual framework;
- core work-place competences.

Workers are taught their employer's beliefs, values and practices. They become 'members' of the company with which they also learn to identify by learning its culture and conforming to its practices:

> The good corporate citizens move beyond performing just the job tasks, rather they act as if they are the owners of the business, desire to satisfy

customers, understand that customer satisfaction comes from how the job is done, and take responsibility for continually striving to do a better job.

(p. 93)

In a sense, this approach to corporate citizenship aims to give the workers the impression that they are part owners of the company but there are few genuine partnerships or cooperatives among the large corporations. However, and more significantly, Meister (p. 93) goes on to say:

> The increased focus on acculturation training is driven by the need of an organization to develop a shared mindset. Gradually more companies are focusing on employees in their vision, values and culture, especially those committed to building a world-class work force.

Corporations are committed to socialising their employees into their own culture and values – a form of tertiary socialisation; a part of the process is creating team-work situations, bonding workers to feel part not only of the corporation but of the more local grouping. This is a significant development at a time when society as a whole has emphasised individuality and individual human rights: corporations have again learned the strength of unity and, therefore, corporate rights. Loyalty to the group and to the company is prized and rewarded. Strength lies in unity. However, there is a flip side to this: an employee who does not foster the company's profitability is not tolerated.[11] Indeed, there are many cases where the corporation has dismissed those employees who have spoken out against their companies and the connotation of 'whistle blower' is one of disapproval rather than one of approval for a brave action making public a corporation's malpractice, as we pointed out above. Such a response is making a public example of these employees and engendering a culture of conformity and fear. Some companies, as a McKinsey, go as far as to expect employees to sign a confidentiality clause (Rasiel, 1998, pp. xiv–xv). Even threats by the trades unions do not always prevent the corporations from dismissing nonconformists and this is increasingly the case as trades unions are weakened, but it is also a reason why capitalism seeks to manufacture its commodities in countries where there are no unions. Fear, or uncertainty about the future is a major phenomenon in contemporary society; this is especially true for unemployment when many people have house mortgages and other forms of personal debt. It is certainly one that corporations play on to ensure that the majority of their employees are loyal to the corporation irrespective of its deeds.

We learn to be loyal to the employing corporation; in other words, most workers are socialised in a culture of conformity to the global capitalist system and the system ensures that the work force are rewarded for conformity but punished for nonconformity. In the information society such corporation actions are newsworthy and so the wider public usually gets to know about whistle blowers or other nonconformists to the system and the publicity itself provides a warning to other potential whistle blowers. The corporations, therefore, endeavour to create a situation where the workers accept the capitalist ethic but punish those who, while they might accept the ethic, do not abide by the companies' own interpretation of it. In other words, corporations are using their power to ensure conformity, something which extends far more widely than with their employees alone.

As we argued earlier, people need to be included but through inclusion they learn to conform and so the sub-structures and governments do not have to exercise as much covert power: individuals learn conformity through group membership. Their learning, however, is incidental and often non-reflective and these conditions give rise to other possibilities.

Conclusion

The argument of this chapter has been that the global capitalist culture is pervasive and that we learn and internalise its aspirations and ideology throughout our lives; we do so freely and often we acquire this information incidentally. Moreover, we can see that the process that we have briefly described here is an education of desire – the desire to have – own the commodities that are produced – is transmitted to us through sophisticated psychological techniques. In this sense, the spread of global capitalism is dependent upon the technologies of the information society, so that power resides in those who can own, and or control, them. It is this, combined with the capitalist system, that constitutes the global sub-structure and so we see that capitalism perpetuates itself through the creation of a learning society – people learn to be part of the system. But the sheer pervasiveness of this culture and the power, economics and persuasion, that is exercised by the global core needs further examination.

Chapter 6

Indoctrination and the learning society

In the previous chapter we saw how the power of the sub-structure of society creates a learning society in which the beliefs, values and practices of capitalism are instilled, thus generating consumers. We noted how people are encouraged to learn, even incidentally, through advertising: fundamentally, the information society is a learning society in which everybody is exposed to the information propagated by the sub-structures of society. By contrast, both in everyday speech and in academic discourse the idea of the learning society is focused upon the need for individuals to learn specific knowledge and skills to enable them to be employable, and so the type of learning society that we have depicted here appears to be a different society. However, it is precisely the same one. In fact they are two sides of the same coin: the one focuses upon the need to be employable and to earn money while the other is about learning the need to acquire and consume the commodities that such a society produces and so to spend the money that is earned. Significantly, the knowledge needed to produce and market commodities is emphasised and given high status – scientific and technological knowledge; it is what Scheler regarded as artificial knowledge because it changes so rapidly. In contrast, those forms of knowledge that would encourage criticism of this form of society are downplayed which suggests that, in the very least, the power of the sub-structure is such that it can control or at least dominate the cultural knowledge of global society – but then it has been recognised at least since the time of Marx that the dominant ideas are always those of the elite.

Consequently, it can be seen that both the concepts of lifelong learning and the learning society are social constructions, biased to reflect those aspects of global capitalism that are seen to be essential to its perpetuation. However, it is claimed here that the forms of learning to which we are exposed in everyday life, in the hidden curriculum of formal education and in the work place are indoctrinational and the type of society that we call a learning society is actually quite totalitarian. The constant accusation at the time of the Cold War was that the communist countries were indoctrinating their populations and even those people whom they took prisoner (Lifton, 1967) were brainwashed, whereas the free West was liberal and democratic, but at the present time it is hard to refute the accusation that Western capitalism performs the same role as did communism in the past. In this chapter, we will examine this thesis in four sections: first of all we will clarify the concepts and relate them to conditioning; second, we will look at learning and brainwashing in the context of advertising; third, we will re-examine the debate between indoctrination and education within formal education; finally, we will look at totalitarianism and freedom.

Indoctrination, brainwashing and thought reform

In a great deal of the literature these three concepts appear to be used interchangeably although they do carry slightly different connotations. The *Collins English Dictionary* suggests that indoctrination is the process of teaching people systematically to accept doctrines uncritically, or to impart learning or to instruct. Brainwashing is defined as effecting radical change in ideas or beliefs by methods based on conditioning, while thought reform does not appear as a separate entry.

Indoctrination is treated here as a form of socialisation in which the individuals have little or no freedom to consent to being exposed to the information – in this sense, indoctrination is about implanting ideas into the mind – whereas thought reform is a form of re-education. Fundamentally, both are cognitive, whereas brainwashing conveys something even more total and incorporates the bodily senses and the emotions as well. At the same time, all three concepts convey the sense that individuals are learners, but the other fundamental element of this debate is that the learners are not accorded a great deal of critical power – they are the recipients of the information or the process and, as a result, they do what is expected of them. In this sense, the learners are not free: Taylor (2004, p. 23), for instance, suggests that brainwashing is 'a collective noun for various, increasingly well understood techniques of non-consensual mind change'.

Freedom, as we have seen is at the heart of the modernity project but there are situations in which we act as if we are free because we are following our desires. However, one of the things that became very clear in the previous chapter is that the information being conveyed to both the young and the not so young was aimed at creating desire, so that when we appear to act freely according to our desires, we are actually demonstrating the power of the brainwashing process.

All three of these terms convey the idea of learning and also suggest that the learners are not free from an environment in which power, both persuasive and economic is exercised and that our learning is non-consensual. In some ways these concepts are closely related to the ideas of conditioning that occur in learning theory. In classical conditioning the learner is taught to associate a desire (food) with a condition (the sound of a bell) in Pavlov's experiments with dogs, whereas in operant conditioning the learners are rewarded (have their desires fulfilled) for 'correct' behaviour. Certainly, operant conditioning can be a form of brainwashing – inducing the response in the learners that the teacher, or other powerful person in the process, wishes. It is perhaps significant that the behaviourist approach to human learning is so prevalent in our society. Indeed, it can be argued that while this is but one approach to human learning, it conforms to the general expectations of contemporary society so that, despite its deficiencies, it has assumed a major place. While this may be a useful therapy, its practice in education, as we will show below, is really morally questionable. Indeed, Kilpatrick (1972, p. 48) suggested that indoctrination failed to respect the person of the learner and that any democracy should reject such processes. While Kilpatrick, and many writers on the topic wrote from an educational perspective and their concern was with children, it is clear that others, such as Lifton (1961), were analysing the processes from a more political perspective and their subjects were adults. Within education, much of the discussion about these processes has revolved around religious education and indoctrination and so in the next part of this chapter we will look briefly at these.

Indoctrination and education

In the traditional debates about indoctrination, the concern of the philosophers was to differentiate it from education, or to ask to what extent was education a process of indoctrination, especially when children are taught religious subjects (Wilson, 1964). Nevertheless, they recognised indoctrination as a form of learning. Clearly, education is to do with aims, content and method of the information communicated in either the formal system of education or even its non-formal and even informal transmission. But, significantly, so does indoctrination. All these three aspects of communication interest us. Wilson (1964), however, touches on each of these points in a most clear manner. Dealing first with communication, he argues that for it not to be indoctrinational, it must be rational. He (1964, p. 33) makes the following point, 'rational communication consists in not putting pressure on an individual in a way which his conscious mind cannot fully resist'. If individuals cannot fully resist the communication or they cannot reflect upon it, then their minds are being closed and their human personality is diminished and we argue here that advertising lowers the resistance of many of its recipients and is a form of indoctrination. Rationality means that truth, evidence and reality are the primary means of communication whereas they are secondary in indoctrination but not in education. In these two senses, advertising falls short of an educative exercise although it still offers learning opportunities. Wilson was also concerned about the method of communication and we will later argue that the method is also indoctrinational. But we are not only concerned with children but with adults of all ages as well and Wilson did touch upon this when he discussed indoctrination in adult industrial society and suggested that: 'In a detribalised society which feels insecure, such as our own society is, indoctrination will generally take the form of pressure towards conformity which is distinguished by a pseudo-liberal attitude' (p. 42). We see this pressure towards conformity through capitalist advertising, although Wilson is careful to recognise that we still have free-will whereby we can make choices, but he concludes that conquering indoctrination in such societies – before the information society with its advanced technology took off – is, necessarily 'a slow process, and entails a lot of hard fighting. Some people who have tried to do it have been crucified or made to drink hemlock: others have had to live their lives in isolation amid the hostility of society'. He admits others give up! Perhaps today it is just as hard, if not harder! More significantly, his discussion was limited to school and school education whereas today we are concerned with a much broader spectrum of learning – formal, non-formal and informal.

In seeking to distinguish indoctrination from education, Wilson has highlighted points crucial to our present discussion, but he also distinguished between getting people to do something, which he regards as conditioning, and getting them to believe things, which he claimed is indoctrination. Not all philosophers agreed with his argument, and we are not convinced of it either: both Crittenden (1972, p. 146) and White (1972, pp. 190–201) also differ from him but also from each other. However, it is clear that while people are persuaded to purchase the commodities advertised – they could be said to be conditioned – but there is also a sense in which they associate the fulfilment of their desires with the capitalist society within which we live and so they are indoctrinated into the virtues of global capitalism. If Wilson's distinction was valid, it could be argued that purchasing specific goods at the supermarket because they have been advertised is a form of conditioning rather than indoctrination, but if we purchase them because we have believed the advertisers' message, or because the message has become associated with the commodities this would be indoctrination. But such a distinction seems unnecessary. In a sense, this form of advertising is also propaganda – as Arendt (1968, p. 43) suggests:

> The strong emphasis of totalitarian propaganda on the 'scientific' nature of its assertions has been compared to certain advertising techniques which also address themselves to the masses. And it is true that the advertising columns of every newspaper show this 'scientificality', by which a manufacturer proves with facts and figures and the help of a 'research' department that his is the 'best soap in the world'. It is also true that there is a certain element of violence in the imaginative exaggerations of publicity men, that behind the assertion that girls who do not use this particular brand of soap may go through life with pimples and without a husband lies the wild dream of monopoly...

More recently, Hyslop-Marginson and Sears (2006) have been less concerned with the distinction between conditioning and indoctrination, reflecting the fact that over the past 40 years the distinction between education and training has also been weakened. They argue that formal education is indoctrinational and they (p. 15) also make the point that: 'Neo-liberal education policy ... reduces lifelong learning to a discursive ideological apparatus that encourages student conformity to market economy dictates by advocating self-regulated training in response to job displacement.' They (p. 15) continue:

> the central aim of neo-liberal schooling is to prepare students as politically passive and compliant workers for the dynamic labour market conditions consistent (with the) global economy. This preparation is attempted through a range of policy and curricular practices that collectively indoctrinate students toward a neo-liberal worldview focused on creating consumers as opposed to citizens.

Here then we see a new hidden curriculum emerging – that the ideology of capitalism is being transmitted to children covertly. Crittenden (1972), for instance, came close to the position that Hyslop-Margison and Sears (2006) adopt when he claimed that if information is presented in such a way as to violate the criteria of inquiry or if the presentation is inconsistent with either the requirements of inquiry or violates moral principles, it is indoctrinational. He (Crittenden, 1972, p. 147) went on to argue that if a teacher is the agent of a governing elite exploiting the country 'to produce a loyal, docile, intellectually benumbed community who believe that the governing elite is equipped with charismatic qualities and is acting for the good of the whole society' then it could be called propaganda rather than indoctrination. However, propaganda is the organised dissemination of information, and when this information is presented in ways that violate the criteria of rational inquiry it falls within the parameters of indoctrination. In addition, White (1972, p. 191) suggests that indoctrination can occur without belief systems, and he is inclined to accept that indoctrination can occur whatever individual beliefs are disseminated, such as belief about a single product.

While there is considerable philosophical debate about the precise meaning of the idea of indoctrination, it is clear that the points made by all of these writers indicate that information transfer must not violate the criteria of critical or rational enquiry otherwise it is an indoctrinational process and that information transfer in any case must be a moral process. It is also evident from this brief discussion that not only is a great deal of advertising falling short of high moral standards, it is also indoctrinational. It is also very significant for our discussion of the information and learning society to recognise that the types of learning being fostered are often incidental and associational, non-reflective and indoctrinational whereas in a more idealist learning society information would be open to critical and reflective thought in order to assess its value. Our society is one in which indoctrination is widely accepted.

We want to demonstrate our argument here under five heads: the intentions of those who transmit information, the techniques used to assist people to learn it, the content of the information, its relationship to 'truth' or to the evidence for its claims and the morality of the process. Even these issues cannot be separated entirely so that the distinction drawn here is for heuristic purposes only.

Intentions

On many occasions advertising agencies claim, rightly I think, that it is necessary to provide information so that the general public can learn about new products and consider purchasing them. If this were the sole intention of advertising and the information was provided in a neutral manner then it would be an innocuous activity and one would wonder why such vast sums of money is spent on it. There is clearly much more to it than this and this is clear when we recognise that there are a number of definitions of advertising:

- to present or praise goods and services, for instance, to the public especially in order to encourage sales;
- to make something publicly known;
- to make a public request;
- to warn or caution.

(Collins English Dictionary)

Advertising is to make commodities publicly known, through acceptable information, open to rational inquiry, and so on. Indeed, Wolfe (1989, p. 97) reminds us that scholars studying advertising in the past concluded that 'early advertising men believed that they were guardians of the public taste, not of business ends, leading campaigns for truth and sincerity, which their own advertisements were undermining'. But we live in a pragmatic age, one in which Lyotard (1984) suggested that the legitimation of knowledge would be performativity, and the intention behind advertising is not just to make something publicly known but to encourage sales, so that they now give people what they want (Wolfe, 1989, p. 103). Perhaps the term 'encourage' is too simple or even misleading. Kellogg's are a company seeking to provide its own information to consumers so that they can decide and choose based on information which, unlike the British Government's proposed labelling plans, is based upon a fact statement about the amount of sugar or salt, etc. in the food rather than a professional evaluation of the amount that is acceptable for healthy food. The British Food Standards Agency has endeavoured to introduce a 'traffic light' diagram on each food to guide consumers with emphasising the scientific facts in the way that the corporations wish to present them. However, the Food Standards Agency claims that its approach is easier to understand and it is this that the food industry seems to oppose. Lawrence (2006, p. 8) makes the comment: 'With red labels[1] on the packets, we might start questioning these health claims. Without the advertising to promote them, we might never know that we need processed cereal and revert to porridge or bread instead.'[2] While industry claims otherwise, there seems to be a widespread agreement that labels and diagrams are more likely to be effective communicators than detailed information in small print. Consequently, we can see here how the techniques of advertising are much more significant than just providing information or encouraging sales. Indeed, Lawrence (2006, p. 9) concludes that:

> the Food Standards Agency is in little doubt that the concerted attempt by industry to derail its traffic light labelling by actively promoting its rival scheme marks the beginning of a new phase in the long battle to improve the UK diet.

Which is the more effective form of guidance is the question, but we can then raise the question about when guidance becomes indoctrinational and we are not convinced that this is an indoctrinational matter but it is clearly an exercise in economic and persuasive power.

Techniques employed in the transmission of information

Analyses of advertisements demonstrate that the information conveyed is rarely if ever neutral. Indeed, very sophisticated psychological techniques are used in the construction of advertisements, using sexual and other emotive connotations of association and about desire, need, happiness, pleasure, and the idealised state of life, appealing to the desire for conformity, self-interest, status as well as the more obvious ones like thrift, getting a bargain, and so on. Not only is the information presented in this manner, it is done repetitively so as to reinforce the message; it is even transmitted in such a manner as to affect the pre-conscious mind, and so on. While the recipients might well be aware of some of the techniques being employed in the advertisements, they may not know all of them nor may they always be able to resist them.[3] Consequently, the claims in the adverts are not rational, not always the entire truth and use techniques of persuasion that are morally questionable, to say the least.

Content of the information

If commodities were to be purchased for their use-value only, then we could expect that information about them would be presented in a rational manner but in capitalist society use-value has been superseded by exchange-value: indeed, it has been argued (Featherstone, 1991, p. 14) that exchange-value tends to obliterate the use-value and so:

> Commodities ... become free to take on a wide range of cultural associ-ations and illusions. Advertising in particular is able to exploit this and attach images of romance, exotica, desire, beauty, fulfilment, communality, scientific progress and the good life to mundane goods such as soap, washing machines, motor cars and alcoholic drinks.

Consequently, many advertisements are not meant to be rational and so the information that they present is not open to rational inquiry, even those social scientists and philosophers can discuss it and the techniques employed in the transmission of the information in a rational manner.

Relationship to truth

It is a significant question at this point to ask what legitimates the information contained in the advertisements. In this world of positivism, scientific and medical discourses provide an almost self-evident 'truth' and so clothed in the rhetoric or science and medicine it presents itself authoritatively, and this is the language frequently employed in adverts. In so doing it relegates other perspec-tives to irrelevancy, and this includes both the humanistic and moral values of society. Not only do they use the language of science, often misleadingly but, frequently they do so with unproven or misleading claims. Indeed, the adver-tisements often move so far from truth that they seek to convince people by the power of persuasion, so that the use-value of a commodity is also relegated to the sidelines. Once the commodity has been freed of its use-value, then the relationship of the information provided about the good to truth becomes a more subjective phenomenon. The extent to which individuals desire an object because of its place in their life-style, the more valuable it becomes so that advertisements are less concerned with truth in this sense and more orientated to subjective value. The advertisement is geared to persuade its recipients that they need the commodity.

Morality

The morality of the process is a complex issue that will be discussed in later chapters of this book, although it is evident from the above discussion that we question the morality of advertising and regard it as a sophisticated form of mass indoctrination – the generation of totalitarianism.

From the above discussion, however, we can see that we are exposed to the processes of indoctrination. The development of global information technology has made this exposure more universal and more life long. The processes of learning that occur in daily life are frequently unintended and not very critical or reflective and it is in these processes that we are indoctrinated: these forms of advertising are themselves processes of lifelong learning. They are also processes of symbolic violence against the person and, as we pointed out in the previous chapter, ethics opposes power with the apparent weakness of responsibility and sincerity. Consequently, we can see that the power of the sub-structure is such that it is undermining rational choice and personal freedom but just as significantly, it is undermining democratic society.

Learning and brainwashing

It can be argued that what is currently practised in the information society is both a form of conditioning and indoctrination that results in people purchasing the commodities that are offered on the market and feeling that the capitalist society offers something of the good life. However, this is an over-simple conclusion since many people seem to believe that we live in a good society in which we are free to act according to our desires but many of our desires are also constructed by the same processes of advertising and propaganda and this, we want to argue here, is brainwashing.

Brainwashing, if it is not used as re-education can mean to effect radical changes in the ideas of people, to condition (*Collins English Dictionary*), and it is in this sense that it is discussed here. Lifton's (1961) research was clearly focused on thought reform in China in which he said there were two processes: confession and re-education. Confession is not an element in this study although the educational processes are: Lifton (1961, p. 17) described these as 'remaking a man in the communist image' and what we are discussing is creating the person in the capitalist image. Under the heading of *Ideological Totalism*, Lifton (1961, pp. 477–497) lists eight criteria for totalism: milieu control; mystical manipulation; the demand for purity; the cult of confession; the sacred science; loading the language; doctrine over person; dispensing of existence. It is clear from the above discussion that many of these points are relevant to contemporary society and that there is a sense in which brainwashing continues throughout life. Of the eight he lists, the following have already occurred in our discussion:

- a great deal of milieu control – as we have seen through advertising and other forms of instruction;
- sacred science – the rationality of modernity;
- loading the language – our language has been colonised by the language of capitalism – human capital, cultural capital, social capital are but a few that we could specify;
- doctrine over person – people are not as important as profit and welfare can only occur within an acceptable financial framework[4];

- dispensing existence – only those who contribute to the wealth of the whole have the right to be and all others are non-persons because they are outside the system and so they can be dispensed with – perhaps!

Basically, the individual life-world is, if not controlled, considerably influenced by the milieu of capitalist consumerism. People were encouraged to conform and dissidence is unacceptable. Fundamentally, the power of the sub-structure is exercised in a wide variety of ways – not always or necessarily coordinated but always acting in the same direction. But power is, as Foucault (1979, p. 73) reminds us, not only a repressive phenomenon; it can also be liberating and even creative and so we need to reverse the direction of our analysis. Indeed, he (p. 48) makes the insightful point about sexuality which is true of capitalism in general that, 'Pleasure and power do not cancel or turn back against one another; they seek out, overlap, and reinforce one another. They are linked together by complex mechanisms and devices of excitement and incitement.' The mechanisms are different but the linkage is similar: the desires have been created and so now the idea of purchasing and consuming can be exciting and so we can now begin to see the power of brainwashing since the desire or need has been created by the same sources as those selling the commodities. Conforming to the expectations of those who have instilled the desires become a liberating (freeing) and exhilarating experience. Our life-world has been colonised and we have learned how desirable it is to conform.

Finally, we need to point to one obvious outcome of this discussion: if we are brainwashed into desires, then it is hard to conceptualise rational and unbiased choice and so many of the arguments for rational lifelong learning and rational choice are already undermined by the processes of indoctrination and brainwashing to which the great majority of children and adults are exposed. Our society is not always based upon rational behaviour, but then it rarely has been, as my own research into superstition showed (Jarvis, 1980) when, in well over a hundred interviews into people's philosophy of life we did not find anybody who was not superstitious!

Global totalism

It must be pointed out again here that power is being used in respect to the economic rather than the political since it is claimed that in global society it is the power to control the economic and technological institutions power that enables the sub-structure to exact conformity to its needs and aspirations. Globalisation has also made it possible to extend ideas of indoctrination and brainwashing beyond the idea of national territories but, as we have already suggested, there are some forces that seek to resist these social forces, so that national and religious policies can cushion or resist the effects of these global pressures.

At least two distinct approaches to totalism can be detected in the literature: the political and the societal. Among the former, Arendt (1976, p. ix) talks of totalitarianism as 'the only form of government with which coexistence is not possible': in her studies of Soviet Communism and German Nazism she is careful in her use of the term and she is well aware that in both of these societies the regime was never monolithic (p. xiv) and that there was a dual authority of the party and the state (p. 93). The absolute authority in both cases lay with the leader and neither party nor state disputed with that authority. What is significant here is the separation of party and state – that totalitarianism is not monolithic. But this is also true globally since the fall of the Berlin Wall: now the forces of the global sub-structure (economic and persuasive) and the forces of law and order (political) provide a dual authority. In many societies, it is clear that the economic and persuasive forces prevail whereas in some, such as Muslim states, the political and the religious prevail. But in those capitalist societies a similar form of totalitarianism exists. Arendt (1976, p. v), is careful to point out that in the first instance both the totalitarian governments of Russia in 1929 and Germany in 1933 rested on mass support.

Lifton's (1967) study is not so concerned with the issues of politics and governance but more with the techniques of brainwashing, as we have noted in the previous section.

In complete contrast to this discussion but still relevant to it, Levinas' (1991 [1969]) approach is very different – one which is also important to the thesis of this book. For him society and its structures are themselves the totalism that have the potentiality to destroy both individuality and human freedom and yet everybody needs them in order to survive. He thus understands the necessity of society and its totalistic structures, as opposed to political totalitarianism, but he recognises that even within his type of totalistic society we can easily lose the human person. His concern is not about capitalism and indoctrination but about the individualism in society that exposes us to the totalistic forces and so he focuses on the richness of relationships. He (1991, p. 38) argues that when the stranger becomes a face, there is the beginning of ethics and of relationship. He sees that totality becomes problematic in the relationship between the same and the Other because the structures make the Other into a stranger so that in some way the totalistic structures have to be broken down for relationships to be created. Nevertheless, structured society is necessary and important since everybody is part of the totality and most have a place within it, but he (1991, p. 61) goes on to say that 'the knowing subject is not part of the whole' because it is the individual who can step outside of the situation. In relationship ethics is born because there is a sense in which the ethical relationship is created at the point where the social structures that separate are broken down. However, once the ethical relationship is formed and the one feels morally responsible for the other, it is not a matter of reciprocity – one behaves morally in relationship with the other because the Other has the potential to become a face, not because the Other can offer reciprocal relationships. The totalisers seek always to place individuals into wholes (systems – if you like) and so individual responsibility for the Other is lost. Almost in contrast to totalism is infinity – to reach for infinity is to transcend the totality in relationship with the Other. For him, it is only in relationships that we can transcend the limitations of both the individual and the totality and reach beyond. What we find, however, in the literature of the learning society (Lave and Wenger, 1991; Ranson, 1994; Longworth, 1999; Wenger, 1998), and much of the current management literature (Senge, 1990) is an emphasis on systems, on totality and totalisers and individuals being members of the group/organisation within the system, rather than on individual responsibility or even on the individual-in-the-world. But we have already pointed out that because we live in groups and systems, it is a form of social inclusion that makes it unnecessary to exercise covert power very frequently.

Conclusion

The question that we might ask, therefore, is to what extent is this global capitalist society a form of totalitarianism? Since there is tremendous opposition to globalisation in some parts of the world, notably the Middle East, it would be wrong to see totalism as global although it would be much more valid to claim that this form of totalism exists in those countries which have adopted the Western way of life, and the same process is occurring in each of these countries, so that it is more than just a state-based phenomenon. Totalitarianism, as we have known it in the past, is a nationalist and political movement based at the level of the state (Arendt, 1976). This form sought to sell its own vision of the nation and eventually of the world initially within its own nation and then beyond: it has its own aims. Clearly global capitalism is neither an overtly political movement, although it is a political problem, nor is it concerned about the national interest but there is a sense in which it is ideological totalism since it tolerates no other form of production or distribution of commodities. There might not even be an overt intention to brainwash or to indoctrinate the population into the belief that the ideology of advanced capitalism is good, but there is an intention to get people – through advertising and propaganda – to practise it through the purchase of the commodities produced by the corporations at the heart of society, and in order to do this questionable methods are employed in these endeavours. Without sales, however, these corporations would fail and so, eventually, would capitalism itself; the success of the system is when the sales are successful and the profits are high and those who own or control the system gain tremendous wealth and live in absolute luxury. But to do this, others must be paid low wages or left unemployed. This is the driving force at the heart of the global capitalist society; it is where a great deal of power lies because these corporations have both been able to manufacture the commodities that people need and also they have been able to persuade people that they need many of the goods that are on the market. This has led to great profits and to the power that goes with wealth.

Over the past chapters we have traced the way in which capitalism has become the global force in, what has now been called, a 'knowledge economy'. Certainly knowledge and learning are playing major roles and we have what is been called, a 'learning society'. In this chapter we have shown how that learning is often a form of indoctrination and brainwashing, whereas, previously we have shown that the learning required for the knowledge economy is scientific, technological and largely instrumental and performative rather than moral knowledge. These are naturally two sides of the same coin – unless there is a circulation of money the capitalist system cannot survive, so that, on the one hand, individuals have to be labourers and workers in order to produce goods but on the other they have to be consumers who purchase those goods or goods imported from elsewhere within the system. They have to be trained to take their place in both production and consumption: this is the learning society. As knowledge is changing rapidly, they have to be prepared to keep on learning so that they can keep abreast of the changes (or at least conform to the expectations of management), and they have to continue to learn to purchase and consume the commodities on the market through the technologies of the information society. This is lifelong learning. But problematically, even if they cannot afford these commodities, they still have to be persuaded that they need them, even to the extent of living in debt through the fulfilment of indoctrinated desires rather than rational behaviour. The same process holds good at the global level through loans, even though the loans are often given in these cases to try to help poor societies develop and become independent. As a result, the corporations might make huge profits and exercise tremendous influence over the world.

People's learning is mostly unintended, incidental and non-reflective and it is far wider than just the cognitive dimension. They respond, almost unthinkingly at times, to the latest information they receive about their areas of interest as they seek to consume more and more. Receiving advertising material, and learning from it, is also a form of lifelong learning – and it fits into the wider picture of the neo-liberal economic society. This is non-reflective learning – merely responding to the stimuli that we receive. Moreover, the control of individuals' learning in such an insidious manner is a major cause for concern since it is a deliberate removal of their potentiality, since it is by learning that we achieve our potentiality. This is certainly not the picture of the learning society and lifelong education that those early education pioneers envisaged and aspired to achieve. They envisaged a different form of learning, one in which the learners might be actively engaged in learning for its own sake, but also in creating a better world in which to live and that entails reflective learning. As we reflect upon the learning society we have described thus far, three things are most apparent: the society that we live in is one where power is exercised both overtly and covertly to the benefit of the elite who control the sub-structural processes, that such power is wielded in an undemocratic manner and its outcomes are immoral so that it is now necessary to discuss the nature of the good.

Chapter 7

Ethics and modernity

In this chapter we want to try to find a basis for a learning society which embodies goodness and in order to do this we have to both enter the field of ethics but also to examine a number of practices and values intrinsic to modernity, and in order to do this we return to the values discussed in the third chapter: scientific knowledge, capitalism, individualism (liberalism), freedom, rationality and pragmatism, and we will now return to them. Before we do so, however, it must be stressed that ethical value is not the same concept as value, as used in that chapter. Philosophers distinguish the two by suggesting that ethical value is moral good while other values are non-moral goods. In my study of ethics and the education of adults (Jarvis, 1987), I distinguished between cultural values and universal goods – ethical value, which reflected Kant's maxim that ethical goods should be universalisable (Korsgaard, 1997, pp. xvii–xxi). However, my position might have been a little too narrow at that point and I want to re-examine it in the first part of this chapter: we will then look at moral development and then we will look at the values of modernity from the perspectives of the six cultural practices and the values built into them from an ethical viewpoint. Finally, we will apply these outcomes in a brief discussion of a modern capitalist society. The reason we do this is because it is important to understand the type of society that has been called a 'learning society' and which espouses, even seeks to control, lifelong learning.

The nature of the ethical good

In this section we will examine six schools of thought about ethical value: deontological, teleological, intuitive, emotionalism, discourse analysis and agapism.[1] It is important to note that, with the exception of agapism, all are grounded in individualism and rationality and the inclusion of the latter tells us something about the nature of modernity itself. The first five emerged in the period of modernity and we can see that we can actually assess modernity by them and see how it is flawed: this we will do in the following chapters. In the final chapters we will focus a great deal more on the final school of thought.

Deontology

Once the idea of the rule of God and revealed knowledge was displaced with the rule of humans and rationality, as we discussed in the third chapter, philosophers were forced to find a rational statement of ethical good and perhaps the most well known early examination was that of Immanuel Kant (see Kant, 1998) who argued that human beings become legislative citizens in the kingdom of ends: all rational beings are members of this kingdom. Consequently, if we are to judge what is good, we would wish that the moral laws that we set ourselves should be capable of universalisation. Kant specified this: 'I ought never to act in such a way that I could also will that my maxim should become a universal law' (p. 15) and this law should be treated rather like a universal law of nature. He then went on to enunciate some hypothetical and some categorical imperatives: a hypothetical imperative being one which is a means to another end whereas a categorical one when the action is deemed good in itself. Finally, he also wrote of practical imperatives which he defined as:

> an end for everyone because it is *an end in itself*, it constitutes an *objective* principle of the will and can thus serve as a universal practical law. The ground for this principle is: *rational nature exists as an end in itself*.
>
> (italics in original) Kant (1998, p. 37)

Human beings are never means, but always ends in themselves; fundamentally, then, Kant is claiming that each individual has moral worth and respect, for that, humanity is universalisable. Since the imperatives are universal principles, then goodness lies in obedience to the laws that are universalisable. However, there are a number of weaknesses with this formulation, such as: the difficulty in finding maxims that are universalisable, although later in this section we will point to one which relates to the thesis that all human beings have moral worth. As an argument, however, this statement of Kant's might be used as something that supports the enunciation of such laws, as on euthanasia and abortion – this argument is based on a principle that might be universalisable, that, the taking of human life is never right although this is also debatable since there are times when euthanasia might be right. Hence, it becomes necessary to qualify the original assertion and eventually it dies a 'death of a thousand qualifications'. But perhaps the most telling criticism lies in the fact that this is an argument of 'duty for duty's sake' irrespective of the outcomes of the action, and that even the taking of life may, in some very rare circumstances be right if the outcomes are beneficial to humanity. It was this decision that led a pacifist, like Dietrich Bonhoeffer, to participate in the failed plot to assassinate Hitler at the end of the Second World War – for which he was hanged. It is, however, an argument that has even wider contemporary applications if we apply it to other cultures and belief systems. Additionally, it is ultimately a motive of obedience that lies at the heart of this argument, e.g. obeying the law even if it is an ass, and so it becomes a cultural and legal value rather than a moral one.

However, perhaps the most well known modern theorist to adopt this Kantian position is Rawls (1971) whose theory of justice as fairness, which is his contemporary statement of the social contract, is fundamentally a universalising process which is based upon the individual's liberties and freedoms. Rawls argues that governments have to satisfy certain moral standards about the equality of individual persons who can be treated impartially but fairly in every situation in order to advance the good of its members. He (p. 11) argues that the principles of justice are those which 'free and rational persons concerned to further their own interests would accept in an initial position of equality as defining the fundamental terms of their association'. Rawls is quite clear that justice is a legal and political concept rather than a moral one. For him justice is fairness between all peoples, even if there has to be some positive discrimination in order to realise justice. Positive discrimination, however, might be viewed as something other than justice in some circumstances. But when seen from a totally different perspective by those who retaliate against an unjust system, since 'justice' as administered by those in authority is viewed with terror because it is seen as an act of retaliation by those who hold power, and its administration 'only perpetuates the violence and prolongs the conflict that afflicts people' (Bell, 2001). In a similar manner Jackson (2005, p. 164) suggests that justice is a Western concept which cannot be universalised which, even if it could, can only be achieved, can only be obtained by those powerful enough to fight for their rights. Indeed, (p. 166) says that 'thinking abstractly about their rights is a luxury the oppressed can ill afford' (p. 165). And so, while Rawls' approach to justice might be a very high-minded approach to social living by those in the West, it certainly does not satisfy the poor and underprivileged in this global world: administering of justice does not re-establish the harmony between peoples and so once the social contract is broken, justice cannot repair it by itself. Justice is not ethical goodness. Arendt (1958, p. 237) makes the point that the only way to bring closure on any wrong-doing is through forgiveness:

> Without being forgiven, released from the consequences of what we have done, our capacity to act would, as it were, be confined to one single deed from which we could never recover; we would remain the victims of its consequences forever...

Rawls (1971, pp. 342–355) is clear that individuals are under a duty to obey these principles once they are embodied in law and so the social consequences of law breaking, for instance, can never be eradicated. Rawls' treatise on the subject, however, is a thoroughly argued case for liberalism – one which he extends in his subsequent book, *Political Liberalism* – which lies at the heart of the Enlightenment project. We will return to his work in the ninth when we look at the idea of democracy. Once more we see weaknesses in the foundations of modernity – this time it is a basic moral tenet, suffice to note that Gray (1995, p. 8) suggests that Rawls' work, like other liberal theorists, 'is the deployment of an unhistorical and abstract individualism in the service of a legalist or jurisprudential paradigm of political philosophy'.

However, in fairness to Rawls, it is essential to define fairness, which he (1971, p. 112) regards as:

- When a number of people engaged in a mutually advantageous enterprise which restricts their liberty necessary for the advantage to be gained must expect that other partners will do the same;
- We do not gain from co-operative labours without doing our fair share.

However laudable this is as a practice in daily living, we know that this liberal principle is incompatible with certain teleological principles, since we never know when the outcomes of the action are completed and so we would have to qualify the principle to the espoused aims of the enterprise. Once we tread the slippery path of qualifying principles we embark upon an enterprise that kills principles by qualifications. This principle of fairness, however, is certainly not in accord with the fundamental aim of capitalism which is to maximise profit even at the expense of pushing down labour costs, and so on. But neither is it a universal moral good since goodness is not fairness and we would be guilty of a naturalistic fallacy if we equated the two, although it is a highly laudable political and economic ideal.

Teleology

The major weakness of the above position is perhaps the strength of this second position. In its most well-known form, Bentham (1978) postulated that the goodness of an act lay in its consequences, so that a good act seeks to produce the greatest amount of happiness for the greatest number of people. However, one might ask why happiness is equated with goodness rather than health, wealth, justice, or something else, so that the traditional formulation is open to considerable question from the outset. Consequently, in its more broad formulation, it could be argued that the goodness of an action lies in its consequences: this, it appears, is rational and reasonable in contemporary society. But this is because instrumental rationality seems to be common sense in modern society: nevertheless it is often used as a justification for action. However, there are a number of quite fundamental criticisms of this position – four of which we will discuss here.

In the first place, we need to ask whether the end always justifies the means. In the above discussion we used an example whereby it might be argued that Bonhoeffer was correct in his action to be involved in the plot to assassinate Hitler, but whether we in the West would use precisely the same argument with the same accord if we were to suggest that this is also true of the Middle Eastern terrorist is another matter. We could go on to ask whether depriving human beings of their rights, if we believe that we have any, is right when the ends are not quite so significant, such as in the case of mis-selling in order for a corporation to make additional profit.

Second, we might ask whether the goodness of an action must depend on its consequences rather than the motives of the actors. Is an action better because it has good consequences, although the original motives were bad, than an action where the consequences were unfortunate, although the intentions of the actor were very good? Clearly, the intention to produce good consequences is more moral than actions which unintentionally produce them, but then we have included a second principle – that of rational intention and so the consequences themselves are not the sole good.

Third, there are unintended consequences of many actions: Bauman (2007)[2] suggests that these might be referred to as collateral casualties: that is, ones that were not intended by the perpetrators of the action. He (p. 117) suggests that collateral means that harm-causing actions can be justified and the perpetrators exempt from punishment since they were unintentional. He cites the terms 'collateral damage', 'collateral casualties' and 'collateral victims' to illustrate his point and later in his study he looks at the collateral casualties of consumer society – the underclass.

Fourth, if we are looking at the consequences of an act, we need to ask at what point in time the action is completed. The short-term consequences of an act might appear to be very good but the longer-term consequences might be disastrous and so which consequence determines the goodness of the act?

These criticisms undermine the whole concept of instrumental rationality, since we cannot determine, say, what are the long-term consequences of behavioural objectives in teaching and learning, neither can we actually control the means by which students learn the content of the lesson. These criticisms are applicable to all forms of education and training, despite official policy which, it must be said, appears to be common sense since the teleological position itself appears to be common sense, even though we have shown it to be invalid.

It might thus be seen that this apparent common sense rational argument for goodness is actually fundamentally flawed and yet, the intention to produce good consequences cannot in itself be classified as bad. These criticisms have been widely accepted for a long while and yet it is the very common sense nature of instrumental rationality and its obvious apparent validity in limited situations that results in its having assumed a very significant place in contemporary society.

Intuitionism

Perhaps the most famous exponent of intuitionism is G.E. Moore (1902) who argued that goodness is goodness and as such it is indefinable: we just know what is good – this is uninferred or immediate knowledge. It could be claimed that revealed knowledge might be regarded as intuitive, although the ramifications of this suggestion take us beyond the scope of this study. Clearly, this position places subjectivity before objectivity and this need not be a weakness, but the idea that the situation can be isolated from the whole in both time and space is much more dubious. Yet it might be argued that knowing what is right in a situation is something we all experience: it is as if common sense prevails, but we have already suggested that this does not automatically lead to correct consequences. Moreover, even if I do think that I know intuitively what is right, there is no logic in this position that compels me to act upon the intuition. However, it is a position that people with certain forms of religious conviction might find easier to accept since they might argue that 'The Holy Spirit told me…', and so on.

However, a more fundamental problem with this position is that Kohlberg (1976) – see below – has shown quite convincingly that our conception of goodness alters with education and experience, so that what might be intuitive at one stage in development might not be so at another and so intuitionism opens itself to the argument that the intuitive goodness might be a relative concept. Consequently, this position in this form does not add a great deal to our understanding of goodness, although we will reformulate it below in a manner that does add more to our understanding.

Emotivism

The difficulty in tying down the concept of goodness, led linguistic philosophers, such as A.J. Ayer (1971) to claim that there is no such thing as goodness, it is merely a sign of approval that we signify about someone or some thing that we like, or conversely we dislike. Ayer (1971, p. 146), for instance, wrote: 'Thus, if I say to someone, "You acted wrongly in stealing that money", I am not stating anything more than if I simply said, "You stole that money"'. But I am saying that I disapproved of it! Hence I am expressing my emotion. This theory was epitomised by Stevenson's (1944) *Ethics and Language*. Emotivism seeks to combine reason with the affective and provide emotive meaning. It also captures the idea that the emotion might be stronger than the reason. This is what Habermas (1990, p. 58) calls strategic action rather than communicative action.

In many ways this theory captures the spirit of the times when everything is conveyed by language, but it does have a number of weaknesses: Urmson (1968), for instance, suggests that it confuses emotion and attitudes in an unhelpful manner and that it ultimately leads to the idea that evaluation is based upon non-rational human behaviour and this is not very satisfactory.

Indeed, the four theories that we have examined thus far seek to locate the moral in different aspects of human behaviour: the first in rules, the second in consequences, the third in intuition and the fourth in language and communication.

None offer a satisfactory answer to the problem for every situation but each contains more than a semblance to the truth and we will return to this below. But, some theorists, such as MacIntyre (1988) and Habermas (1990) locate the whole problem of ethics within the framework of the Modernity and the Enlightenment project itself, as we have done in this discussion thus far. Habermas' theory of discourse ethics is an attempt to overcome some of these problems, although his position appears to be stronger than some of the others, it is not without its criticisms.

Discourse ethics

Habermas' theory emerged naturally from his theory of communicative action although it can also claim its origins in Kantian thought. For Habermas, discourse ethics is about procedure rather than substantive orientations (Habermas, 1990, p. 122). He claims that 'none of the competing ethical traditions can claim prima facie general validity any longer' (Dews, 1986, p. 248). In looking at Habermas' position we move much closer to the debate about democracy, but we also move to a theoretical position which is consistent with life-long learning and the learning society. Indeed, in his early work, he also used the work of Kohlberg (1976) on moral development and Outhwaite (1994, p. 50) makes the point that:

> As soon as we treat communicative competence as something that has to be acquired, it begins to look as if we have to deal with cognitive and learning processes at both the individual and the social level, since the individual capacities presuppose a social context, including a necessarily public language...

However, Habermas (1990, p. 67) is not as concerned about universalisabilty per se as was Kant, since it is in the competence of the communication that the truth claims of the discourse are tested. In this we see Habermas approaching, but not mirroring, the type of position held by Mill (1910) many years earlier. He (Habermas, 1990, p. 68) makes the point that discourse ethics stands or falls by two assumptions:

> (a) that normative claims to validity have cognitive meaning and can be treated like claims to truth and (b) that the justification of norms and commands requires a real discourse to be carried out and this cannot occur in a strictly monological form, i.e., in the form of a hypothetical process of argumentation occurring in the individual mind.

But Habermas also differentiated between ethical understanding which can be reached through argumentation and moral norms that can be regarded as good for everyone. Unlike Kant, Habermas' (p. 67) position is that: 'Rather than ascribing as valid to all others any universal maxim that I can will to be a universal law, I must submit my maxim to all others for purposes of discursively testing its claim to universality.' It is, therefore, the universal agreement between those who can rationally discuss, in an ideal speech situation, the maxim with normative expectations that determines its validity and the agreement lies in the discourse between people: hence he calls his work discourse ethics. The fact that the relations of communication have to be ideal suggests that he 'sees the social relations of communication as putting unjust restrictions on the emancipatory potential of intersubjective understanding' (Honneth, 2007, p. 69). In this formulation Habermas is breaking away from the basic Kantian position and also undermining the fundamentality of liberalism. Communicative participation is an important step in seeing how Habermas develops a conception of discursive democracy which we will discuss later in this work.

Habermas (1990, pp. 96–97) has four rules for discourse ethics:

1   A definition of a universalisation principle that functions as rule of argumentation.
2   The identification of pragmatic presuppositions of argumentation that are inescapable and have a normative content.
3   The explicit statement of that normative content (e.g. in the form of discourse rules).
4   Proof that a relation of material implication holds between steps (3) and (1) in connection with the idea of the justification of norms.

He recognises that the discourse contains, within it, intuitive and pre-theoretical knowledge which need to be made explicit so that participants are aware of the basis of some of their propositions through a process of rigorous questioning. Habermas is clear that this discourse is a learning discourse for the participants. While he recognises the significance of conceptual development in the development of morality, he is faced with the problem that not all people may develop their moral conceptual understanding to its highest levels, and so, it is difficult to locate the moral good in individuals' developmental processes and their dialogue since they may not all be sufficiently developed to enter enlightened moral discourse. Indeed, it may be wrong to locate it in morality in knowledge itself.

One of the main strengths of Habermas' position for learning theory is that it is through the process of communicative interaction that we undergo processes of learning. Through discussion between people, we all learn and so we can learn our ethics in relation to other people, but one of the weaknesses of such a position is that it can be 'the blind leading the blind', since it is possible for misguided people to reach an agreement through an apparently rational discussion and yet they could both be wrong! Clearly, his work is not without its critics: Benhabib (Rasmussen, 1990, p. 67.), for instance in an argument similar to the one just presented, suggests that rational discourse occurs about norms when they are endangered and not when they are taken for granted and so rational discourse might not be a realistic way of reaching a universalisable ethic. Indeed, Rasmussen (1990, p. 73) summarises the problem thus: 'can one sustain the claim that basic assumptions regarding the communicative resolution of truth and validity are given in the language as discourse?'

Habermas' position is dependent upon his views of communicative action and the ideal speech act, which is an idealistic position assuming people will not only speak the truth in a rational manner but that they will use the discourse for the good of the whole group. Fundamentally in order to create the conditions for such an act to occur requires other values to be present, such as trust, love, etc. between the participants. In accepting the idea of rational language he has not really taken into account the emotive elements that we have previously recognised. Additionally, agreement in discourse need not result in action or even in morally good action. It does seem, however, that there is something very important in the idea of discourse to which we will return, since the dialogue between people is always a learning experience and so, underlying his ideas is the concept of a society whose members keep on learning. At the same time, his assumption that discourse is always reasonable is based upon a rather restricted view of the person as a rational being.

MacIntyre (1985, p. 56), from his rather conservative position, highlights a major problem in the Enlightenment ideas of morality since they are all based in reason rather than human nature:

> morality did in the eighteenth century, as matter of historical fact, presuppose something like a teleological scheme of God, freedom and happiness as the final crown of virtue as Kant propounds. Detach morality from that framework and you will no longer have morality; or, at the very least, you will have radically transformed its character.

This change in character, resulting in the disappearance of any connection between the precepts of morality and the facts of human nature appears in the writings of the eighteenth century philosophers themselves. For although each of the writers ... attempted in his positive arguments to base morality on human nature, each of his negative arguments moved towards a more restricted version of the claim that no valid argument can move from entirely factual premises to any moral and evaluative conclusion – to a principle, that is, which once accepted, constitutes an epigraph to their entire project.

While Habermas defends the Enlightenment to some considerable extent, MacIntyre (1985) feels the whole project is flawed and has failed. Since the individual is an individual and a member of a number of social groups, we are confronted with a complex situation which results in a loose and rather incoherent set of moral attitudes that do not embody a coherent conception of human good – as the above five positions have demonstrated. Now there appear to be no possible simple formulation of moral rules. Baudrillard (1993, p. 10) reached very similar conclusions:

The glorious march of modernity has not led to the transformation of all values, as we once dreamed that it would, but instead to a dispersal and involution of value whose upshot is total confusion – the impossibility of apprehending any dominating principle, whether of an aesthetic, a sexual or a political kind.

In a sense there is a pessimism here about the future of society that reflects some of the concerns of late modernity. There is a sense that modernity has not achieved its promises. However, this does not rule out the possibility of holding a moral stance about contemporary society, although we are forced to recognise that it is not a simple one – nor is it one that can be reasoned out:

> Morality is not safe in the hands of reason, though this is exactly what the spokesmen for reason promise. Reason cannot help the moral self without depriving the self of what makes the self moral; that unfounded, non-rational, unarguable, no-excuses given and non-calculable urge to stretch toward the other, to caress, to be for, to live for, happen what may. Reason is about making correct decisions, while moral responsibility precedes all thinking about decisions as it does not, and cannot, care about any logic which would allow the approval of an action as correct.
>
> (Bauman, 1993, pp. 247–248)

While morality may not be safe in the hands of reason, the political rules which govern society should be based upon such reason and, as we will argue later in this book, such reasoned political discourse should always be judged by an ethic, by a moral good. Indeed, we might go as far as claiming that any form of structured society should be built upon ethical values and so political thought should always be assessed by ethical arguments. And, at the same time, we will show later that it is the structures themselves that inhibit moral behaviour.

However, before we seek to assess the current society, as described in the previous chapters, we do need to extend Bauman's point and also that implicit in Habermas' position – that the relationship between people is significant if we are going to grasp the meaning of ethical value in the contemporary world – but it is the complexity of the relationship between the individual and the group to which we keep returning.

Agapism or situation ethics

By way of contrast to Habermas, this final position is about substantive orientations rather than procedure but, from the outset, we are aware that failure to specify procedures might lead to its not always producing good results. *Agape* is one of three Greek words for 'love': the first is friendship, the second is sexual love and this is the third and it means 'disinterested love', 'concern for the other'. It is argued here that this form of love is the sole moral good – there is never a time when it is wrong to be concerned for the Other. Yet we have to recognise that acting upon this concern does not mean that our actions will always result in the good since we may act out of ignorance or forethought. This form of love is disinterested concern, but it does not imply lack of interest, only lack of self-interest. In this sense it is the very antithesis of modernity. It is paradoxically a sense of commitment – to the other; at the same time it does not deny that we have a self-love, only that in relationship with the Other is not the place to manifest it.

We have been confronted with a number of problems in our quest to understand the moral good. In the first instance, if we start with the idea of society as a whole and solidarity, we may argue that it is good to protect the integrity of the whole, but when we see how the unity of the people has resulted in ethnic cleansing, and the like, then we can question this as a logical starting point. In the process of emphasising the whole we can lose our individuality in this process we lose something that is at the heart of humanity. But if we over-emphasise our individuality we play down our responsibility to others and ulti-mately to the whole group/community and this is selfish. It seems that this is the fundamental human dilemma or as Jackson (2005, p. 43) would claim: 'all modalities of inter-subjective reasoning are steeping in an awareness that one's humanity is simultaneously shared and singular'. As so, we have seen that it is impossible to locate the moral good in the specific aspects of human behaviour: rules, consequences, intuition and language and communication. Finally, we have suggested that it may not be possible to locate it in reason and so we are faced with major problems: how can we protect both the individual and the social whole, how can we formulate a theory that protects reason but does not locate value within it, and so on? This, clearly, is one of the major problems with modernity itself and perhaps the liberal response to the solidarity of the pre-modern times was the pendulum swinging too far in the opposite direction to that of the unity of the community: there is a middle way. It is argued here, however, that this moral good lies in inter-personal relationship itself, in some form of inter-personal concern: in what Buber (1958) called the 'I–Thou rela-tionship' which, he argued, underlies all human being for 'in the beginning is relationship' (p. 18). However, once we begin to discuss the idea of relation-ship, then it is hard not to see the influence of power and its misuse (Adorno, 1973). But this is the issue: the misuse of power is immoral but relationships can ideally exist without the exercise of power and, herein, lies the sixth and final ethical position that we are examining in this chapter – that love is the univer-sal good whereas all the other values which we have examined are cultural goods and relative to the age. Here, we would agree with Taylor (1991, p. 17) who clearly makes the point that 'some forms of life are indeed higher than others, and the culture of tolerance for individual self-fulfilment shies away from these claims' and we believe, that this position offers a more moral form of human living because it takes the best from all the others and reaches beyond them to something even more profound.

Understanding relationship lies at the heart of the ethical problem – for ethics are fundamentally about social situations. Significantly, we can see that relationship potentially precedes knowledge, since we are confronted by people before we know them! The Other is always there but we may not, or indeed need not, enter relationship but once we recognise the potentiality of relationship Levinas (1991 [1969]) argues is the beginning of ethics. However, even this might be rather narrow, since knowledge of the mere existence of the other – the stranger – may be the demand for ethical relationship since that knowledge can be transmitted through the media so that the Other may never become a face. Indeed, the existence and personhood of the Other is sufficient justification for ethics – that the Other is a living being demanding relationship. As Levinas (p. 43) writes about the relationship between individual freedom and ethics:

> A calling into question of the same – which cannot occur within egoist spontaneity of the same – is brought about by the other. We name this calling into question of my spontaneity by the presence of the Other ethics. The strangeness of the Other, his irreducibility to the I, to my thoughts and my possessions, is precisely accomplished as a calling into question of my spontaneity, as ethics. Metaphysics, transcendence, the welcoming of the other by the same, of the Other by me, is concretely produced as the calling into question of the same by the other, that is, as the ethics that accomplishes the critical essence of knowledge.

Here then lies the heart of ethics – not in the denial of individualism but in its acceptance since it is in a voluntary foregoing of the freedom that it offers to pursue a potential relationship but ethics begins when the stranger crosses our paths and we become aware of the stranger's humanity – it is a desire to enter a relationship of care and concern for the sake of the Other. But it is very easy to exercise power in such a relationship since we might do what we think is good for the other without reference to the other's wants or desires: this is a well-intentioned mis-use of power in the relationship. Bauman (1993, p. 124) suggests that:

> (m)oral behaviour is triggered off by the mere presence of the Other as a face: that is, an authority without force. The Other demands without threatening to punish, or promise rewards. The Other cannot do anything to me, neither punish nor reward; it is precisely that the weakness of the Other lays bare my strength, my ability to act, as responsibility.

It is the presence alone that always demands the response of love, or concern (Gaita, 2000). But we might want to ask, why should we be concerned for the Other in this way? The answer must lie in the very existence of the Other: we must be concerned for the Other because the Other exists and for no other reason – this is the moral worth of humanity: indeed, the human person is the embodiment of life itself. Sometimes the Other can exercise power over us, can hurt us, but it is not the power possessed by the Other that triggers off the moral response, it is the very being of the Other, the face, that signifies the presence of one with whom we can enter into relationship and for whom we should be concerned, irrespective of whether or not the Other seeks to exercise power over us. Now, the possibility of relationship with the Other is mediated to us through the structures and inhibitions of society and to some extent is not controlled by the actors themselves. Harvey (1993, p. 106) points out that: 'Relationships between individuals get mediated to me through market functions and state powers, and that we have to define conceptions of justice capable of operating across and through these multiple mediations.' The social processes operate but the moral demand is still placed on each of us as individuals since the Other inhibits our freedom just by existing. Since we all live in relationships, then this demand to care for the other is always placed upon us and, in this sense, it is generalisable but not in the Kantian sense – it is generalisable because of the nature of humanity in relationship and this has no need of a social contract because individuals should see themselves as members of a community as well as individuals. MacMurray (1961, p. 122) claims that:

> To act rightly is ... to act for the sake of the Other and not for oneself. The Other ... always remains fully personal; consequently its objectives must be the maintaining of position personal relations between all agents as the bond of community.

At the heart of this position is the claim that there is only one moral good and it is always good – that is being concerned for the Other because the Other is a human person, the embodiment of life itself. This position embodies all the other theories that we have discussed but it is not based upon informed logic or rules. It is never wrong to be concerned even though in the exercise of concern we may well make mistakes and do wrong things. But moral actions are not mindless, nor antinomian, nor are they contrary to reasoned thought, but they are guided by the love or concern for the Other, irrespective of who the other is. The intention to love or care for the Other is never wrong. Agape means disinterested love but concern for the other is an intention or a principle rather than a practice.

Agape is grounded in human experience and we can see it in the ideas underlying intuitionism. Indeed, intuitionism can be re-formulated in terms of learning theory and, as such it can be seen to strengthen this position. It starts from the presupposition that human beings are not born individuals but in relationship: we are initially developed in a womb, born at the end of a physical cord and in a dependent relationship in which we are loved and cared for before we have the level of conceptual development to grasp what is occurring. In fact we experience loving concern and learn pre-consciously and we internalise that learning without ever bringing it to our conscious minds. However, in situations where such pre-conscious knowledge is learned and it can be brought into the conscious domain (see my discussion in Jarvis, 1987 and in Jarvis, 2006). Everybody has learned pre-consciously of the value of loving concern and so in situations when expressions of it are appropriate it comes to the surface – almost as if it is immediate knowledge rather than knowledge learned pre-consciously as a result of experience. In this sense, this approach to intuitionism has a strong case – but it is pre-conscious knowledge based upon experience rather than direct and uninferred knowledge that is the basis of 'the intuition'. Humanity could not exist without this learning, but perhaps it needs the individualism that we learn as we mature in order to progress and develop it. Only through development can we recognise the significance of individual responsibility but while we might feel responsibility for the Other, we may not act for the good of the Other – this is because we do have freedom and that freedom allows us to act immorally. Ethics, however, is not contrary to human freedom but intrinsic to it and the moral good lies in a value that will act for the good of the Other but not exercise power over the Other; indeed, the exercise of power is contrary to the moral goodness of love and concern itself.

But what are the implications for this rather nebulous theory?

At its least, it means that foregrounding self-interested individualism is fundamentally flawed since the individual always lives in relationship so that it is the relationship between individuals that comes first. Then it means that to be concerned for the other results in our always endeavouring to treat the other justly, be honest to the other and establish a trustworthy relationship but it is more than just an instrumental phenomenon. In human relationships these are the principles that can establish the community. Gaita (2000, p. 190) writes, 'We need truth in politics just as I have argued we need justice. Like justice, truth is *sui generic*, even in politics'. Whether it is good in itself or merely good because it is encapsulated within the concern for people is debatable, but what is not debatable is that we need truth and justice if we are to 'learn to live together' – one of the pillars of learning – in the Delors Report (1996) on life-long learning. But even more significantly, since justice is a political concept it has to be based on moral concepts that underlie relationships.

Once we recognise the significance of the relationship, then the value of dis-interested love, or concern, for the Other can form the basis of many different practices and political systems – it allows for a pluralism that liberalism does not. In addition, we may seek to put our principles into practice but circum-stances might prevent the outcomes for which we had hoped. However, we do not just acquire principles and so in the next section we will look at this process.

The utopian vision lies in a world in which this value rules supreme and people matter because they are human beings, so that everyone should exercise both concern and freedom in a responsible manner for the good of the whole and, as a result, all individuals grow, develop and fulfil their own human potential in relationship – what Levinas refers to as Infinity. But the vision may not be realisable so that a function of utopian thought is to point us to the fact that we have not achieved perfection: that the City of Man, or the New Jerusalem, is still a vision and perhaps an eternal hope but one which, we will argue later, cannot be achieved through the ideas of modernity which endeavoured to construct it through individual effort and knowledge.

This, then, is another approach to the moral good: that there is only one moral good that is unchanging and unchangeable – that is always good. In this it fulfils Kant's maxim, it recognises that the value lies in the motive rather than either means or ends, that it is not intuitive but learned pre-consciously and reasoned, and that it lies beyond language and even agreement between peoples. Each of these theories of modernity has considerable value although the only one that appears to be the most satisfactory is agapism – but this is a principle and not a specified way of behaviour or a law: it has no power and yet this is its strength. But the agreement between peoples might point us to another concept that we need to explore later in this study – the idea of democracy in a learning society. But before we do this, we also have to recognise that there are stages in moral development – both personal and social.

The stages of moral development

If morality was to be based on the cognitions and rationality, as Habermas and other theorists have suggested, then it is possible to see how philosophers and educationalists have combined to produce realistic theories. Rawls (1971, pp. 462–485), for instance, suggests that there are three stages in this process: authority, association and principles. In the first stage he recognises that children need to learn moral rules from their parents whom they recognise love them and provide them with clearly stated rules. In the second stage, he suggests that individuals associate moral rules with their own roles in different associations and groups. In this way, as we have already pointed out, we learn to conform to different groups' norms and values in such a way as to make the exercise of overt power unnecessary. However, Rawls (1971, p. 473) suggests that 'the morality of association quite naturally leads up to a knowledge of the standards of justice'. He (1971, p. 478) goes on to discuss this process and suggests that the outcome of adopting a morality of principles is twofold: 'one corresponding to the sense of right and justice, the other to the love of mankind and to self-command'. Here we find Rawls' morality of principles approaching the agapistic position suggested in the previous section but quite unable to reach it because he actually fails to develop the first stage.

In a similar manner, since he located his ethical theory in communicative discourse, Habermas was forced to recognise that people develop conceptually and that the appreciation of morality is learned. Consequently, he turned to a theorist of moral development – Kohlberg (1987) whose work was developed from Piaget's (1929) classical analysis of conceptual development in children. However, Kohlberg took Piaget a little further because he did not see each conceptual stage clearly demarcated in the way that Piaget did. Kohlberg's conceptual stages are as follows:

It is very clear from the outset that there is considerable overlap between these two statements of moral development and that human learning occurs in the process of personal moral development. Indeed, it is suggested here, that this is a form of lifelong learning since individuals grow and develop their moral principles throughout their lives. Additionally, it should be noted that the different theories of moral good mentioned in the first section do correspond to some of these stages. For instance, we can see that the deontological position is reflected in the first, fourth and sixth stages of Kohlberg's statement; that the teleological position is to be found in the second and fifth stages; the intuitional

Table 7.1 Kohlberg's model of moral development[3]

Level 1 Pre-conventional
Stage 1
Heteronomous morality
– sticks by the rules in order to avoid punishment and has an egocentric point of view.
Stage 2
Individualism, instrumental purpose and exchange
– right is what is fair, individuals only follow rules when they are in self-interest in order to serve the needs of self, concrete individualism and aware that people's interests conflict.

Level 2 Conventional
Stage 3
Mutual interpersonal expectations, relationships and interpersonal conformity
– lives up to what others expect in order to be a good person in the eyes of self and others, puts ones self in the other person's shoes.
Stage 4
Social system and conscience
– fulfilling agreed duties and contributing to society in order to keep the system going. Considers individual relationships in terms of place in the social system.

Level 3 Principled
Stage 5
Social contract, utility and individual's rights
– upholds relative rules in the interests of impartiality, abides by the rules for the welfare of all and in order to protect people's rights since the actor is a rational individual aware of values and rights.
Stage 6
Universal ethical principles
– following self-chosen ethical principles even when they conflict with laws because they are omitted to those principles and because the actors recognise that this is the nature of morality and that the people are ends in themselves and should be treated as such.

has few clear relationships except that its intuitional values are usually conventional; since emotivism denies that there is a moral good, then we would not expect to find its parallels in these schemes; discourse ethics finds its place in most of the stages of development; agapism is really only to be discovered in the sixth stage.

However, this theory is based only on a conceptual theory of learning and we have suggested that learning is pre-conceptual, even pre-conscious, and so we feel that it has limited value. Indeed, we would dispute this approach based on the fact that we are born in relationship and our first experiences and learning is about relationship and so the starting point of the individual, as Kohlberg's first stage suggests, is fundamentally flawed. Conceptualising moral values may well be a developmental process but learning them through experience is not.

We are now in a position to look at the values of modernity discussed in the third chapter and to evaluate the extent to which they reflect high levels of morality.

Ethical values and modernity

It will be recalled from the second chapter that we isolated a number of features that typified modernity: scientific knowledge, capitalism, freedom, liberal/individualism, rationality and pragmatism: it is now our intention to analyse all of these from the perspectives developed in this chapter – both the theoretical and the developmental. At the same time, it must be noted that this is a subject that demands a whole volume rather than a section of a chapter, so that the following section can only highlight some of the major issues with which we are confronted.

Scientific knowledge

It is often claimed that scientific knowledge is value free but this is an over-simple claim. It is true that facts have no values but then they also have no meaning. Once meaning is given to a fact we have introduced a non-empirical dimension to the situation and have diminished the significance of the empirical. The meaning is always cultural and as such it is not factual but because the meaning given is associated with an empirical fact it tends to achieve the status of objective knowledge. No meaning is objective, it is always cultural and so scientific knowledge is always cultural and is often employed to make false, or unproven, claims. We have already noted how many advertisements make reference to scientific knowledge in this way and often do so immorally because they use this knowledge claim for their own capitalist ends and not for the ends of human good.

Capitalism

Capitalism is clearly a teleological form of life: as we saw in the third chapter at its crudest it is the pursuit of profit by rational and legal means and, as such, functions at a low level of moral development in Kohlberg's scheme. However, its end is one of the criticisms made of teleology in the third chapter, precisely, what are the ends of capitalism? It could be said that they are the profit accruing to the owners of capital (including the shareholders) as a result of the production of goods which scores very lowly in Kohlberg's scheme – indeed capitalism is not a highly developed one in terms of human values! But it is an approach to life that does appeal to the lowest common denominator.

However, the one specified end does not mean that it is the only end product of any intended action – there are often many other products and these are often unintended: other ends could include the impoverishment of the workers, the impoverishment of the suppliers of the raw materials, addiction to consumerism, and so on. These are the collateral damages of consumer society! As we asked of utilitarianism – why should happiness be the only good? There are others! This is true of capitalism in which profit is the articulated end-product but we rarely assess its moral value by any of the other end-products, both short-term and long-term, and so we are presented with a false view of the phenomenon. Profit is certainly not the only outcome and while it may be a cultural value it is certainly not a moral good but it is the one upon which the dominant rationality of contemporary society focuses and upon which the news media present. But the profit for the few may be the exploitation of the many which is also a potential outcome of the capitalist system.

In precisely the same way, we pointed out that there are moral issues about the means as well as the ends, and these are also underplayed in any discussion of capitalism. For instance, in order for profit to be maximised – supplies of raw materials have to be obtained as cheaply as possible, the production and retail costs have to be minimal, the sale price has to be as high as the market will take and the amount of sales must be maximised. Each of these four points is open to moral considerations:

- Raw materials have to be obtained as cheaply as possible. This now becomes an end and the means of obtaining raw materials, such as: offering the producers the lowest possible price and forcing it upon them if there is a monopoly situation; denuding the planet of essential natural phenomena – like forests; stealing community property or community rights to natural phenomena – like water from indigenous peoples; and so on. Perhaps the biggest fundamental problem that modernity faces is when the resources run out – a world destroyed by capitalism.
- Production and retail costs have to be minimal: Consequently, technology is brought in to replace labour since it is apparently cheaper and more efficient; wages are forced down to the lowest possible level at whatever costs

to the workers; production is moved to countries where labour costs are lower and where the workers are not organised to fight for workers' rights; and so on. Even on the day when I was writing this there was a report from the OECD that globalisation has reduced the power of the unskilled workers and that governments need to improve their 'social safety needs' – or welfare state provision (Seager, 2007). Moreover, looked at from the perspective of the poor, capitalism is seen as having won the battle to dominate modernity and it is often referred to as 'savage capitalism' (Bell, 2001) in which the poor are becoming superfluous – not just as labour power but as people.

- Sale price has to be as high as possible. The greater the need for a commodity is felt the higher the price can be, so that if advertising can create a need, then the price may be as high as the market can carry; that the prices are high can be seen when discount sales bring down the price by a great deal.

- Sales have to be maximised. This has been achieved through discounted sales but also through mis-selling. Many people, including myself, have been deceived by the sharp practices of the expert sales person and rogue traders in which the feelings of the purchaser are not considered in the pursuit of the maximisation of sales. But sales are maximised through advertising, indoctrinating children and continuing to provide information – both true and false through the media to entice people to consume – this was fully discussed earlier in this study.

Now each of these means puts the pursuit of profit before any other end, such as the purchasers' needs or the suppliers' and workers' standard of living, and so on. None of these is concerned primarily about the Stranger, the Other who can become a Face. Consequently, it may be seen that there are many situations in which the ends of capitalism are not justified by the means and so it becomes an immoral practice. Indeed, it most frequently is! But the question might be asked – is it always immoral? Here the answer is more equivocable.

It could be argued that the masses which purchase the commodities of global capitalism are made happy by their purchases and, therefore, this system produces the greatest happiness for a great number of people and so it is true to the utilitarian principle and is, therefore good. However, in so doing we have suggested this process seeks to control and even to diminish human potential so that the ends do not justify the means. Moreover, all the other moral objections to capitalism still demand an answer: in almost every country in the world there is also a growing poverty and the development of an underclass, and so, the gratification of the desires of an elite minority appear to outweigh the enforced impoverishment and dehumanisation of the remainder. But one other interesting criticism remains: it is sometimes forgotten that Hobbes (1968 [1651], p. 185) argued that there are three principle causes for people quarrelling and the first of these is competition – without a controlling force this could lead to 'a warre, as is of everyman against every man' and so we can expect those who are impoverished to fight for their share of the cake. However, Habermas' focus on discourse begins to answer this problem – but only if the rich and the poor speak to each other as equals. Once again we are forced back to the intention of the actors. Consequently, capitalism per se could become a moral practice but before it can it would need to rethink most of the basic assumptions of modernity – indeed, even the basic assumptions of pre-modern capitalism. At present, we are forced to conclude that the practice of global capitalism does not achieve moral goodness.

However, as capitalism is about private ownership, and, it will be recalled that Abercrombie et al. (2000, p. 37) suggested that among the five features of capitalism is private ownership, it requires further discussion here. As we mentioned in the third chapter, Locke regarded property rights as one of the fundamental rights of human beings. This now seems common sense although it is neither a simple nor a straight-forward matter: it might well be argued, for instance, that when individual entrepreneurs develop innovations, plan the production of the commodity and market it, then they have the right to own the production process and profit from it and that will be the starting point of this discussion. Innovations are frequently individual and often thought and fought through at considerable cost, and in this sense, the developer is an individual who stands outside of the group and if the product is beneficial to the social group, then that individualism is justified: indeed, it may be a universalisable action. In this sense, we can see that the position of Hayek (1944, 1979) is perfectly valid.

However, this is not always the case because we have seen the structural readjustment policies implemented by the World Bank and foisted upon governments of poor developing countries because of their debts in which community resources, such as water, have been taken from the community and given to private enterprise in order, so it is claimed, to manage the resources more efficiently actually amounts to stealing of communal ownership and rights. It is the failure to recognise communal ownership that has led many moderns to assume that indigenous people did not own their property and we now see it in World Bank policies. This is true of many forms of the West taking from the indigenous peoples (Gaita, 2000). Hence, to turn Nozick's (1974) argument on its head – this is the government being forced to steal from the people in order to implement the World Bank's economic policies. Not only is it a misuse of power but it is an action that one could not wish to be universalised and, as we noted in the second chapter, it is not surprising that Joseph Stiglitz (2002) the World Bank's former chief economist and Nobel Laureate in Economics has recently claimed that the time has come for major changes in the World Bank's economic policy and the values that it reflects – he (2002, p. 252) writes that 'development is not about helping a few rich people get richer ... it is about transforming societies, improving the lives of the poor, enabling everyone to have a chance at success and access to health care and education' (cited from

Bawden, 2006, p. 113). Consequently, the question needs to be asked about how the private property was acquired and whether it has a degree of moral legitimacy about it which it is clear that some of the structural re-adjustment policies do not have.

While we have not produced many case studies here to illustrate all of these points (space does not allow this in a book of this length) it is possible to do so and such studies as Korten (1995), Monbiot (2000), Gaita (2000) and Pilger (2003), and many examples produced in the newspapers can be used to illustrate all of these points.

Freedom

Freedom, as we are beginning to see is intimately connected to fundamental aspects of the modernity project: we will now briefly examine it in relation to the ethical theories that we have already discussed.

Freedom is almost self-evidently good but this was not so in the thinking of Hobbes (1968 [1651], p. 185) who feared a 'war of every man against every man' – as we mentioned in the third chapter and so the social contract, and therefore, the state, is a necessary institution to prevent this happening. Consequently, he would argue, freedom has to be restricted. But the war has not happened and it has not been averted because of the power of the state although the state may need to regulate capitalism for other reasons. In utilitarian terms, we might be asked just how free can we be? Should we be free to destroy other people's freedom? (Berlin, 1991 [1969]). This is a point that we discussed earlier when we questioned the idea of positive freedom. Clearly freedom needs to be limited and we might want to ask questions about whether we can universalise the intentions of the free actor or whether they are egoistic. There is a sense in which freedom has to be used responsibly and this means that we have to acknowledge the weakness of the utilitarian position and also recognise that the deontological position needs to be qualified. Consequently, the intuitive position that freedom is self-evidently good becomes problematic.

Habermas' starting point in discourse ethics is his theory of communicative action which maintained that at the heart of society is communication which he specifies as being when 'participants coordinate their plans of action consensually, with the agreement reached at any point being evaluated in terms of inter-subjective recognition of validity claims' (Habermas, 1990, p. 58). Hence, freedom becomes a debateable point and, as such it is open to all the previous points that we have raised.

From the agapistic position, it could be argued that it is the Other's being free that impinges upon my spontaneity (freedom) and this is where ethics actually begins: we can see that the responsible utilisation of freedom per se lies at the heart of ethics and, as Habermas' theory of discourse ethics demands, freedom has to be used responsibly in cooperation with others and for their own good. For, as Buber (1947; 1959) argued, relationship is the beginning – for him the I–Thou relationship is at the heart of human living. We are always in relationship with Being itself, with our own being and with others, and our relationship with others assumes many dimensions. Consequently, we will see here that the relationship is the realm of ethics – which is the problem that we have been aware of from the outset. For Buber, there can be no 'I' without a 'Thou' because it is only because of relationship that we can exist as separate beings but the relationships they form, apart from those at birth, occur because people live at the same time and occupy the same space.[4] As Levinas (1991 [1969], p. 66) argues so forcefully, the stranger is free but 'Discourse is ... an original relationship to an exterior being.' The first stage in relationship is an exchange in words but once the stranger has appeared on our horizon our own freedom in respect to the stranger is curtailed. For Levinas, when the stranger becomes a face there is the beginning of ethics. Bauman (1993, p. 124) summarises Levinas' position clearly when he writes:

> (m)oral behaviour is triggered off by the mere presence of the Other as a face: that is, an authority without force. The Other demands without threatening to punish, or promising rewards. The Other cannot do anything to me, neither punish nor reward: it is precisely that weakness of the Other that lays bare my strength, my ability to act, my responsibility.

Freedom, then, is something to be used responsibly and for the good of the Other – and in pursuing the good of the Other we forego our own freedom but we are also free to ignore the Other: this is something that modernity has downplayed and, as we will see in the next section, similar arguments apply for individualism.

Individualism

We have already criticised the individualistic position earlier in this chapter in which we argued that we are born in relationship, live in relationship and almost the only time when most of us are entirely alone is at the point of death. Naturally, we develop as individuals but individualism is an ethical form of egocentricity. Having said this we do have to recognise that the individual has moral worth; the individual embodies human life and it is the individual, the Stranger, whose very presence makes moral demands on us. We need to be an individual when we love those whom others despise, and when we care for those who are the underclass and disenfranchised. But, this is the theme that runs through the whole of this study: in a sense, it is the problem of humanity itself – the problem of the individual in relationship with other individuals.

Learning as a process individualises us and through learning we develop self-identity, lifelong learning reinforces the process, we need to be individuals to achieve, we need individuals to behave responsibly, we need to step outside of the group to do things that will improve the quality of life of the whole of humanity. Individualism is not wrong. But how we use our individuality is the question since once our focus turns in upon the self, the potentiality for enriched relationship for the good of the whole disappears. Once, the desire for self-satisfaction and self-gain take precedence, then the high moral values that we have referred to here disappear. Once we respond to the advertisements to fulfil our desire, even our own potential, we are distracted from the Other – the Stranger who could become a Face. But not responding to the Other is not only an offence against the Other – it is more fundamentally an offence against community itself – an offence against the people and so we are brought back to the social contract.

Individualism is not wrong in itself, indeed, individuals in relationship is the ideal, espoused by Buber and Levinas, and many other thinkers. But individualism without relationship is problematic because there can be no loving concern, no concern for humanity, no wish to universalise our actions and no consideration about bringing the greatest benefits to the greatest number of people. The capitalist system has fostered the latter form of individualism and the few gain great wealth – perhaps even some happiness! – but apart from learning to be producers and consumers, where that is possible, the majority remain Strangers who might never become Faces.

Rationality

Of course rationality is good: it is what academic argument is built upon; indeed, it is what society is constructed upon – but is it sufficiently good? We believe that we can obtain all knowledge rationally and by scientific inquiry. Again, it is a common-sense position that few will dispute. But the only trouble is that human beings are not entirely rational: none of us are. Logic and rationality might be for the computer and the computer model. We might try to control people and make them behave according to the model. But people do not always behave rationally. In a little piece of research on superstition (Jarvis, 1980) we interviewed many people and discussed with them their philosophies of life: everybody we talked to had at least one superstition. Handy (1989) called this *The Age of Unreason*. In that book he argued, correctly, that a great deal of creativity comes from upside-down thinking and a great deal of this does not happen to order in the way that many research contracts are framed, and so on. Those early computer scientists, who coined the phrase 'fuzzy logic', recognised that human beings are not and never will be computers – for they are machines, designed to act according to the laws of electronics and process information accordingly and we human beings do not do this.[5]

In contrast, it might be argued that the rational person follows the laws of logic: indeed, Brown (1988, p. 184) suggests that the classical model of the rational person demands that 'the notion of a rational belief is fundamental, and the notion of a rational person (i)s derivative'. Indeed, this suggests that the rational person is just like a machine! But Brown himself disputes this and

146 Ethics and modernity

he suggests that not only argument but also experience has a place to play and that 'rationality provides reasons for accepting claims' (Brown, 1988, p. 226). In this sense, he has underlined Weber's distinction between instrumental and value rationality. If we can understand why an action is undertaken or if we know why we have acted in a certain way, then it is hard to claim an action is irrational.

But then to be concerned for the Stranger, especially if the Stranger can offer us no benefit does not seem rational either – but this response assumes that instrumentality is the only form of rationality and we would argue that being concerned for the Stranger because strangers are human beings is rational but not instrumental. In this sense, value rationality is fundamental to our argument that in the learning society, we learn to understand and behave rationally. But because we live in a society in which the dominant ideas are instrumental, ethical ones are made to appear irrational rather than non-instrumental and downplayed – but they are not irrational.

Pragmatism

James' (2000, p. 113) distinction between rationalism and pragmatism is important at this point: 'The essential contrast is that *for rationalism reality is ready-made and complete from all eternity, while for pragmatism it is still in the making, and awaits part of its completion from the future*' (*italics* in original). But James is really only discussing instrumental rationality and so this claim is of limited value. Earlier in this same work, James (2000, p. 34) makes the point that pragmatism is about empiricism while rationality is about abstraction but that pragmatism can accept a number of truths since they 'are not real truth' (p. 34). Truth for the pragmatist 'is a class name for all sorts of definite working-values in experience' (p. 34).

This distinction is clearly one that Brown might possibly accept in his later theory of rationality, but the significant point is that pragmatism is open to future learning and future developments. Consequently, it is a theory that can incorporate lifelong learning and the learning society, since it seeks to reconcile and it is in this openness that we can endeavour to bring together a variety of theories of the good and see the value in each as well as the weaknesses. This is also a reasoned approach.

The ethics of a modern capitalist society

As we draw this chapter to a close we can conclude that global capitalism is not built on the value of moral goodness but on the other values of modernity – freedom, individuality, rationality and pragmatism – which both allow for people to be good or to fall short of goodness. We are, therefore, confronted with an interesting moral dilemma – since individuals choose to conform to such a system does this make them evil? Perhaps the question sounds a little outrageous but if we are more specific: what of the advertising executive who produces advertisements that are deliberately misleading? What of the employees of the tobacco company who continue to work for the company and promote its sales even though they know that the product they produce will send some consumers to an agonising death? What of the policy maker who deliberately prevents people from obtaining their traditional rights by privatising community facilities, such as water in parts of central Africa or land in North America and Australia? And so we could go on – and clearly there are many fundamental arguments here that are beyond the scope of this book, although we would conclude that they are all morally wrong since they fail to be concerned for the people who suffer. But are all of the people who have lived in such societies, and benefited from them, evil? Are we in the West all evil because we live in an advanced capitalist society?

Before we answer this point, it is important to note that no society has been perfect; in this sense every society's culture has fallen short of the high ideals of the ethical society. It is for this reason that people have looked back to an imaged earthy Paradise and who then look forward to the New Jerusalem – the City of God or the City of Man. Both lie beyond the bounds of time – both are utopian, dreams in a dystopian world. And so, our modern capitalist society is morally just like other societies – dystopian.[6]

But why do people conform to it? We have seen the arguments for being socialised into the culture of the group; we all are. It was Marx (see Bottomore and Reubel, 1963) who highlighted the ideas of the dominant classes being the dominant ideas; it was Gramsci (Joll, 1977) who discussed the significance of hegemony – the covert exercise of power that we have discussed throughout this book. We are all part of such a society in which the cultural values are institutionalised – even if they fall short of moral goodness. Perhaps Arendt (1964) provides us with a further clue when, in her report on the Eichmann trial, she concluded that evil is banal. While her report caused great consternation among many people, especially Jews, who had experienced the Holocaust (see Young-Bruehl, 2004), since she did not depict Eichmann as the embodiment of some evil monster but as a rather ordinary person who just saw himself as doing his duty – conformity to the system but to a system that was very bad. But the Holocaust is rightly seen as an horrendous phenomenon and global capitalism might not appear to be so for those in the West, and so ordinary people go about doing their duty! But we live in a world in which the banality of evil is institutionalised and to which we nearly all conform.

However, not all evil is banal: there is an evil beyond the banality which devises and perpetrates all forms of wrong doing and about which ordinary people are appalled. It is both the existence of this greater form of evil which perhaps hides the moral banal forms from us – it is the evil depicted by the evil monster which people expected Arendt to describe. However, this is not the place to pursue this subject any further: merely to note that banality is not the limits of evil.

Conclusion

In this chapter we have tried to demonstrate that the ethical dichotomy lies between the individual and the group: the highest ethical value is one in which people in relationship count as supreme and that their freedom and individuality are important but that that freedom and individuality can be used either for the good of humanity or to its detriment. We have suggested that contemporary society tends to emphasise the ego-centric use of these terms and judges the success of our actions in terms of the wealth acquired, but we have disputed the validity of this position ethically. We have recognised that there are no simple answers since we are not machines and so we do not always act rationally nor should we unless we take value rationality on board, but we are participants in human living, which involves relationships of loving and caring. Such values are downplayed in a contemporary society that emphasises the individuality, freedom and rationality present in contemporary global capitalism: indeed, we have recognised that the values of such a society are socially constructed whereas the ethical values transcend the cultural ones and relate back to human living itself – to the very basis of our humanity which is the individual in the social. We have also suggested that global capitalism does not measure up to the high ethical standards of humanity, but the question must still be raised as to whether modernity has failed by its own standards. If neo-liberalism is the logical outcome of modernity, then morally and politically it has failed. Clearly, even the city of man cannot be built on the values of neo-liberalism, but it is within this society that lifelong learning and the learning society have become dominant ideas, and so it is to these ideas that we must now turn.

Chapter 8

The ethics of lifelong learning and the learning society in global capitalist society

Of course contemporary society is not perfect: no society has ever been, but nearly every society has its myths and aspirations about the perfect society, and so our analysis of lifelong learning and the learning society takes place against a backdrop which is both familiar and unfamiliar. It is familiar because we are looking at lifelong learning and the learning society in a social context which influences its policies, procedures and practices but it is unfamiliar because the power structures are much more overtly economic than political. Yet, it is the type of society which some scholars had great hopes that the learning society would be more democratic and more idealistic, e.g. Hutchins (1968) and Husen (1974): the former looked to a new Athens and the latter believed that it would happen as a result of the introduction of computers. More recently, Ranson (1994), looked forward towards a new democracy and Welton (2005) asked whether it might be a just society, both were concerned about the same problems upon which this study focuses – the gap between the world in which we live and the politics and morality that we would espouse. In this chapter, we will analyse both lifelong learning and the learning society and we will look specifically at these two latter studies that point us towards our analysis of the concept of democracy and the creation of a better society. Other writers, e.g. Longworth (1999, 2006), have merely embraced the status quo without critical analysis. Longworth, however, has clearly and positively described ways in which the learning society can be developed; however, he does not demand our attention here although we examined him and other similar writers in the previous volume (Jarvis, 2007b). Our intention is to continue this critical analysis and place lifelong learning within its current social context, one that suggests that modernity has not succeeded, and then look beyond to what could be.

Lifelong learning

In the EU policy documents of lifelong learning we are introduced to four aims: employability; active citizenship; social inclusion; personal fulfilment (EC, 2001a), but in the Delors Report (1996) we have four pillars of learning – to be, to know, to work and to live together. The comparison between these two sets of aims is actually very instructive, as we saw in the second chapter: the former reflects the individualism of modernity in work, citizenship and personal fulfilment, whereas the latter is concerned about the whole society learning to live together. Lifelong learning per se has no aims, only those who are its exponents have aims for it and it is these that may be analysed from a moral and/or political perspective. The latter is much more acceptable than the former, although even this requires at least one additional pillar. Rather than taking each organisation's aims and analysing them individually, although we started to do this in the second chapter, it is felt here that we should just look at the components of lifelong learning and analyse them; thereafter it can be seen how each organisation measures up to the overall analysis.

We have already pointed out that there are two major strands in lifelong learning: the process of human learning throughout the lifetime and the recurrent education provided by the state or business and industry or even by private providers, so that this part has two sections – the first deals with human learning itself and the second with recurrent education.

Human learning

The human being is of inestimable value: as we have argued learning is the driving force of our humanity. Learning is both the process of being and of becoming; it is about achieving our potential. In this, it is nearly always good, but it is not universalisable since we can learn things that inhibit our growth. As the body grows and develops through the ingestation of food and drink, the whole person grows through learning and experiencing and the process continues almost from the time of conception until the time of death. Much of that learning comes from the processes of daily living through informal and non-formal processes but society has always recognised the significance of this process and has for the last century or more provided more formal means of nurturing the precious potential of children, as well as ensuring that they were disciplined, controlled and prepared for their place in society; this was undertaken through institutionalised learning or education. More recently, this process has been changed both through the processes of individualisation and the emergence of the mass media: the first indicates where we have lost the source of a great deal of the informal learning that occurs in community and the second has become a dominant non-formal learning process and so we will further sub-divide this section into three – informal, non-formal and formal lifelong learning.

However, before we embark on this it is necessary to draw a fundamental distinction between reflective and non-reflective learning. In the former the learners are gullible and accept what they are told as we have seen in previous chapters, while in the latter, learners reflect upon their experiences and might well be critical of the situation in which they find themselves. At the heart of a great deal of adult education has been critical learning which is very distinct from the adult learning that occurs in some aspects of contemporary society.

Informal lifelong learning

From before our birth until we die most of us live in some form of relationship with others: from the earliest life in the womb we are in a relationship – in a loving relationship and we experience this through our senses but not cognitively in the first instance. We internalise this sensation and learn pre-consciously. Only later in life do we conceptualise it or act upon it. It is the universal human experience and lies at the heart of moral relationships. In this very small and taken-for-granted event lies the major moral criticism of the individualistic system within which we live.[1] It is our very first learning and it occurs before consciousness. We continue to learn pre-consciously after birth and as our consciousness develops so we learn first of all through our senses and then through our cognitions. We continue in that relationship and learn in a loving environment for the first years of our lives – in this sense we learn the moral good, as we argued in the previous chapter. It is a form of continual socialisation through which we learn what it means to be members of a group/community, but as we pointed out earlier, it is through these relationships that power is exercised both covertly and overtly. But in early childhood, it is also through relationships that we gain our first understanding of the world and through which we also learn about our place in society and gain our identities – both social and personal. It is through this informal learning that we embark upon the process of becoming persons – persons who are of moral worth. Learning then is not just the universal process by which we become persons and members of a people; it is a moral process which drives our human formation. It is essential to our being and becoming and as such it is nearly always good, but when the relationships in which this learning are disturbed and when the content of what is learned is dysfunctional, then learning becomes questionable. Learning is always potentially good because of its contribution to our humanity and to the human community but there are times when this is just not so – Dewey (1938) referred to this as mis-education[2] – since the product of these learning processes need not be a good person. This does not detract from the fact that the person who is not good is still a Stranger who can become a face and should be loved, but it does point to the fact that learning is a moral process which takes place within a social context and as such it always has the potential to be morally good but it is not morally good in itself. The morality itself still lies in the nature of the relationship in which the learning occurs, as we showed earlier, and so the parent or the teacher has first to enrich the relationship that exists and only after that to exercise power in a loving manner when it is necessary if that learning is to have good outcomes.

At the same time, children learn a great deal in their formative years through interaction with their environment, through individual play and then in play with others. They learn about empirical facts and then they learn how to associate their learning with language and meaning – but learning through the sense experiences is certainly a different form of learning from that which occurs through the cognition: this former type of learning is just as essential to human development, and as such, it is still a moral process. Informal lifelong learning, because it happens within a global capitalist culture, will almost inevitably result in learners reflecting many of the values of that culture but since we are also free individuals who have the ability to think and question, we are able to reject aspects of that culture in part or in full.

Non-formal learning

Non-formal learning is more organised and even institutionalised but occurs outside the formal context of the school, even though it might be organised by it. It usually has specific aims and is a means of learners discovering for themselves or through which information is transmitted to them in less formal situations – a great deal of what passes for experiential learning, and even the hidden curriculum, in formal education is actually non-formal learning. The social context within which that learning appears is crucial to the development of the person and all aspects of that learning – its content, means of transmission, the intentions of those who organise it, and so forth – are open to moral evaluation. We have already investigated one of the major sources of human learning in the information society – the media. But learning in non-formal situations is not restricted to the learning through the mass media, although it is crucial to our argument here.

We have shown earlier that advertising is a form of indoctrination and although the concern of the scholars we discussed was with religious indoctrination within a school setting, we also looked at brainwashing which was political and we concluded that nearly all children in Western society are subject to the processes of economic indoctrination and brainwashing, which we concluded is an immoral process. As we pointed out earlier, Wolfe (1989, p. 97) reminds us that:

> Early advertising men believed that they were guardians of public taste, not of business ends, leading campaigns for truth and sincerity, which their own advertisements were undermining. A generation later, even while paving the way to a modern, consumption-orientated, capitalist society were, in Roland Marchand's [1985] view, continually shocked by the gullibility of the very public they were trying to influence, as if greed and acquisition, rather than being essential moral features of capitalism, were somehow unseemly.

Two things concern us here: the one to which we have already referred is the gullibility of the recipients of the advertising. This is non-reflective, acquiescent learning and it is this to which we want to make further reference later in this study. Second, the advertising people probably have never been guardians of public taste, although they might wish to think that they have, but whether they were or were not, the whole process of advertising needs always to be examined from a moral perspective. Had they ever been guardians of the public taste, we might have felt inclined to praise the outcomes of their activities although the methods they used might still have been of dubious moral worth. But now many advertisements could not claim to be guardians of any taste since they use many questionable images, displays and innuendos, associational techniques and appeals to egoism in the pursuit of their message.

However, it is not only the tastefulness of the content of their message that we might want to question, it is its relationship with truth, the lack of rationality, the psychological techniques that are used – in all of these they are not concerned about the recipients of their message but only about the pursuit of profit, and so on. Advertising, as we now know it, utilises emotivist techniques to suggest what is desirable and by so doing it implicitly denies that there is a moral good beyond the cultural values of capitalism. It falls short of offering anything that could be universalised and it falls into all the traps of utilitarianism offering ends but not moral means nor necessarily truths. Its messages cannot be questioned rationally and implicitly its message is that profit is more important than people. In short, it is hard to find any moral support for many of the practices for commercial advertising. It is an indoctrinational technique when the learners are moulded and consumers are created. However, it might be argued that this is a rather sweeping condemnation for two reasons: anybody can turn off the television or not be concerned with the advertisements that appear on the screen and also because the consumer society brings happiness to many people.[3] While the first is true, if we have been socialised into the advertisements as we suggested earlier, then it becomes harder not to look at them and it is not really a chore to see them since they can titivate desire, make us laugh, and offer us even more potential happiness. But the happiness of those in the West is not the only end-product of the system – indeed, in the West there is already the creation of an underclass and in the underdeveloped world poverty just continues to increase and the ecology is gradually being undermined: these are the outcomes that all consumers have to learn about. Fundamentally advertising is also about the misuse of power: it is using economic and persuasive power for the ends of profit and the enrichment of the few at the expense of the many. Clearly this type of non-formal learning falls short of high moral standards.

By accusing advertising within global capitalist society of being a practice that falls short of high moral standards, we are not condemning all non-formal learning nor even the uni-directional transfer of information: information transfer is a legitimate and important process. Information sharing is also part of the educational process – enriching the person within the wholeness of society. Information sharing need not be an exercise in power, although it frequently is, especially in children's education since it is the power of the representatives of society to socialise children into the culture of the wider society.[4] This form of power might be regarded as legitimate because it protects the unity of the whole and it may be exercised in love, although if not exercised in a moral way it becomes questionable.

Formal learning

Formal education is always social and in a sense instrumental because schools are created to prepare children for adulthood and to take their place in society. But the significant thing about them is that they should exist for children and for the whole of society, their legitimacy becomes debateable if their ends differ from these: they have universalisable ends since they exist to assist the learners develop into mature individuals and to integrate them into a society and by so doing they can enrich society as a whole. However, with the way in which global economics has permeated schooling, both in the ways that formal education is organised and the content of what is taught casts some doubt upon the fundamentals of schooling as to assist learners to achieve their human potential and to enrich society as a whole. Education organised as a commodity in the learning market has been forced to cut the costs necessary to offer a comprehensive education, despite all the claims that more money is spent on education than ever before.[5] But it could be argued that more children are getting to higher education than ever before, although the standards achieved are on the whole lower.[6] The market place has not improved education, although the majority of the teachers no doubt have the same high ideals as they ever had and teaching remains a moral process. It will be recalled that when we examined indoctrination we suggested that each of the following is a moral constituent of the teaching and learning process:

- the intentions of those who teach;
- techniques used in the teaching and learning process;
- content that it taught and the extent to which it is open to examination;
- relationship to the truth – the content must be true and valid.

In contrast to advertising, education should differ in each of the above four points: those who teach do so because they have a calling to serve society and the learners in their charge; the techniques employed in teaching should always endeavour to build a caring relationship in which the learners feel free to question and explore; what they teach should never be above question and contradiction and its relationship to the truth – whatever that is – should always be transparent. This may be the ideal and we probably all know or have known schools, colleges and universities that endeavour to achieve these standards, but as we showed earlier in this study formal teaching and learning institutions are being diverted in some ways by the exercise of economic power and so the education content is partially directed towards subjects that might be considered useful for future employment. We have also shown how there is a hidden curriculum in schools and how universities are becoming increasingly dependent on finance provided by business and industry – often at a price of providing opportunities to influence the learners to the benefit of the commercial organisations' ultimate profits and so it is the situation within which the formal learning occurs which needs to be questioned.

Now it can and should be asked whether everything that commercial organisations do beyond their actual commercial tasks should be seen as attempts to indoctrinate in this way and, clearly, the answer must be in the negative: many corporations take their corporate responsibility seriously, give funds to needy causes without seeking undue publicity, and so on, and this is to be lauded, although it is right that motives for such action should always be assessed. But the contrast between education and advertising must be seen along the lines of, at least, the above four points.

There are other types of formal learning, such as liberal adult education and even senior citizens learning: the former of these has been reduced considerably in the UK by the present government but the latter has grown tremendously as the population ages. At the present time, universities of the third age in the UK are free from external pressures and, consequently, can be more true to the ideals of human learning. Human learning, then, is both the process of learning to be but it is also becoming and is discussed very thoroughly in the Delors Report; it is also about fulfilling our human potential, as the EU policy documents stress, but Delors crucially recognises that we do need to learn to live together. However, citizenship education, human relationships and ecological education do not play significant roles in the practice of much formal lifelong learning.

Recurrent education

The other aspect of lifelong learning is recurrent education – formal teaching and learning provided by universities, colleges, work places and private institutions. Perhaps there is no need to expand the analysis that we undertook in the above section here, except to point to the fact that if education is so essential to human growth and development at one level and to career development at the other, then these functions have moral significance. The fact that a great deal of recurrent education is offered in the market place of learning means that there is rarely equal opportunity to access it; the market always favours the wealthy, most frequently males and the young or those whose employers will sponsor them. Entry is restricted to those who can afford it – something we have already claimed is open to a number of criticisms in respect to its morality – or those who can be sponsored. It is impossible to universalise the practice that recurrent education should only be made available to those who can afford it. It is impossible to defend it on the grounds of the moral worth of each citizen since the market implies that those who can afford to pay are worth more than the poor. Intuitively it also seems contrary to common sense. In short, even by the cultural values of modernity, it is impossible to defend many of these practices.

Certainly, recurrent education does not exist because those who organise it care for the strangers who might become their students.

In addition, the market always assumes that the providers are in competition in order to be efficient, although we have repeatedly claimed in this study that the ends do not justify the means and if there is to be community and togetherness in society, then competition that divides becomes a more questionable enterprise in itself. This is certainly true in knowledge production and dissemination, and questions need to be asked about the morality of refusing to offer opportunities to learn unless the educational enterprise will make a substantial profit, since such a refusal denies the potential learners opportunity to enrich their lives, develop their humanity and even to enhance community living.

In response to this it can be pointed out that the provision of educational opportunities for adults costs the state money and that the state has only a limited budget, so that while 'education for all' might be a popular slogan, it is an unrealistic practice. While this is the claim often made, and clearly there are other major expenditures that the state has to make – such as health, it is not often proven beyond reasonable doubt that the state cannot afford to contribute more than it does to education, as some of the Scandinavian countries show in their educational policies. Clearly education is regarded as a welfare provision and offered to those who are least able to help themselves, i.e. the unemployed, and this could be argued as one feature of a just society.

But recurrent education also functions in a completely different manner in the work place: its provision is also a means of social control rather than the provision of opportunities. One of Coffield's (2000, vol. 1, p. 8) characteristics of the learning society is social control, and he cites Hewison's (Coffield, 2000, vol. 1, pp. 167–197) research, which he (Coffield, 2000, vol. 1, p. 16) summarises as: '"opportunities for lifelong learning" were viewed by many of the participants in their study as a threat or an obligation imposed by employers rather than a promise....' A similar sentiment was echoed by Field (1999, cited by Coffield 2000, vol. 1, p. 18) – there is: 'Without anyone much noticing it, a great deal of professional development and skills updating not because anyone wants to learn, but because they are required to learn. Contract compliance, regulatory frameworks and statutory requirements are the three main culprits.' This is an immoral use of recurrent education since it is the use of coercive power to enforce workers to attend educational opportunities.

The provision of recurrent education is not self-evidently a good thing but there are many occasions when it is good for individuals since it does provide opportunity for self-growth, career advancement and social development. These are the things frequently cited by many who espouse the idea of continuing learning and they are perfectly valid but they have to be seen from within the broader picture in which it is impossible to universalise the assertion since recurrent education is not always a good thing.

The learning society

Lifelong learning, as we know it today, is a direct result of the Enlightenment and the Industrial Revolution – it is the product of modernity. It contains, therefore, many of the flaws of such a society: for instance, learning has become a commodity to be sold in the market place and providers compete with each other to sell their commodities at the highest price to as many individuals as possible. Many academics have expressed their concern about this situation as we have already pointed out. It is as if the higher ideals of education have been overtaken by the lower values of the market and the concept of the learning society with the implicit high moral values of learning might be being used to hide the reality of the place of education in global capitalist society.

The debate about the nature of the learning society was explored in the second volume of this trilogy (Jarvis, 2007b) and in discussing the concept itself we are confronted with a major difficulty: the learning society itself. For any society to exist in a stable form its people must learn either to be compliant or to participate in the political processes but even the latter can be destabilising. Consequently, the society that we have been discussing throughout this book – the global capitalist society – is the present manifestation of the learning society. The thing that makes this society different is the types of knowledge that constitute the basis of its economy. Yet in European policy another form of learning society also exists – one that emphasises the ideals of Europeanisation – learning to live together.[7] Here we are discussing the creation of a new form of society – people coming together – and in this it is an almost complete antithesis of the learning society used within the global capitalist concept. In Europeanisation, there is an ideal of a people learning to live together rather than one in which individuals pursue their own ends: it is the group rather than the individual. In a sense, there is a looking forward to a high ideal. Europeanisation is about people not competing with each other in war but learning to co-operate in a great adventure, to use Bauman's (2004) phrase, of bringing people together. It is a looking forward. Indeed, the concept of the learning society is a futuristic one. As we pointed out at the end of the first volume (Jarvis, 2006) the fact that humanity continues to learn illustrates the point that humanity is an unfinished project and so we can begin to stop looking back and begin to look forward to what the learning society could become. It is this futuristic aspect that Freire (1972b) recognised when he claimed that there is both a denunciation and an annunciation in the role of education.

However, we can see that social change is not linear, as Sorokin's (for discussions on Sorokin, see Timasheff, 1965; Merton, 1968 *inter alia*) theory of social change over a half century ago suggested. He argued that change involved a swing between sensate and ideational cultures. A sensate culture is one in which ultimate validity is attested by the senses whereas the ideational suggests that reality has a deeper meaning. Sorokin actually suggested that when the two combine we have an ideological culture but if they merely co-exist we have a mixed culture. Sorokin's sociological theories lie beyond the scope of this chapter and will not be discussed here except to suggest that it also reflects Schiller's 'bent twig' (Berlin, 1991 [1969], p. 251) in which there is a backlash: the pendulum effect of cultural change is a fundamental idea of action and reaction – even thesis and antithesis. We may be witnessing a movement away from a sensate culture in the direction of a more ideational form – or a backlash against global capitalism. In this we may be seeing a reappraisal of values in a number of different ways – that is a re-thinking of the Enlightenment project. In the first place, the anti-globalisation movement may merely be reflecting a traditional radical anti-capitalist position. But there is more to the change than this: we are seeing capitalism itself beginning to take notice of these concerns; politicians and 'celebrities' are aware that there is a popular movement away from the extremes of global capitalism with which they feel it wise to be associated; there is a focus on Africa where the extremes of poverty have been experienced and most vividly portrayed to the affluent West by the media; the idea that the good society is a wealthy one is beginning to be questioned; people are beginning to become the ends rather than the means; a broader spectrum of knowledge is beginning to be recognised; there is an increasing emphasis on citizenship and citizenship education, and in some ways the curriculum is being adjusted. Change does not happen overnight but there may be significant signs of change. Perhaps this promise of a better society was also one of the driving forces behind books like Ranson's (1994) and Welton's (2005) – perhaps, even an indication of an annunciation – in which the hopes and aspirations of people like Hutchins and Husen are being recaptured.

Towards the good learning society?

The two studies upon which we will focus here have both had almost a sense of disappointment with what is the learning society and they have both looked towards a better society.

Towards the learning society

Clearly this title suggests that Ranson still sees the learning society as something to be achieved in the future rather than suggesting that we need to reform the one that we have. Starting from a different place and having different intentions to this book, his (1994) study looks at some of the changes that have occurred in British society that have affected education. However, he reaches the same point as we have reached here: education in the market place. He is concerned with a technical problematic – an administered market – which is something he suggests has been the government's initial attempt to produce. In a sense, this concept both tries to catch the apparent advantages of the market – stimulating the productive and innovative processes while controlling the excesses of the market. He examines how legislation has tried to achieve this but he reaches a point where he is forced to offer a critique of the market. He concludes that actually the market reinforces the status quo – Bourdieu's (1973) thesis of social and cultural reproduction of education. He points out that the only democracy in the market is the power of choice – although we would add, a limited power and a very limited concept of democracy. Ranson crucially recognises that the problems facing society are public since our society does not encourage people's participation in public affairs and so to have an educated public is crucial. He (1994, p. 102) claims that:

> The challenge of our time is to renew the purposes and institutions of democracy, which allows citizens to participate in the creation of a society that enables each to develop as a person but also contribute to the good of the community as a whole. Civic responsibility and individual responsibility are perceived as mutually reinforcing, creating the conditions in which 'anyone might do best and live a flourishing life'.
>
> (Aristotle)

He cites MacIntyre's (1987) pessimistic, although for different reasons we think correct, claim that 'what modernity excludes is the possibility of the existence of an educated public'. However, he wishes to dispute this position and sees the creation of a learning democracy as the way forward: for him, now is the time to create a new 'moral and political order that responds to the needs of society that is undergoing historic transition' (p. 105). He (p. 106) rightly argues that:

> It is only when the values and processes of learning are placed at the centre of polity that the conditions can be established for all individuals to develop their capacities, and that institutions can respond openly and imaginatively to a period of change.

Consequently, a learning society needs to create conditions in which the processes of learning are put at the centre, although in a democracy the learners should also be at the centre. Ranson would claim that he has done this since he is concerned about the learning self. His two organising principles are the creation of citizenship through the processes of learning and practical reason and it is his emphasis on the latter that shows that his is a modernistic model of the learning society. Having said this there is much in his discussion of the conditions for a learning self with which we fully agree: self as agent; unity of a life; the self as person in relation. In addition, his social conditions for learning – civic values, creating a moral community and widening horizons – lead into a discussion of the conditions for polity – justice, participative democracy and public action. He also outlines what he sees to be the way to reform government for such a society that will be for the public good, enabling civic participation, progressive decentralisation and multiple accountability. Thereafter, he makes suggestions for the reform of the structure of central government, local government and educational institutions – here we see his vision of the demo-cratic society.

In a sense this is a very reasoned dream of a learning society in the same tra-dition as Hutchins' study some 30 years previously. But it is a vision within the framework of modernity, it is based on reasoned argument and is centred on the state, he does not pursue the power of the market sufficiently, so that while it is concerned about the moral community – based on a form of discourse ethics (pp. 109–110) – it is assumed rather than argued. Here then is a utopian vision of a democratic society that is both reasonable and rational that accounts for both its attractiveness and popularity. Indeed, there is much in it with which we will agree in our final conclusions although because it is written from within a framework of modernity, assuming a rational ethic and neglecting to look fully at the human learning process that ultimately it does not succeed in being fully convincing. This is perhaps because his approach to the political is separated from a rigorous analysis of the ethical and it is maintained here that ultimately the political must be evaluated by the ethical. Having said this, it is much more convincing and holistic than most policy statements about the learning society and it does offer us a way forward. Welton (2005), by contrast, starts from the question of justice in examining the learning society – but like Ranson's it looks to the future rather than assuming the present.

Designing the just learning society

Welton's book starts with a concern for justice. It is more specifically orientated towards adult education than is Ranson's and he starts with reference to the world conferences on adult education. He concludes the first chapter that the learning society finds fulfilment in the information age, in a similar manner to that which we argued in the second volume of this trilogy (Jarvis, 2007b). Simi-larly Welton is concerned with industrialisation and agrees with the argument that we have produced in the third chapter about the market achieving a 'god-like' status (Welton, 2005, pp. 187–197), although he omits any major discus-sion of globalisation so that he does not appear to lay sufficient foundation for the worldwide learning society but he does focus on how businesses learn and unlearn. He (p. 212) also makes the fundamental assumption that for the learn-ing society to be realised 'the business enterprise must be a social good' – some-thing that this study has questioned because global capitalism works for its own ends rather than for the good of the planet and it peoples. In a number of chap-ters he looks at the behaviour of organisations and he focuses specifically on empowerment and concludes that empowerment of workers would only be of value if it opened up the macro-level ethical debates, as this does not happen we need an informed and active citizenship. He (p. 178) concludes that 'Propo-nents of a just learning society should try to help youths and adults to acquire the know-how and the skills of active citizenship as they participate in various groups.' This would be fine, if there were sufficient groups in which this could occur but the society in which we live is individualising and there are fewer groups, apart from schooling, in which this could happen. Thereafter, Welton examines a curriculum for the life-world based, to a great extent, on Habermas' work. We will also examine Habermas' work on democracy in the next chapter but Welton opens up Habermas' work with many interesting references to Honneth (1995) who also criticises Habermas' work for being too cognitive. Welton completes his study of a curriculum for the life-world by looking at therapeutic culture as a way of overcoming social fragmentation that leads him into a discussion of the elemental learning dynamic in the contemporary world. Welton's emphasis is on the individual's life-world and so he never reaches out to the politico-economic situation in which this process is occurring. Finally, Welton does not really engage in a fundamental discussion of justice although through empowerment and mutual self-recognition he begins to embark on the process, and so he (2005, p. 219) concludes with the utopian hope that:

> The just learning society paradigm is offered, then, as a counter-utopia to the commodity paradise utopia of globalising capitalism. We end with the modest hope that human beings have the intellectual and spiritual resources to create another world, one anchored in the indigenous learning capacity of our species.

Consequently, he outlines his own curriculum for a realistic utopia – a concept used by Rawls (1999). Welton's hopes lie in humanity's own capacity to learn and this is a position with which we have sympathy although he does not really analyse human learning. Since he neither analyses justice nor human learning sufficiently rigorously he has unfortunately not produced a compelling argument although his hopes are extremely attractive.

For both Welton and Ranson, the learning society is a future hope – for Welton a realistic utopia and we will return to this in the chapter after next. However, it might be asked whether they actually need a concept of learning in their final deliberations because they are asking questions about the nature of society itself. Neither of them really explores the concept of the learner (the person) nor the nature of the society in which the learning society, as a concept, has appeared. Indeed, it is not just society that has to be changed but the people; they have to desire to see changes in society or have to see that changes are inevitable as the Enlightenment project is seen to be non-viable in the very near future.

Conclusion

Learning is fundamental to humanity and is the driving force for human growth and development, but it can be misappropriated and used for the benefit on the minority against the good of the whole. In itself, therefore, it is a natural phenomenon but it is one in which almost everybody learns the moral good pre-consciously through experiencing a loving relationship. However, the teaching and learning relationship can be manipulated through the power plays of wider society so that not all learning is good in itself and we can be socialised into a world that denies the moral good. Indeed, we would argue that the universal moral good has been downplayed since the Enlightenment but that the values of modernity are now being questioned and individuality has taken precedence over the community. Hence, the learning society, as we know it at present, is the product of contemporary society with its questionable values. It is no wonder, therefore, that some scholars look to the future: Ranson looks to the future of a democratic society in which people can learn to be active citizens and play a major role in the creation of a better world while Welton looks to the future and hopes that human beings can learn to create a just society. In the next two chapters, therefore, we turn our minds to the concepts of democracy and utopia.

Chapter 9

Democracy and the learning society

We finished the last chapter by looking at two studies by Ranson (1994) and Welton (2005) that focused in their different ways on the idea that a learning society should be both just and democratic. Indeed, it would be true to say that in adult education we have always accepted the democratic principle within both its pedagogic practices and also it theoretical formulation; the work of Freire (1972a, 1972b) is perhaps the most well known in this respect. At the end of his life he (Freire, 1998) returned to the subject in a penetrating study of pedagogy and freedom, to which we will return in the final chapters of this book, but many of us have always taken for granted the idea that education should be democratic but once we recognise this we acknowledge the political nature of both the institution and the process of education: education is always political! It is significant in this respect that among the aims of the European Community's (EC, 1995, 2000, 2001a) policy statements citizenship has a significant place but because of our concern about global capitalism and employability we have neglected to analyse the European documents from a political perspective.

The aim of this chapter, therefore, is to examine the ideas of democracy: we will conclude that it is a concept that in its 'pure' form cannot be realised in time, i.e. that it is a utopian. Since we also see its formulation as a product of the Enlightenment, which we have already suggested is a flawed project, we will be critical of the practicalities of the idea. In the first part of this chapter we will explore the concept itself and, thereafter, we will look at some different types of democracy including Rawls' (1999) major concerns for liberal democracy and Habermas' criticisms of his work. Rawls' work is significant to this study since both Ranson's (1994) and Welton's (2005) theories of the learning society are fundamentally liberal in a Rawlsian sense. We will relate the discussion in this chapter to ideas about the learning society and lifelong learning through opinion formation, will-formation and public reason.

The concept of democracy

The title of this volume was clearly influenced by Dewey's (1916) famous study in which he (p. 87) wrote:

> The devotion of democracy to education is a familiar fact. The superficial explanation is that a government resting upon popular suffrage cannot be successful unless those who elect and obey their governors are educated. Since a democratic society repudiates the principle of external authority, it must find a substitute involuntary disposition and interest; these can be created only by education. But there is a deeper explanation. As democracy is more than a form of government; it is primarily a mode of associated living, a conjoint communicated experience. The extension in space of the number of individuals who participate in an interest so that each has to refer to his own action to that of others, and to consider the action of others to give point and direction to his own, is equivalent to the breaking down of those barriers of class, race, and national territory which kept men from perceiving the full impact of their activity.

For Dewey, then, democracy was both a form of government and a way of life: Hoffman (1988, p. 140) notes that as a result of the industrial expansion following the American civil war, democracy came to stand for the American system as a whole. Hence, in this statement of Dewey we find a classic American liberal statement about the ideas of democracy, but what precisely is democracy? In the first instance, the answer to this is straightforward – it is the rule of the people by the people but certainly this was not what it meant in the United States in those early days since neither the indigenous peoples nor the Afro-Caribbean people had a political voice. And so, who are the people and what do we mean by rule? In Athens, only males, citizens and landowners were able to play their part in government, so that the people were limited to a specific class. If it were to be extended to all the people then the women and slaves would have a place and this was unacceptable to the Athenian mind. In order for this to occur Athenian society would have had to have been re-ordered. This was beyond the conceptualisation of the thinking people, and so, it was unachievable. Even today this raises major problems: for instance, if the people were everybody, then we could argue that not everybody is qualified to address the complex issues of our day and, therefore, some should be excluded. Alternatively, there needs to be lifelong learning about specific issues for all the population in order to produce a learned population that could pronounce on the issues of the day. But however much learning they undertake, they could still not be sure that the decisions that they took were right for the future and so it was always a risk (Beck, 1992). But, it could be argued that in humanitarian terms, everybody who is free and rational should have the opportunity to participate in the rule or else they are not free citizens, irrespective of the level of their learning, because learning does not always result in wisdom nor does it result in correct decisions – both points are true. But in a knowledge society ignorance might be more likely to produce incorrect decisions so that it might be argued that the learned have a better chance of getting it right. However, it could then be argued that unless people have bothered to become informed then they should not participate, and so the argument goes on, and while this is a political argument for lifelong learning it does not prove that learning is essential for a people to reach the best decisions on issues that concern them. However, we do not actually have a situation where the people actually hold power – all that they hold in the most democratic countries is the power to elect their leaders, and we would hope that they are more knowledgeable! But, as we will explore later in this study, we also need to understand what learning, knowledge or wisdom is the most appropriate for making decisions that might approximate to 'correctness'.

But also we need to ask, who should rule? Lively (1975, p. 30) suggested seven possible answers to these questions:

- All should govern.
- All should be involved in crucial decision making.
- The rulers should be accountable to the ruled.
- The rulers should be accountable to the representatives of the ruled.
- The rulers should be chosen by the ruled.
- The rulers should be chosen by the representatives of the ruled.
- The rulers should act in the best interests of the ruled.

As we have already pointed out the first of these is an impossible ideal which if it was ever tried would almost certainly result in anarchy or 'war of all against all', but the second that implies that referenda should be conducted is much more possible in the contemporary technological age, although governments tend to reject the idea once they are in office since they themselves want to exercise power. Indeed, the same objection may be raised about the level of knowledge of the people to make an informed decision and among the implications of this is that every democracy should be a learning society. But, even if we accept the idea that all the people are sufficiently learned to vote on a resolution, they will not always all agree about the outcome and the question must be asked as to whether the majority decision is actually a valid way of thinking about democracy since the majority can be and often is wrong. And so, should numbers be the basis of democracy? This is often the basis in Western societies but as we saw with the prophet earlier in this study – the majority were wrong and so it is difficult to make out a case for equating democracy with numerical strength. Yet the inclusion of everybody in an election or a referendum might provide a moral or ethical framework within which people make their decisions. Uniformity of beliefs is only likely to occur in a totalitarian society where everybody has been indoctrinated.

However, many societies in the West are not direct government democracies but representative democracies in which the people elect their rulers for a specified period of time, such as four or five years. But the same argument about the ability of the voters to understand the complex issues still obtains, as it does for those who are elected. It is very clear that many of the elected, even the most powerful people in the world, are also ignorant about many of the issues about which they pontificate. There are other dangers in elected leaders since they can, and do, lose contact with the people for much of the time and they often rule in response to their own party's programme or in response to pressures placed upon them from other sources, such as from the economic and technological institutions of the sub-structure, and so on. In these cases they cease to represent the needs of the people, so that representative democracy loses a lot of its democratic flavour.

As Lively (1975, p. 51) pointed out, this leaves us with three major issues:

- The extent to which all constituent groups are involved in decision making.
- The extent to which government decisions are subject to popular control.
- The degree to which ordinary citizens are involved in public administration.

Then there is the question of what do we mean by ruling? Clearly this is a matter in the exercise of power, but we have already seen something of the different forms of power and how it operates. Who should have what type of power? It is argued by liberal democratic thinkers that reason should prevail over power, although clearly public reason needs the support of state power if it is to play a role. But once again, we are confronted with this major issue for democracy, and for any learning society: should non-learned people have the right to exercise power? If they do not have the right to exercise power, they should at least have the right to influence it!

Consequently, we can see that we are beginning to point to the need for a moral framework for democracy and this is precisely what Rawls has introduced into the debate.

While democracy is about political power and the powerful are, to some extent, accountable to the electorate, it can be seen that the type of society presupposed by my model of globalisation suggests that a great deal of power, certainly economic and persuasive power, lies with the unelected who control the sub-structures of the world, but they are supported by the USA and its elected system. But it might be argued that the market is a controlling force: that the people may influence some of the corporation decisions by purchasing or not buying the company's products is a genuine possibility since the market is the one point at which the people can exercise rational choice. Clearly, the other way of influencing any corporation is by becoming an owner and purchasing shares, but those with only a few shares in a corporation have little power. In addition, we have already seen how the power of advertising and of the media in general means that the market is not a level playing field and neither do the people choose rationally as a result of their reflections since they are gullible and tend to adhere to the suggestions that have been made to them through the advertising media, as we pointed out earlier. Indeed, the question remains as to whether the political power of the elected politicians can control the economic power or vice versa – or whether on some occasions the politicians have actually sold out to the economic forces of their society, as such writers as Monbiot (2000) imply. Much of the argument of this volume suggests that while politicians still play an important role, a great deal of actual power now resides beyond the political realm. At the same time the equality of humanity can only exist within the limits of the political and moral realms: globalisation has enabled those with economic power to by-pass the political and moral processes in many countries and has privileged the wealthy and has rendered politicians and the arbitrators of morality relatively powerless in certain areas of everyday life. This has brought about a considerable degree of scepticism about politics and politicians and also about the churches among the general public. It has also, probably, helped to lessen the desire of the public to participate in the political processes. This must be coupled with the fact that if people's desires are satiated by what they are offered in the market, then there appear to be fewer reasons to participate in the political process and fight for their own and, even less important, other people's rights. Hence, we have seen in recent decades the growth of political apathy in which the public sphere has been weakened and atrophied: this form of society is one in which fewer people are likely to participate in the political processes and that it is fundamentally ego-centric and individualistic, and once this occurs. Then this form of society becomes even more anti-democratic when others do fight for theirs or other people's rights and the battle impinges in some way upon the lives of the apathetic, then they decry those who are politically active. Once again this latter point relates back to the liberalism of modernity and ideas of the common good appear to play little part in the minds of many people and they only want to get involved in the political process when their own individual interests are threatened. Individual self-interest reigns and this is a rational outcome of the liberal position but this picture of society is certainly not the one that the Enlightenment thinkers had although it does portray something of the failure of the Enlightenment project. It also highlights reasons why the European Commission made active citizenship one of its aims for lifelong learning and the learning society (EC, 2001a, *inter alia*).

However, the idea of 'active' can be contrasted to activism and it can be argued that the type of society in which we now live demands activism as much as active citizenship. Society needs both active citizens and activists if we are to establish any form of democracy or to exercise our own humanity. Indeed, we would want to argue that being an active participant in the processes that govern our own lives is fundamental to our own humanity and that we undermine our own potential if we become politically apathetic. To have the experience of participation is to have a learning experience that enriches us as human beings, but participation offers even more than this. Being involved in such processes make people aware of the common good, of the community beyond our individuality, and of the needs of others, and it this latter process which is about learning more about the moral dimension. While this may be the outcome of many who participate, it has to be admitted that for some it is a way to achieve their own aims in a selfish manner and this undermines the ideas of the social contract, which is itself at the heart of Enlightenment thinking.

Democratic participation is a desirable phenomenon, as Dewey suggested, but it is still a process of working towards an ideal state. Because it is ideal some of the values of the Enlightenment, such as freedom and individualism, need to be questioned once again. Perhaps people need to have their freedom curtailed for the common good – but by whom? Perhaps the answer must be 'by the people themselves', but this demands a degree of moral constraint that is foreign to the idea of liberalism, that it is the pursuit of self-interest in the market. Alternatively, perhaps the group/community is more important than the individual, but then we need to ask what group and what is the relationship between the group and the individual – but this is where we began our discussion in the third chapter, and the idea of democracy does not appear to solve it. But several prominent theorists have tried to defend the idea of democracy from within the framework of modernism and so we need to turn to them in order to examine what they have argued.

Models of democracy

Habermas (1998, pp. 239–252) offers three normative models of democracy: liberal, republican and deliberative politics based upon his own theory of communicative action. In this section we will describe briefly these three positions highlighting their strengths and weaknesses. In this we will rely to some extent on his outline, but we will then relate this discussion to the ideas of lifelong learning and the learning society.

Liberal democracy

The state (instrument of public administration) is programmed in the interests of society (a system of market structured interactions of private persons and their labour). In this instance, individual citizens have rights and freedoms that are protected by the government provided that they pursue their interests within the framework of the law. These rights include political ones so that the citizen can determine whether government acts in the best interest of the citizens, but the law determines which citizen is entitled to what rights, and the legal order is conceived of in terms of individual rights. Consequently, politics is a struggle to gain access to political power and to hold on to it by convincing others that they who gain it will use it in the citizen's interests: in this sense it is a reflection of the market. At the same time, theoretically the citizens have sovereignty since they determine who will exercise power over them for a limited period of time.

We can see in this position that there is no fundamental conception of society, so that Mrs Thatcher, as Prime Minister of the UK could famously proclaim that 'there is no such thing as society' since it is the struggle of self-interest: this is the very antithesis of the republican approach. Since self-interest prevails in this view it is easy to see how capitalism can secure a firm foundation here since the process of politics resembles the market place. Fairness is supposed to be guaranteed by compromise, through the ballot box, in which all citizens have an equal right to vote, although this assumes that the market is a level playing field which, as we have already pointed out, it rarely is. However, the outcomes of the elections give legitimacy to the political power of government, the use of which government has to justify at the following election. The public can, and should, seek to influence power through the formation of interest groups that initially target government on issues of policy and practice and, also, seek to influence public opinion in such a way that the debate should influence the outcome of the following election.

Republican or communitarian democracy

Politics is a reflexive form of substantial ethical life – members or communities become aware of their inter-dependence and act as citizens to develop their community. In this instance, it is the sense of community that is an integrative force. At the heart of this approach lies the public sphere and civil society that provides the context within which the public debate occurs and this is integral to administrative power.

Citizens are politically responsible within a community of free and equal members, and their rights are dependent on the law that has priority over individual rights. In this sense, sovereignty is to be found in constitutional law. At the heart of this position lies the need for the formation of political opinion and will to act in the public sphere, and those in power are expected to respond to this public debate. In this debate, the people exchange views and make their opinions known in such a way that it affects the exercise of power.

Putting society first means that the communitarian has an ethical responsibility that might be considered both a strength and a weakness of the republican position since self-interest is a rather dominant phenomenon in the lives of many citizens. However, the realism of this position is that citizens acquire from the outset a sense of social identity as well as one of self-identity that is not so apparent in liberalism. In theory the market is subsidiary to the political debate but if the public sphere is weakened it is possible to see how economic power can play a significant role and the market assume a dominant place. At the same time, the strength of this approach lies in the rational discourse of ethical self-understanding that members of the community have. One of the strengths of this position is that since the public sphere can span the whole of society, society becomes a political community engaged in debates about public issues (a learning society), and interested individuals or groups can ensure that there is public debate about the issues within the context of the social group's interests.

Deliberative politics

It is clear that the above two positions start from opposite extremes: the one from the individual and the other from the community, but Habermas' third theoretical position seeks to elucidate something of a middle way, although it is closer in many ways to the communitarian position. This is based upon his own theory of communicative action and the ideal speech act, which we also discussed when we examined discourse ethics. At the heart of this model of democracy is discourse through which, Habermas claims, rational results can be produced. The strength of this position is that it combines both the possibilities of the fairness that lies in liberalism with the community's sense of self-understanding and justice. In a sense, it seeks to combine both human rights with the communitarian spirit of the republican position and provide procedures through which public debate can take place. Sovereignty, Habermas maintains, now rests not in the people or the constitution but in the associations of civil society and in this he comes close to Dewey's position with which this chapter commenced. Significantly, Rawls (1999, p. 139) adds to this debate by suggesting three elements of deliberative democracy: public reason, a framework of democratic institutions and the knowledge and desire on the part of the citizens to follow public reason. We will discuss public reason later in the chapter but we can see how Rawls has moved closer to deliberative democracy by fusing his ideas of liberal democracy with those of deliberation.

Having seen the differences between these three positions, it is not surprising that two of the major exponents of democratic thinking in contemporary society come from different starting points, but since both function within the framework of modernity, their positions do approach one another and we will look at this debate in the next section before we return to the issues of lifelong learning and the learning society which are inherent in the models of democracy.

Rawls' theory of liberal democracy

Liberals have not always been supporters of democracy – often they were its opponents and so why did the two ideas become fused? Hoffman's (1988, pp. 158–159) summary begins to explain this paradox by going back to Locke who conceptualised abstract individuals exchanging goods and services as a natural state. It was in the exchange process of single commodities that led us to see people as individuals although we have pointed out that in the history of ideas individualism existed long before this debate occurred. But as Marx argued, the value of a commodity lies not in labour itself but in the price mechanism of the market that hides the social aspects of the production process. The participants in the exchange, like the commodities involved in the sale, appear as independent agents involved in making a social contract. As Hoffman (1988, p. 160) says:

> The only force that stands above these abstract individuals is the impersonal workings of the market – the theological laws of a supreme nature – so that, as Marx and Tocqueville stress in their different ways, the classical liberal view of the individual translates very easily into religious terms.

In the market situation there is a degree of abstract equality between the players, irrespective of who they are but the actors have the equal rights of the market in exchange and even at the ballot box. However, this does not give them equal political power. In this sense, liberal democracy gains its legitimacy in the market place of contested values and ideologies, resolved only through the ballot box without according equality of anything other than rights to the individual.

This is certainly true for the most prominent exponent of liberal democracy in recent times: Rawls' (1971, 1993, 1999) writings have been tremendously influential and in these he has also tried always to fuse the ideas of the political with those of ethics, so that the first of his major works referred to here is a theory of justice. His attempt to build justice into his theory is of major significance, since his, is among the first to try to incorporate a moral dimension into a theory of liberal democracy. This is a significant step in political theory but we also feel that there is a place for human learning which he might argue is to be found in his discussion of public reason. He (1999) regards his conception of a liberal democracy as a realistic utopia and here we find echoes of Dewey's (1916) classic book. For Rawls (1999, pp. 12–16), there are six conditions for a realistic utopia:

- Justice must be realistic – it must rely on actual laws and achieve a form of stability that these laws allow.
- Justice must be utopian – use moral ideals, principles and concepts to specify a just society.
- The political must contain within itself all the elements essential for a political conception of justice.
- Constitutional democracy must have political and social institutions that effectively lead citizens to acquire the appropriate sense of justice.
- As religious and political consensus is not necessary for social unity, the unity should be rooted in a reasonable conception of right and justice.
- There should be an accepted reasonable degree of toleration.

It is clear from the above six points that Rawls' liberal position incorporates some of the ideas that we discussed within communitarian democracy, indicating that he has already qualified the original liberal position, which is not surprising considering some of the debate about liberalism was firmly rooted in America, which is a constitutional democracy. In addition, in response to his critics, such as Gray (1995)[1] and Habermas (1998), he has developed his ideas even further – even beyond the Western ideals of democratic liberal living by later discussing 'decent peoples' who do not live under liberal regimes but who can also achieve high forms of social living, although his initial conceptualisation rarely breaks away from the western (American) model of democracy and he certainly does not radically change his initial position although he does extend it.

In the fourth of these six conditions, it would be possible to replace the word 'acquire' by 'learn' and so we see the basis of a just learning society within the framework of liberalism. Indeed, in his discussion of public reason where we find his thoughts about how such democracy might operate, his main focus seems to be that it is something that holders of, and candidates for, public office should exercise within an accepted constitutional democracy. But when he moves into deliberative democracy an idea he has developed as a result of the criticisms lev- elled at his *Political Liberalism* by Habermas he focuses also on the active citizen and he returns to the contentious subject of the knowledgeable citizen, he (Rawls, 1999, pp. 139–140) writes:

> Deliberative democracy also recognizes that without widespread education in the basic aspects of constitutional democratic government for all citi- zens, and without a public informed about pressing problems, crucial politi- cal and social decisions cannot be made. Even should far-sighted political leaders wish to make sound changes and reforms, they cannot convince a misinformed and cynical public to accept and follow them.

Here, then, in the political analysis of deliberative democracy we find the con- ditions of a future learning society that neither Ranson (1994) nor Welton (2005) would dispute. Indeed, Rawls' political liberalism and the liberal educa- tion of Welton and Ranson converge at this point. Indeed, he argues that it is public reason that may 'determine a constitutional democratic government's relation to its citizens and their relation to one another' (Rawls, 1999, p. 132). In other words this should be a 'way of life' in such societies, as Dewey would have argued. Citizens should have learned sufficient to be able to understand and judge that the arguments presented are derived from the principles of justice and satisfy the criterion of reciprocity (p. 133).

The problem lies in the fact that Rawls is clear that he is only discussing the political realm which he argued should enact justice through fairness but this could only happen if the political realm had the power to enact it, which in global capitalist society it does not have. Coupled, then, with the other criti- cisms of liberalism by writers such as Gray (1995) we see that this is in reality an unrealistic utopia and when this conception of democracy was exported from the USA by force to Iraq, an apparently utopian vision turned into a hellish outcome. Democracy cannot be transplanted in this manner since it is not a universally valid idea.

Rawls' idea of public reason which is crucial to our thinking about the learning society and lifelong learning and once he extends this discussion he also approaches deliberative politics. He suggests that any well ordered constitutional democracy should be based on public reason since we are all confronted with a reasonable pluralism. Public reason 'specifies at the deepest level the basic moral and political values that are to determine a constitutional democratic government's relation to its citizens and their relation to one another' (Rawls, 1999, p. 132). He (p. 133) suggests five different aspects:

- the fundamental political questions to which it applies;
- the persons to whom it applies;
- its contents;
- the application of these conceptions to the coercive norms enacted in law for a democratic people;
- citizens' checking the principles derived from their conceptions of justice.

Basically this is a public deliberation because the citizens are free and equal and can/should join the debate about the extent to which public issues are enacted in a just manner. It is a discourse for those who are office holders or those who aspire to office, but one might want to add that the media and the general public should also be part of the discussion, but in this way Rawls would be pushed into a position which he might not be able to accept. He admits to its being an ideal and says that the ideal is realised when not only office holders think in this way but when the general public can put itself in the place of the office holder and think in the same manner and judge evaluate the outcome. Rawls (p. 136) is concerned that when people do arrive at different conclusions about issues as they do in a pluralist society, there should be fair cooperation between them. The social contract of justice as fairness is then worked out through the representatives of the people in a cooperative manner:

> the content of public reason is given by a family of political conceptions of justice, and not by a single one. There are many liberalisms and related views, and therefore many forms of public reason specified by a family of reasonable political conceptions. Of these, justice as fairness, whatever its merits, is but one. The limiting feature of these forms is the criterion of reciprocity, viewed as applied between free and equal citizens, themselves seen as reasonable and rational.
>
> (Rawls, 1999, p. 141)

He suggests that rights, liberties and opportunities are the main features of political liberalism, as are the assignment of priorities of these in relation to the general good. Finally, citizens should have the means to make use of their freedoms in a fair and cooperative manner.

Rawls feels that it is necessary to distinguish public reason from secular and religious reason and he claims that political doctrines are not moral ones – but he does feel that laws should be governed by justice as fairness. Public reason is grounded on the political concept of justice and its justification must be public. The whole of this debate depends upon the fact that the participants are reasonable and that they will abide by the consequences of their actions.

Such a high view of citizens is one of the utopian concepts about Rawls' work: indeed, his conception of the person is another weakness of his position. The idea that reason alone can bring about unity in a pluralist world places too much significance on reason which, as Habermas (1998, p. 93) points out, assumes that everyone shares the same view of the political world and that political values have priority. There are other apparent weaknesses in Rawls' very extensive formulation of democracy, such as, that it is fundamentally liberal, that justice and goodness are not the same, that reasonableness is not truth and also that despite its claims to offer a universalistic perspective, it is based to a considerable extent on an apparent defence of the American conception of democracy. Despite these criticisms, this approach does offer a relationship between political perspectives and morality which is more acceptable, although we would want to argue that political systems need to be evaluated by ethical values, although, as we pointed out in an earlier chapter, it is fundamentally impossible to univeralise the major ethical theories that emerged from the Enlightenment, except agapism.

Rawls' position clearly approaches that of deliberative politics in its final version and it is in deliberative politics and practical reason that we find a basis for the learning society and lifelong learning.

Democracy as a learning society

Ranson (1994) and Welton (2005) were clear that the learning society should be a democratic society in which the people are engaged in learning opportunities. This was the hope that Hutchins (1968) espoused when he envisaged it to be a society when educational opportunities were open to everybody and that society would be rather like a modern Athens. There are many things about ancient Athens that might not be acceptable to contemporary society but one can understand something of Hutchins' sentiments and we will examine his work a little more fully in the next chapter. However, Plato was also well aware of the problems between government and learning which he worked out most extensively in *The Republic* (Cornford, 1941). But for him:

> it was the rulers who had to be prepared throughout a life of learning in order to undertake the task of ruling. Only the older people are fit to rule

since only they will enter dialogue for the sake of seeking the truth, since their own reasonableness will bring credit in the pursuit.

(Plato in Cornford, 1941, p. 255)

Then when they are 50:

those who have come safely through and proved the best at all points in action and in study must be brought at last to the goal. They must lift up the eye of the soul and when they have seen the Good itself, take it as a pattern for the right ordering of the state and of the individual, themselves included. For the rest of their lives, most of their time will be spent in study; but they will all take their turn at the troublesome duties of public life and act as Rulers for their country's sake, not regarding it as a distinction, but as an unavoidable task. And so, when each generation has educated others to take their place as Guardians of the commonwealth, they will depart and dwell in the Islands of the Blest.

(Plato in Cornford, 1941, p. 256)

First, we see here that for Plato those who rule must regard it as an irksome duty that interferes with their studies but that it is the wisdom that comes from knowing the good that guides their deliberations. Plato sees the moral good as at the heart of political deliberations. However, he is not writing about a liberal democracy but about an oligarchy, and the philosopher king's power is that of an artist working with a model that constrains freedom. For Plato, then, knowledge of the Good, which is itself an understanding of the moral and physical universe, lies at the heart of government and herein is his utopian vision. Philosophers can sketch a constitution which could embody the ideals of justice, goodness, temperance, and so on (Plato in Cornford, 1941, p. 205), but the philosophers would only be acceptable to the general public if it could see what the love of wisdom means.

In a sense, then, Plato's *Republic* needs lifelong learning to produce rulers fit to govern and also an education that can prepare the general population to appreciate the wisdom of the philosopher kings. But he is forced to admit that the ideal state may never have existed and its first degenerative form is timocracy – the possession of private property as the first criterion for participation in government rather than knowledge of the good. Indeed:

perhaps there is a pattern set up in the heavens for one who desires to see it and, seeing it, to found one in himself.[2] But whether it exists anywhere or will ever exist is no matter, for this is the only commonwealth in whose politics he can ever take part.

(Plato in Cornford, 1941, pp. 312–313)

The utopia is unrealisable!

But in both Rawls and Habermas we are confronted with a similar debate to this – public reason must be the order of the day in any form of democratic government and this demands that society is a learning society: those who govern must be aware of the issues and be able to make their views known, those who aspire to government must also be able to articulate the issues in a way that the electorate will have confidence in them and there must be opportunity for public debate in the agora. It is not just the idea but the ethos of society must be one in which people want to learn about issues, want to debate them and respect learning. It must be one where informed public opinion is listened to and responded to by government.

Learning, philosophising about things for oneself is fundamental to the man of understanding who seeks to establish the commonwealth within himself, in Plato's terms, but this becomes an individual dream. Lifelong learning must have outcomes – it demands that the learners act upon their learning and in this instance to become active citizens. But unless the agora exists that permits the debate then the citizen can play little part, but even where it does it may be no more than seeking to influence those who have power or even to resist those who have power – economic, persuasive, political or moral – so that the debate is enjoined. But once there is resistance – or quarrelling, as Locke pointed out so many years ago – there can be no ethos of reciprocity. It might be reasonable to expect the debate to decide, but reason does not always produce compromise between people of strongly held commitments, especially those commitments that further self-interest.

Here, then, we see the problem with individualism and with liberalism. Liberal democracies are realistic utopias as Rawls (1999, p. 11) acknowledged at the start of his *The Law of Peoples*, but they only seem realistic to reasonable people and while public reason might be part of the political dimension of democracies and lifelong learning an element in the practice of citizenship, it is perhaps unrealistic, especially in a global capitalist society which provides people in the West with their material needs to expect vast numbers of people to seek to be the philosopher kings, or for them to want to engage in the public debate. And yet, we are beginning to see a new agora appear – the media, especially the Web, is a way on both engaging people in contemporary debates and even mobilising people to protest against injustice in society – this is a new public arena.

It is not surprising that Thompson (1995), writing about the media, takes up this argument in respect to deliberative democracy. He (p. 255) defines deliberative democracy as a society that:

> treats all individuals as autonomous agents capable of forming reasoned judgements through the assimilation of information and different points of view, and which institutionalizes a variety of mechanisms to incorporate individual judgements into collective decision making processes.

As he points out, it is the process of deliberation by which people reach their viewpoints, and this is lifelong learning. The media offer opportunities for vast amounts of information and a forum for open-ended argument. However, Thompson (p. 256) makes the important point that deliberation does not demand dialogue and so it can happen through the media. In this way, deliberative democracy does not imply participative democracy – in a sense we now have a distance learning format – and provided that the media offer both a forum and a way by which individual's deliberations can get fed into the decision making process we are now faced with a new approach to democracy – a mediated democracy. Clearly this perspective offers a new dimension to the idea of public reason. In addition, it begins to point us beyond traditional pictures of democracy. While it offers some hope for a liberal approach to democracy, even Thompson (p. 258) is forced to conclude that it 'would be ingenuous to suppose that these proposals for a deliberative democracy would succeed in overcoming, or even ameliorating to a significant degree, the problems confronted by democratic politics in the modern age'.

Clearly the media can help sustain a liberal form of politics and give it a semblance of democracy: they certainly affect public opinion and can help focus it on specific issues and, in this way, affect the decision making processes and even the ballot box, but it is actually placing more power with another set of professionals – those who control the media. In public broadcasting these can be relatively neutral but commercial broadcasting is owned by society's substructure which raises questions about the extent to which the media can be a genuine market place for ideas or a forum that can translate these ideas into public policy.[3]

Yet the Web, as opposed to other media, apparently allows for a freedom of expression that does not demand editorial sanction and is not owned by society's sub-structure; it does offer a means by which people can protest against all forms of power – economic, persuasive and political – and the fact that it is protesting against power indicates that the people do not have power, and what is called representative democracy may actually be a form of open society that allows people to protest without the elite ceding any power to the citizens.

Conclusion

Ranson (1994) and Welton (2005) suggested that the learning society should be democratic and paradoxically political theorists have been suggesting that democracy should be a learning society – the only trouble is that democracy is unrealisable. Indeed, we have pointed out that the nation state no longer has sovereignty over its own territory because of the processes of globalisation and as Connelly (2007, p. 37) nicely summarises it:

> Familiar debates in International Relations theory between imperialistic and anarchistic readings of a world order either place too much control

over events in a dominant power or reduce the world to a quasi-autonomous system exerting constraints on sovereign states. The contemporary world assemblage is marked by two tendencies: (a) neither state authorities, corporate elites, market mechanism, nor international agencies possess sufficient foresight to govern the world internationally as a system: (b) every state, corporation, labor movement, and supranational movement is nonetheless enabled, constrained and restrained by the larger world assemblage in which it is set. Ambiguities and uncertainties become magnified as its sites are extended to encompass the world.

The outcomes of modernity are ambiguity and uncertainty. Reason is not god. We are confronted with what appears to be a reasonable vision of society but it is one that now seems to be unrealistic. Before we move on to ask what type of learning does this contemporary society demand, we do need to look at utopian thought since, we will argue, that the learning society is itself utopian.

Chapter 10

Utopia deferred

As the title to this chapter suggests, we have not reached the end of history (Fukuyama, 1992) and, indeed, his title reflects the same type of millennial beliefs that many contemporary fundamentalist religions espouse. In the words of the old hymn 'It began with the tale of a garden and ends with a city of gold' – both of which are myths that lie beyond history. And so, through the ages human beings have asked questions about why God did not create a perfect society in which everybody could live together in peace and harmony. The ancient Hebrews told a profound myth[1] of the Garden of Eden where the writer(s) battled with these problems and recognised that if human beings were to have free-will they could not be slaves to either a divine law or the law of nature. Hence in the myth Adam and Eve eat from the tree of knowledge and learned. It could not be God's fault that people are not perfect – it must either be their own or the fault of another mythical entity that tempts them. But they were also concerned for the future and long before the Christian era they were telling of a future time when the good society would occur at the behest of God (Isaiah 40).[2] The reality of the present – the reality of time – was sandwiched between a mythological past and an unrealistic and mythological hope for the future. Both myths lie beyond time when human beings had to work out their lives for themselves and occasionally the prophets, like Jeremiah, would warn them that they were not on track to realise this good society. From the beginning of recorded history this religious thought has profoundly influenced Western thinking – but also other nations of the world have their own religious myths trying to explain the same phenomena. We find this insoluble problem of combining human free-will with the good of the community being recognised. People learned to live with the religious myth since it 'answered' some of their profound human hopes for a better society and 'explained why we live in this present state'. In Christianity itself, we find three dominant strands of this: Christ told many parables about the Kingdom of God – the reign of God in the good society of the future; after Christ's death, the belief that Christ would come again to establish his rule on earth; a repeat of the Old Testament myth of the City of God descending to earth (Revelation of St John).[3] And for as long as Christianity was dominant in the West, it was possible to leave the problem within the confines of mythological and religious belief, but with the Enlighten-ment and the overthrow of the influence of the religious explanations of the world, intellectuals in the West confronted these problems seeking more 'ratio-nal' answers, as we saw in the third chapter of this study.[4] But, at the same time, a multitude of utopian, eschatological and millennial beliefs and movements emerged (Wilson, 1967),[5] especially among the underprivileged – of which contemporary capitalism has created even more. More significantly, while we can claim that the religious versions of utopia are faith-based and not grounded in reason, we cannot deny their significance or lasting influence.

As we saw in the third chapter of this book and also in the Appendix to the second volume (Jarvis, 2007b) this problem has been dealt with in profoundly different ways. In the millennial belief systems, religious myth has prevailed but in the literature from the Enlightenment onwards there has been the idea of 'The City of Man' – a utopia constructed by human kind, the perfect world, the good society and the thinkers pursuing this path have naturally, but perhaps unwisely, neglected the early religious thinkers who sought to answer this problem and returned to the early Greek thinkers whose influence on the West has been almost as profound.[6]

And so, is utopian thinking the result of a rather futile hope, a profound reli-gious belief that there is a creator who has left humankind to work out its own destiny, or a political aspiration for the good society that the Greeks first began to explore that human beings can create by their own efforts? Is it a City of God or a City of Man – or is it neither? Does it start from the community or the indi-vidual or is there a middle course? Does education have a place and is it a learn-ing society? Is it about communitarians or about self-interested individualists building their own community? Or are we confronted with one of the profound mysteries of human being: how can free people, with their individual needs, learn to live in harmony? However, this might actually be the wrong question since it starts with the individual! Might the question also have been how does a people retain its unity when individuals seek to realise their own potential or ambitions? Perhaps there is a middle way!

One of the Delors (1996) Report's four pillars of learning is learning to live together – the other three are learning to be, to know and to do. Exploring the place of learning within this complex maze of ideas is the aim of this chapter.

We will briefly review the concept of utopia in the first part of this chapter and we will see how it is something that lies outside of time – not at the end of history but beyond history. In Baudrillard's (2006, p. 62) words, 'Utopia is the deconstruction of every unilateral finality of man or history.' In the second part of the chapter we will review our discussion on the political ideas underlying utopian thought and in the third we will return to global capitalism. We will then look at the educators' utopian concepts and re-examine the place of edu-cation and learning in this complex world. Humankind has always looked to the future, often thinking utopian thoughts and so the final part of this chapter will examine the education of desire. Thereafter, we will reach the conclusion that the utopian concept serves a number of other purposes but that it will always be deferred so long as we have historical existence. Consequently, human learning and the learning society need to be re-conceptualised.

The concept of Utopia

As Marin (1993, p. 16) reminds us, the paradoxical meaning of this complex term can be displayed by playing with the spelling:

> three terms in which the 'e' of happiness (*eutopia*) is substituted by the 'o' of nowhere (*outopia*) to cross the infinitely small but infinitely great distance which separates the geographical fiction from a political and social one; where the permutation of a 'p' and a 't' (potia/topia) makes time and space equivalent. Displaced letters, displaced names (displacing their significations) – a displaced map displacing all maps and really finding none – Utopia as process is the figure of all kinds of frontiers, displacing, by the practice of it travels, all representations, secretly duplicating any kind of real geographical voyage and any kind of historical and temporal change.

And so utopia is nowhere and in no time – it is a hope, an answer to a very prevalent question about how do we create a better society and an answer to an unasked question about the meaning of humankind to which religion had provided an answer, but as a hope it can be conceptualised into an ideology which people endeavour to enact in the real world and at a specific historical time. As ideology, as Marin (1993, p. 13) makes clear – it becomes a totality and 'when political power seizes it, it becomes a totalitarian whole'. This we have seen both in Soviet communism and American imperialism – among so many other endeavours – but which we have also argued in this book has occurred as a result of global capitalism. In almost all of these endeavours it is ruthless power that has brought it about and education has often been a significant tool in the process.

In its broadest and least controversial meaning – utopia is the vision of the good society that human kind has always had but the vision varies from people to people and culture to culture – it is a plurality which is itself a negation of the liberal ideas that have prevailed in the West and, as such, an implied criticism of modernity. However, the word has carried disparaging meanings, such as something being unrealistic, when criticising one or other of the ideologies that have been futuristic in nature, and so on. One of the reasons why Marx criticised religion was because its utopian ideology distracted the working classes from realistic political activity:

> *Religious* distress is at the same time the *expression* of and the *protest* against real distress. Religion is the sign of the oppressed creature, the heart of the

heartless world, just as it is the spirit of a spiritless situation. It is the *opium of the people.*

(cited from Birnbaum and Lenzer, 1969, p. 93)

It was sentiments such as these that combined, with radical Christian beliefs constituted liberation theology – a position from which Freire (1972b) was to offer his *Pedagogy of the Oppressed* and the many other writings that pointed us to a way for a better world. But Marx himself was a utopian, offering a vision of a better world: but like the other visions, his classless society was unrealistic – but it was a political vision and claimed some scientific basis.

Political visions of Utopia

In the previous chapter, we examined one of the classical political utopian visions in Plato's *Republic* and we noted that even Plato doubted that it could ever be realised because individuals would seek private property and so destroy the vision. Marx also offered a political vision – the classless society, and like the New Jerusalem, this was a society that lay outside the bounds of time. Rawls (1999, p. 6) also recognised the utopian enterprise on which political philosophers embarked:

> Political philosophy is realistically utopian when it extends what are ordinarily thought of as the limits to practical political possibility. Our hope for the future of our society rests on the belief that the nature of the social world allows reasonable just constitutional democracies existing as members of the Society of Peoples.

He hoped that his vision would transcend the unrealistic in utopia and offer a realistic model of the good society. As we saw in the last chapter, he constructed his democracy on a moral principle of justice as fairness. At the same time, we pointed out in the seventh chapter that justice is not goodness and so while he was offering an exposition of democracy based on a moral value, it was not based upon the only one value that could be universalised. Moreover, it is grounded in the liberal idea of human rights but one might want to ask whether there are any human rights and if so, on what grounds? Consequently, we see an inherent problem in his formulation – while he argued that liberal democracy was the ideal that should be universalised, his concept of justice cannot be universalised as a moral good and neither can the liberal idea of human rights be assumed to be self-evidently correct. While the god of reason came with the Enlightenment, it was a god that was fallible and not capable of being universalised, so that it is not surprising that his approach was criticised by those who have considered that the Enlightenment project has failed (Gray, 1995).

Rawls' model of democracy is grounded in American liberalism and as we pointed out in the first chapter, the USA is part of the global sub-structure and, like most powerful entities, it has endeavoured to extend its rule. This has been most evident since George W. Bush assumed power, since not only did he adhere to the American beliefs of power and the constitutional liberal democracy but he combined these with a faith-based Christian fundamentalism that led to his seeking to impose, by force when necessary, the American view of the good life on those parts of the world that did not accept his ideas.[7] While Bush's position is not necessarily always overtly religious his fundamentalist beliefs and the support that he received from the right-wing have provided the bases for his actions; it is grounded in the idea that the liberal democracy that America enjoys can be exported to those 'less-privileged' countries but Gray (2007, p. 161) reminds us that Robespierre warned his fellow Jacobins of the perils of seeking to export revolution by force of arms. Gray (2007) has ruthlessly exposed the fallacies of the American liberal democratic position espoused by George W. Bush showing that the complexity of human affairs is 'too complicated and difficult for any one kind of government to be universally practical or desirable' (p. 126).

Additionally, Gray highlights the corruption of the American regime – something that he suggests 'dwarfs the scandals that surrounded the oil-for-food programme during the Saddam regime' (p. 171) and this takes us back to our model of globalisation in the first chapter in which we pointed to the interrelationship of the political and the economic. It also demonstrates how the pursuit of self-interest has excluded morality from the practices of much daily living, including that of the 'respectable' wealthy classes. Like the religious myth, the political myth of utopia is unachievable and reason is not the universal god.

Fatal flaws in modern economic thought

Throughout this study (Jarvis, 2006; 2007b) we have shown how the ideas of the human being as a rational being – rather like a machine – bears little relation to humanity, even though scientific thought would urge us to think in this direction. Human beings are not rational creatures, they are emotional and possess a 'fuzzy logic' that means that aspirations built upon pure rationality are not actually realisable, or desirable in our human world. But it is not rationality per se that is the problem – it is instrumental and economic rationality – it is the type of rationality of which Simmel was afraid and to which we made reference in the third chapter when he considered that money is god.

This kind of thought offered us an economic utopia – visions of which began to appear in fourteenth century England, visions that were far less sophisticated than the visions of Hayek and Nozick. For instance, in the poem mocking the monasteries and their indulgent life-style we read:

There are rivers broad and fine
Of oil, milk, honey and of wine
(*The Land of Cokaygne*)

Kumar (1987, p. 9) also notes the *Big Rock Candy Mountain* reflects the same sentiments.

O'Neill (Kumar and Bann, 1993) points to another more contemporary food manifestation than the monastries – McTopia, which seeks to relate fast food to some aspects of utopian thinking, although it may also be dystopian since its lowers the levels of aspiration of the 'milk and honey' for all to consuming the food that the poor, in the West at least, can afford – in this sense there is a democratisation of eating and making us all obese. However, it has always been necessary for fast-food chains to make sure that customers do not dally too long over their meals since they occupy space that might be used by another paying customer and that would reduce both profit and growth.

But eating to satiation is not the whole picture. We can as easily point to the super-rich of economic globalisation and be as mocking, cynical or con-demnatory of them as we see in *The Land of Cockaygne*. Clearly, they see their wealth as earned by their own individual efforts but the Rowntree report on poverty in 2004 has indicated that 'poverty on an unacceptably large scale is still very much part of today's Britain'. However, the next report on segrega-tion continued the theme. The report that came out in July 2007 highlighted a crisis and highlighted the poverty 'clustering' while the wealthy flee to the outskirts of the city. With the personal wealth of the richest 1 per cent now controlling 24 per cent of the national share, Hunt (2007, p. 28) suggests that we are heading towards Victorian levels on inequality. He goes on to say that Engels noted how the rich could take the shortest route to their places of work without ever being aware of the poverty around them and that this still exists today. This is something that is also easy for the middle classes to do as they drive through, or around, poor districts and not see or understand the poverty in which many people live. Engels postulated that a revolution in Victorian England would have been easy. But it is not just the third world, it is also the third world in the first that is the product of neo-liberal economics. If we can say this about Britain, one of the wealthiest countries on earth, the same can be said for all the rich nations of the world, as the OECD reports. Seager (2007) commenting on the report notes how globalisation has reduced the bargaining power of unskilled workers throughout the OECD membership and, surprisingly enough, the OECD has urged governments to improve their safety nets for these people. This is contrary to the economic neo-liberalism embraced by OECD. If this is the picture within the rich nations, then the gulf between the rich and the poor nations is even worse. We do not have to look beyond the poverty of Africa, to the billion people who live on under one dollar a day to realise that global capitalism is not working for the benefit of everybody and that it is not that these people have had employment and have become redundant but that they are redundant people to the global capitalist world. And so, what of the economic utopia offered by Enlighten-ment thinking? Gray (1995, p. 155), commenting on globalisation makes the point:

Market liberalism is at its most utopian, however, in its conception of a global market society, in which goods, and perhaps people, move freely between economies having radically different states of development and harbouring very different cultures.

But, it is this that has generated and exacerbated global poverty. He goes on to suggest that the global economic developments of the 1990s have subjected both developed and developing economies to massive strains and job disloca- tion which destabilises societies, but this destabilisation is integral to the global process:

> Communities are scattered to the winds by the gale of creative destruction. Endless 'downsizing' and 'flattening' of enterprises fosters ubiquitous insecu- rity and makes loyalty to the company a cruel joke.[8] The celebration of con- sumer choice, as the only undisputed value in market societies, devalues commitment and stability in personal relationships and encourages the view of marriage and the family as vehicles of self-realization. The dynamism of the market process dissolves social hierarchies and over turns established expectations. Status is ephemeral, trust frail, and contract sovereign.
>
> (p. 149)

The kind of economic rationality that pursues economic growth at all costs will soon result in further growth being unrealisable in this world of finite resources – this is an apocalyptic vision. At the point the utopian hopes of growth will finally be destroyed and with it there could be many other unfortunate con- sequences. The values of modernity have destroyed a great deal of community life while they have given wealth to the few. But the outcome does not measure up even to the ethical values that emerged in this modern period itself, let alone to any higher ethics. For instance, the practices of capitalism cannot be universalised, human beings are not treated as ends but as means, the final outcome of this practice could be the destruction of the planet. When viewed as a whole, the world of global capitalism is far from good for the greatest number of people, it is not intuitively good but intuitively bad. Indeed, the way that the planet is being destroyed is intuitively 'bad'. Yet the individual interests of the progenitors of this condition remain dominant and the values of modernity remain in place at the ultimate cost of, possibly, humanity itself.

However, there comes a time when these divisions between the rich and the degrading circumstances of millions of people are no longer acceptable to human being: the poor rebel and when this happens the wealthy label the rebels terrorists[9] and claim not to understand why the poor are doing it. But 'terrorists' also have a desire for a better life for their people and they are aware that it is the power of the wealthy West that prevents them from obtaining it so that their ideals can turn from utopian to ideological and they seek to obtain their share of the world's goods by violent means.

Economic and political policies throughout the Western world have sub-scribed to liberal democracy and economic capitalism. Moreover, they have all seen lifelong learning as the way, whereby, the working people can continue to be employable and avoid being socially excluded. Considerable finance has been poured into lifelong learning by governments and by the sub-structural institutions of Western society so that people can play their part in the know-ledge economy and educators who have for so long been on the margins of society have enjoyed their place in the mainstream and, unfortunately, there have been few voices in education that have protested at the social conditions that global capitalism has produced: education has in many cases either been colonised by the sub-structure or it has sold out to it. But then, this is the nature of power rather than utopian thinking.

Education's Utopia: the learning society

Education has nearly always been provided by the powerful institutions in society: both the Church and the state, and now by the new global sub-structure. As global capitalism has become the dominant force in Western society, it has either utilised the state and its resources to fund the type of edu-cation that it has demanded or it has provided it for itself if the state will not comply. Some states have been much more compliant and have been used by the global capitalist institution by colonising the state education system, as we noted in the second chapter, but others have resisted and some may be suffi-ciently strong enough to utilise global capitalism to their own ends, namely Russia and China. But throughout education's history there has always been another more critical approach to society and it has found its foundations in critical theory and become a recognisable force in adult education. To put it crudely, there were two major approaches to adult education: liberal adult edu-cation and critical adult education. However, lifelong education did not really have its origins in either of these: rather it emerged through the extension of mainstream schooling into adult life because of the demands of the sub-structures of society and it has displaced liberal adult education to a consider-able extent. Liberal adult education always had a humanitarian, even a utopian dimension whereas critical adult education always recognised that society was imperfect and that education might be seen as an instrument in changing imperfect society for the better. In other words, there has always been a utopian dimension to education but it is one which has frequently been sub-sumed by the political demands of the state. Hence, we see that a great deal of the education of adults in the West at the start of the twenty-first century can only be described as an extension of global capitalism and learning is some-thing demanded by the system and, as such it has no independent ideology – it merely reflects the demands of global capitalism. But both traditional adult liberal and critical adult education were much more utopian and it is to these that we now turn.

Two major writers, in the liberal tradition, saw education as an end in itself rather than a means to another end – that of employability – were Hutchins (1968) and Husen (1974). Schon (1973) also looked at education from a futurist perspective but his enterprise was much more seeking to predict the directions that education would/should take in response to rapid social change and he would certainly not have seen his work as utopian.

Hutchins (1968) thought, wrongly, that education would come into its own in the twenty-first century, whereas we have seen that only one aspect of it assumed importance. He recognises that the labour market would be a very significant player but he did not see it as dominant as it has become – but then he started from a classical American liberal position before global capitalism had really taken off. For him, everybody must be educated – but not as the same rate or in the same way or to the same extent (p. 37). But all who learn should be assessed on their learning which indicates that he still had an instrumental dimension to his understanding of learning rather than regarding learning as something to be undertaken for its own sake.

However, he thought that liberal education, something that used to be limited to rulers, could now be extended to everybody since in a liberal democracy 'all men are rulers and all will have some leisure, liberal education can be extended to all' (p. 39). Not only could everybody have the opportunity to learn, he claimed that as a result of the education offered by the Soviet system it showed us that anybody could learn every subject. However, true to his American perspective, he was still concerned about the totalitarian elements of the Soviet system and so he hoped for a 'civilization (in which) all men are citizens of the world republic of law and justice and of the republic of learning' (p. 77). Liberal education should be for all – he wanted universal education (not universal schooling). Basically the curriculum that he suggested in his seventh chapter was very similar to the liberal approach offered in the UK at the same time, he advocated an educated person with a broad rather than specialist education.

In his final chapter, Hutchins outlines his vision of the learning society. He is clear that the educational systems cannot do it all and that technology could compensate for the shortage of teachers that this new system would create. But people will have a lot more leisure time in this new age, a common fallacious belief of that period, people would have more time to benefit from the education and learning offered. Consequently, the learning society is one that offers part-time education to everybody at every stage of grown-up life. It will succeed 'in transforming its values in such a way that learning, fulfilment, becoming human, had become its aims and all its institutions were directed to this end' (p. 133). It would be something like his understanding of ancient Athens and he reminds us that the Greek word for leisure is the word that we translate as school. Citizens only had the leisure time that they did because Athens was a slave-owning society but he thought that machines would be able to do for modern people what slaves did for the Athenians. For him, the learning society is an educative society with changed values.

The other educationalist who tackled this subject was Husen (1974), although his writing was almost completely orientated to schooling. For him, '*educated ability* will be democracy's replacement for hierarchical positions gained as a result of social prerogatives: it will be an individualistic, meritocratic society and education will play an important role in helping individuals in the process of social upgrading. The technicians, experts and scientists will become important persons not only on the strength of their know-how and proficiency in planning, but because the information they provide policy makers with will be so complicated that the latter will increasingly tend to waive their authority (pp. 238–239).

He recognised that this is an information society and the distribution of information will be increasingly facilitated by electronic and technological means and that this would change the structure of the work force, and this was especially true of schooling where work practices in the school would have to change and the emphasis would be put on learning and not on teaching. This would lead to a more or less complete individualisation of learners.

Both of these writers in their different ways emphasise aspects of liberalism in which individuals can learn and achieve: for both the learning society is an ideal that comes within the modernity project. In both cases it is utopian, but so, in a completely different way, is critical adult education which has both criticised liberal adult education and also the society in which it emerged: it exists as a critique of the present society and points to the hope of a better society since it is based on the Marxist utopian dream of a classless society. The critique is based on a different set of values that different utopias demand and the critical pedagogy offered by McLaren (2005), for instance, is in line with much of the content of this study. We will return to this topic in the final part of this chapter. More recently, however, we have seen lifelong learning and the learning society as a new social movement (Jarvis, 2007b) and in the writings of Longworth and Davies (1996, p. 145), for instance, we find the language of utopia being used:

> What we have tried to describe ... is the end of the age of education and training and the beginning of the era of lifelong learning. As a necessary companion to the age of information it will allow us to understand better its implications for the lives of everyone of us to allow the human race to develop its potential in more positive ways than hitherto. Already commentators are looking at the world as it is and predicting descent into a new dark age of the human spirit – mean-minded, aggressive, parochial, utilitarian and without the ideals which allow us to reach a more civilised way of co-existing on this small planet.
>
> We believe that lifelong learning offers an alternative to that bleak scenario.... Lifelong learning is not just desirable, it is a survival issue for us all.

Given that they were trying to convince their readership of the desirability of lifelong learning, they are using the language of the apocalypse to warn them and then offering a utopian way forward. It is a better world they offer and life-long learning is the way forward; the problems are with us but through learning we will conquer them. At the same time, Longworth (1999, 2006) has written some extremely readable books about learning regions and learning cities, describing what is happening in various parts of the world. However, these books assume that the values of modernity with its neo-liberal basis, and so they are open to all the criticisms that we have levelled at modernity.

Lifelong learning is essential to our humanity (Jarvis, 2006) and is the basis of our growth and development but in its individualistic formation it sees society as an agglomeration of individuals all striving for self-development and then attempting to learn to live together by rationally constructing a demo-cratic way of living. Like all the other manifestations of utopian thinking that we have discussed these formulations of lifelong learning and the learning society offer an unrealistic future based on the dubious foundations of moder-nity. In a sense, they are fulfilling two of the major functions of utopian think-ing – directing us to an unachievable future that is better than the present but also telling us that the present is not good enough. Moreover, we have suggested that there are very many things about the present which are undesirable such as human poverty which, if not created by neo-liberal policies in the dominant West aids and abets it and the ecological disasters that are currently being generated by the over-use and destruction of the planet's resources. But, as we argued earlier in this study – the global capitalist system generates/indoctrinates potential consumers by creating a desire to consume and then it reinforces this desire among consumers through its advertising campaigns. These are outcomes of the learning society that we currently experience and perhaps we have to learn to resist them. As E.P. Thompson (1977, pp. 790–791) wrote:

> And in such an adventure two things happen: our habitual values (the 'common sense' of bourgeois society are thrown into disarray. And we enter Utopia's proper and new-found space: *the education of desire*. This is not the same as 'moral education' towards a given end: it is rather to open a way of aspiration, to teach desire to desire, to desire better, to desire more, and above all to desire in a different way.
>
> (*italics in original*)

The education of desire presents us with a paradox since we have already exam-ined a way in which consumer desire is being created through indoctrination and brainwashing and while it would be false to claim that critical adult educa-tion has ever appeared to be indoctrinational, it would be true to say that criti-cal adult educators certainly desire a different society and they would see their work as a critique of the values that are the foundation upon which contempor-ary society is built.

The education of desire

Desire need not be utopian as we have already shown; indeed, capitalism is most persistent in educating desire in the direction that it needs and in the process it is creating a far less than perfect society. Other forms of desire can take us in the direction of other forms of self-interest and people can have these desires trained or supported or realised in a wide variety of different ways. But the desire for a better world is one which was manifest in the religious myths of the new Jerusalem but also in Marxism as it attacked the Christian position by offering an apparently less mythical alternative – the classless society. Based upon a weak view of social change and a weaker understanding of the rationality and the human being, its attractive offer was seen as an alternative to Christianity, although many scholars especially from liberation theology, such as Freire, endeavoured to combine the two. A major part of the attraction of radical Christians and others to the Marxist perspective was that it also attacked capitalism and offered some form of emancipation to the oppressed – but Marxism offered an alternative utopia that is just as unachievable as those others at which we have looked in this study. Radical adult education, supported by Marxist utopianism, has rightly been critical of much of contemporary education, as well as modern society. It might also be claimed that it was, therefore, being used to educate the desire of people to bring about the classless society. Paradoxically, if we talk about education of desire, we are in danger of regenerating the process of indoctrination that we have fully discussed earlier. Educating emotions and feelings is a difficult undertaking but the question needs to be asked as to whether we do need this form of education since we have always longed for a better society.

Education has always played a dominant role in preparing people for their place in society rather than one of preparing people to be creators and innovators, and even in teaching people the values that they need to learn to perform their roles within it. In this sense, education normally performs a subsidiary function, but nevertheless crucial one, in most societies of the world. We are confronted with a very interesting ambiguity at this point – traditional education has fulfilled the function educating (socialising) children into the order of society in order to preserve it (conservative) – that is educating children into the perceived best or most utilitarian values of the society into which they are born, whereas liberal education starts with the individual and seeks to educate the self-interested individual into the culture of the society. It is necessary to find a middle way.

However, Dewey offered another aim for schooling which is most appropriate at this point. He (1916, p. 51) wrote:

> It is commonplace to say that education should not cease when one leaves school. The point of this commonplace is that the purpose of this school education is to insure the continuance of education by organising the

powers that insure growth. The inclination to learn from life itself and to make the conditions of life such that all will learn in the process of living is the finest product of schooling.

Schooling should prepare children for lifelong learning but more than this, it should prepare them to want to learn in their later life. Perhaps this is the education of desire that we should foster and this is in no way a process of indoctrination. If we are to generate a genuine democratic form of society in which people are prepared to play the role of knowledgeable citizens, then we do need to help them to love learning and perhaps this comes by a society or a community embracing lifelong learning and celebrating it in as wide a variety of ways as possible. Perhaps social events like learning festivals, when whole communities celebrate learning and engage in joint learning activities, where the young and the old join together in such learning activities, are ways by which the young may develop a desire to learn because it is fun[10] and learning is celebrated as a fun event. For this to occur, however, we need to put the community before the individual and socialise children into the desire to learn per se rather than the desire to consume or even the desire for utopia.

Conclusion

Utopia is deferred – indefinitely – since it lies beyond history rather than at its end. But utopian ideas so have genuine functions of making us aware of the imperfections of the present society and pointing us to something which is better – we all desire a better world. Indeed, utopian ideals have almost always appeared as a reaction to an oppressive world and they have normally taken root among the oppressed peoples of the world. We have shown that force cannot bring about utopia, and it often does not bring about a better world, as the case of Iraq most recently has demonstrated. Utopian ideals cannot be exported! But we still have this ideal of a better world.

In precisely the same way we have discussed an ethic that also points to a better world – agapism. When people are concerned for people, without self-interest, but only out of commitment to the Other, we might also see a better world and this, as we have argued is contrary to the fundamental, but flawed, bases of modernity and the belief in individual advancement. This ethic of agapism, however, has no power, except the power of the Face – the person whose very presence makes demands on all of us. It is in relationship that we can discover something of the better society that we desire but educating emotions and feelings to desire such a society is a difficult undertaking. But the question needs to be asked as to whether we do need this form of education since we have always longed for a better society: life other non-science non-instrumental subjects no place was found in the past but perhaps now we need to recognise what is missing from our very lop-sided modern curriculum which emphasises science and instrumental subjects. But schooling should also have another aim.

We need to re-discover the truth that Dewey taught us about schooling – schooling should generate people who love learning – this is the learning society, when a culture of learning has been created and if this is coupled with an ethic of care and concern for all peoples throughout the world, it might be possible to envisage a world that is moving in a more utopian direction.

Chapter 11

Back to the beginning?

If the Enlightenment project is flawed as we have suggested, then we are confronting a pretty pessimistic situation: civilisation, as we know it in the West, has taken some wrong paths and some of our taken-for-grantedness is without foundation. Can we go back to the beginning of the processes that we have been discussing here, or even earlier – to pre-history to which we have made reference earlier in this book? Of course not – but this does raise issues about how change in society occurs and this will constitute the first part of this chapter. In some ways MacIntyre's solution in *After Virtue* was to look backwards and we will look briefly at his position in the second part of this chapter. But it may be that we have to seek an ethic that is not merely a reasoned argument for the good, and this is something that Habermas has pointed us to; perhaps communicative action and deliberative politics is a signpost to something even more significant, which in their different ways Mead (Strauss, 1964) and Buber (1958) among many others have investigated, and that is relationship itself. We are not born as individuals but we are born in relationship and then have to learn how to be individuals – we may not have individual rights in this sense but we are members one of another which is a moral relationship and so we will investigate agapism as a foundation for morals and, therefore, as a foundation of politics. But the important thing about this is that while we can universalise the principle, it is not experienced in universal but specific situations. Indeed, the insurmountable difficulty is that agapism cannot be translated into a legal code – it is not possible to command people to be concerned about other people. However, as a principle, it neither gives priority to the individual nor to the group. At the same time, this is not just an intellectual formulation but is grounded in everybody's experience, and so it is not unrealistic. It is from our experience that we learn and seem intuitively to know that it is good to care for other people: this form of learning was discussed in an earlier volume of this trilogy (Jarvis, 2006) and is also discussed in earlier chapters of this study. This will constitute the fourth part of this chapter. Finally, we want to ask what the implications of these discussions are for contemporary society and so we will look back to some of the issues raised in this book, which will lead us to the final chapter in which we look at the revolution demanded in learning to move society along in this direction.

Time and change

If the moral debates that we have investigated can find their origins in pre-history, it calls into question the notion of progress and coupled with this it asks fundamental epistemological questions. In his differentiation of knowledge into seven categories, Scheler (1980 [1926]) suggested that the final two – mathematics and science and technology are artificial because they did not have time to become embedded in a culture before they become out of date and this implied that the other forms of knowledge always appear to be dated but this does not mean that they also have to be neglected. One of the main reasons why science and mathematics and technological knowledge change so rapidly is because the capitalist system needs new knowledge to produce new commodities or older ones more efficiently and this demands research in specific areas of knowledge: current knowledge is no longer acceptable or legitimate because new knowledge can be used to produce the goods more efficiently, and so on. Progress has been related to these changes. But if these are the only bases upon which progress is judged, then they are extremely limited. Indeed, if we look at some of the social issues to which we have referred in this book, such as the number of people who are living in poverty, those who are disenfranchised, the questions of universal justice, equality, governance, and so on, it is difficult to think that we have progressed socially a great deal at all. Once we base our discussion on the other categories of knowledge we are forced to raise questions about humanity's progress. Some scientists have claimed that these other categories of knowledge are dated, but the point remains that while some peoples of the Western world are better off materially, this does not mean that humanity has progressed. These other categories of knowledge do not change very rapidly. Even, for instance, the concept of justice on which Rawls based his formulation of democracy does not change like scientific knowledge. If, however, utopia is an end of time state, then progress could have been seen as moving in the direction of the end of history, but this is a difficult thing to demonstrate. Consequently, we actually question the idea of progress and suggest that it is a Western, scientific concept and not one that has universal validity. We are, therefore, discussing the idea of change and process through time; whatever sociological theory of change we adopt, it does not pre-suppose progress but only process through time.

From the argument in this book, we can see that one of the major driving forces for social change has been the global sub-structure, which has generated change throughout many societies of the world. Social change might, therefore, be seen as something that is evolving as the market generates new demands and the production system, including new knowledge, produces new phenomena which become embedded in society's cultures. By contrast, however, it could be argued that such a system has generated opposition and so with Marx and his many followers considered that change would come when the system and its antithesis clashed and a new classless society would be born through a revolution. Using the Hegelian dialectic of thesis/anti-thesis/synthesis, Marxists see that as a result of over-production and the sentiments of injustice experienced by the working classes by the system, the capitalist system will be destroyed and be replaced by a classless society. As we have already seen, however, this classless society is a utopian myth that is, like other utopian myths, unachievable within time. While there have been many other theories of social change, this is not really the place to explore them, but one thinker has pointed us in a useful direction as far as this study is concerned.

Without accepting uncritically his total theory of social change, Pitirim Sorokin,[1] the first professor of sociology and founding chairman of the Department of Sociology at Harvard University, devised a theory that helps us understand the current situation in the Western world. Some of Sorokin's work was concerned with the meaningful interaction that occurs between two or more individuals and he regarded society as comprising either interacting individuals or interacting groups: society is the totality of interacting groups and culture is the totality of meanings, values and norms possessed by interacting human beings. He saw a group or society as a causal-functional unity in which all components are mutually and functionally interdependent. Culture is everything that is created or modified by interacting individuals and groups are themselves parts of the whole society that comprises a number of sub-systems within which we function. He postulated four such sub-systems:

- Sensate – in which people experience the world by their senses.
- Ideational – in which people believe that behind the sense experiences is a deeper reality which he regarded as ideational.
- Idealistic – the system of truth arrived at through reason.
- Mixed systems – when the ideational and the sensate are juxtaposed.

Change, he suggests occurs when culture flows from the sensate to the ideational and back again and in so doing it passes through a mixed phase. For him, every cultural sub-system is incompletely integrated and when one of these systems becomes too strong then there is a change in direction towards the other. While there are criticisms of this system, it seems that there is another similar system of change that is occurring and that is between the mixed and the idealistic. Society was, throughout the modern age, moving away from the mixed system towards the idealistic but as we have shown in the previous chapter, the idealistic is unobtainable and we are now beginning to see that there is considerable value in a system that combines the sensate and the ideational. In this late modern world there is a swing in this direction and away from the idealistic for the many reasons that we have discussed in the previous chapters and so we have to look for a new way of understanding culture.

After virtue

One writer who recognised the need to change and who also began to look back was Alisdair MacIntyre (1985). He reviewed very thoroughly some of the moral arguments to which we have made reference in the seventh chapter and concluded that modernity had to fail. He (p. 56) is quite clear why the Enlightenment had to fail:

> morality did in the eighteenth century, as a matter of historical fact, presuppose something very like the teleological scheme of God, freedom and happiness as the final crown of virtue which Kant propounds. Detach morality from that framework and you will no longer have morality; or, at the very least, you will have radically transformed its character.
>
> This change of character, resulting from the disappearance of any connection between the precepts of morality and the facts of human nature already appears in the writings of eighteenth-century moral philosophers themselves. For although each of the writers ... attempted in his positive arguments to base morality on human nature, each of his negative arguments moved toward a more and more unrestricted version of the claim that no valid argument can move from entirely factual premises to any moral or evaluative conclusion – to a principle, that is, which once it is accepted, constitutes an epitaph to the entire project.

We have also shown how the thinkers at whom we have looked have only based their arguments on reason but MacIntyre argues correctly that moral reality is more than reason, so that the whole project is bound to fail: reason is not god!

MacIntyre then turns towards another way of looking at morality – he looks back to Aristotle and the idea of virtue, which is more than a duty or an obligation. He immediately recognises that there are a multitude of concepts of virtue and he classifies them into three: a quality that enables individuals to fulfil their social roles; a quality that enables them to fulfil their human roles; a quality that enables them to achieve earthly or heavenly success. Clearly then, virtues are to be discovered in practice, which he (p. 187) regards as 'any coherent and complex form of socially established cooperative human activity'. In this sense he is discussing standards of excellence that achieve their status in a tradition of practice. He (p. 191) defines virtue thus:

> A virtue is an acquired human quality the possession and exercise of which tends to enable us to achieve those goods which are internal to practices and the lack of which effectively prevents us from achieving any such goods.

This is an individualistic formulation but it is one acquired only through participation in the community of practice: he recognises that in any field of

practice, the individual is entering not only a community of contemporary practitioners but one that also has a tradition to which the current practitioners
endeavour to aspire. Consequently the virtues are not grounded in human
reason but in the traditions of excellence in the community. MacIntyre also
approaches the idea of lifetime experience when he suggests that the unity of a
single life is that of the unity of the life-story that emerges from a quest that is
pursued within that living and uncompleted tradition. Indeed, an individual's
search for good 'is generally conducted within the context defined by those traditions of which the individual's life is part' (p. 222).

The strength of this position is that people define their good in relation to
others within their tradition, which is the authority from which individuals
have to learn. The tradition only exists for as long as it is a living tradition and
members of the practice exercise its virtues. However, this is precisely what professional practice has always emphasised, but it has certainly been downplayed
as professionals are instructed to achieve competence rather than expertise and
wisdom: competence is itself an ideology of individualism. Yet the traditions of
the practice are not written in tablets of stone and there is continuous debate
within the community as to precisely what the community is or ought to be. It
is at this point that MacIntyre appears to be confronted with a major difficulty:
if there is always debate about what constitutes the practice and, therefore, the
living tradition, it either demands a relationship in which members trust one
another and share their ideas in a sense of equality and accept whatever verdict
is reached by whatever means the community decides or else it opens itself to
the exercise of power by those who are its designated leaders.

MacIntyre recognises that republicanism is an attempt to restore something
of what he regards as the classical tradition which inherited an ethos of equality
– members of guilds and societies had equal rights (p. 237), so that the republican conception of justice is defined mainly in terms of equality and only second
in terms of public merit. For MacIntyre, love, fraternity and equality form the
basis of the virtues. This position has its attractions, many of which we have
neglected at our peril since the Enlightenment, and it comes very close to our
own position in many ways but we are still unhappy with the emphasis on individual virtue. However in a very rapidly changing society, tradition might also
inhibit change that might actually be good for the community. In addition,
once criteria for the development of the good of the community are specified, it
might begin to re-enact the Enlightenment debates yet again. Consequently, we
feel that while the strengths of this position need to be incorporated into lifelong learning and the learning organisation/society, it does not really answer all
the problems with which this study commenced. But it is in the community, as
Habermas, and even Mead (Strauss, 1964) before him, has highlighted, that we
might find some more satisfying answers: not so much in the communicative
action but in the relationship itself.

The agapistic relationship

The paradox of social living *par excellence* is that of how to be an individual in a group or alternatively how can any group, let alone a people, survive when individuals each seek their own interests? The stories of the Old Testament to which some reference has been made previously record some of the problems the ancient Hebrews faced in this respect. The story of modernity is one in which the individual has been prevalent and we have seen how the group has been torn apart and early sociologists such as Toennies (1957) and Durkheim (1933) documented the process. From Durkheim's (1915) studies it is also clear that this is a fundamental problem for all the religions of the world: religion has primarily been a unifying force. With the advent of modernity and secularisation the individual has become the centre of attention. In studies, such as MacIntyre's (1985), there is a genuine attempt to return to the whole group but in Habermas' deliberative politics there is an attempt to find a middle way. However, what is now needed is to go beyond discourse ethics and deliberative politics to discover another approach to this question and in the remainder of this chapter we want to explore one that has profound implications for education and learning theory. This approach seeks to locate the act of goodness in the relationship itself and the good as being disinterested concern of one person for the other. Honneth (2007, p. 101) suggests that Derrida, relying on Levinas, goes beyond the conceptual horizons of discourse ethics, and offers a morality based on a phenomenology of moral experience – friendship. Honneth (p. 115) says that Derrida claims that every friendship relationship has two intersubjective attitudes:

- relationship to the other as a concrete, unrepresentable, individual person;
- responsibility, bearing asymmetrical features since the person is obligated to respond to the friend's need without considering reciprocal duties.

But if the relationship is determined entirely by the asymmetrical, one-sided obligation that would no longer be friendship but love, which is where our argument begins. Without exploring Derrida's ethics further here, since it would take us beyond the parameters of this argument, Honneth (p. 125) concludes that Derrida's argument has taken us a little beyond the Kantian tradition and 'care has again been awarded a place in the domain of the moral'. That it should ever have been denied a place demonstrates the way in which Enlightenment reason has been flawed. Moreover, we want to argue here that a fundamental weakness in this position is the emphasis on the individual. Buber[2] (1958, p. 22) argues that in the beginning is relationship and in his thesis 'I–Thou' he argues that unity of the living relationship is captured in speech and also in a spiritual connection of human life through which *I* becomes an *I*. Buber then proceeds to a theological interpretation of the relationship which I do not wish to pursue here but which I think has considerable validity. Something of the same depth of understanding about relationship is to be found in MacMurray (1961, p. 116) who argues that 'the moral rightness of an action ... has its grounds in the relation of persons'. In other words, it is in the relationship itself that the moral justification of action is to be found. This moral concern might be termed 'love'.

However, love is a confusing word and it is necessary to understand it: there are at least three different words in Greek that can be translated as love – the one related to friendship, the second to emotional and erotic love and the third to a disinterested concern for the other. It is this final form *agape* that constitutes the basis on much of the following discussion. This linguistic clarification is necessary if we are to refute some of the assertions that deny love a place in the moral vocabulary (Honneth, 2007, pp. 171–179). Love, then, is disinterested, but committed, concern for the other – it is in Derrida's sense an asymmetrical relationship, but as a moral good, or even the only moral good, that transcends cultural values and yet it fulfils many of the criteria of those other approaches to ethics which we discussed in the seventh chapter.

- To care for the other is never wrong, so that it can be universalised and it becomes a moral duty but it can never become a law. As we can universalise the imperative to love the other, then we can argue that it transcends cultural relativism.
- To be concerned about the outcome of one's actions in relation to the other is utilitarian but in this case we do not look to the happiness outcome but to the response of the *I* to the *Thou*. The good lies in the relationship between persons not the act, although acts should be the outcome of the good.
- We feel intuitively that we should be concerned for the other.
- To claim that the word has no empirical meaning is true, but then neither do the linguistic arguments upon which much of the linguistic debate is conducted.

But it is possible to claim that to act in the interests of another and not out of self-interest, as the liberal argument claims, is not rational – but then love is not grounded in rationality but in the relationship between people. Neither is it about the power that one person can wield over another, the taking away of the other's autonomy, it is in being with the other and being concerned about the other – and respecting the other's autonomy is also an element of that concern. Disinterested concern is, it is argued here, the sole universal moral good and so we need to justify this position and we will do so not so much from the arguments of logic and reason but from those of natural life, learning, experience and the science of the brain.

Towards a justification of agape as the universal basis of morality

In order to justify our argument we need to return to Buber's 'In the Beginning is Relationship' but in this case the beginning is the beginning of every human life: no foetus develops in the womb as an individual detached from its mother. We are all physically attached and when we are born into this life, we are still attached at the end of a cord. Even when the cord is cut, we are still totally dependent upon our mothers and cannot become individuals during our earliest days of life: in the beginning is relationship. We all experience this relationship – it is a universal phenomenon. Moreover, it is nearly always a relationship of love, care and concern, although we recognise that there are times when this relationship is traumatised by a mother's or another significant other's failure to exercise that concern. The significant other, or others, is also an important factor in this emerging relationship, as Mead (Strauss, 1964) demonstrated. The child develops within a relationship of care and concern – one that puts the child before the mother and significant others in most cases. In the beginning of life for most children there is a genuine and deep experience of a loving relationship. It is this love that we learn pre-consciously through experience and which appears quite intuitive when it surfaces without our consciousness in later years.

The anthropologist, Michael Jackson (2005, pp. 35–36), discussing the everyday patterns of social interaction and inter-experience assumes that:

> the elementary forms of intersubjective reason have their origins in the pre-reflective protolinguistic, sensuous, and embodied patterns of the human infant's relationships with its mother – an ebb and flow of synchronised rhythmic movements and noise-making, of touching, smiling, looking, holding, clutching and playing.

Here, we see love experienced in relationship before we are able to learn consciously: this is at the heart of pre-conscious learning about relationship.

There are at least three more perspectives that support this argument: first from neurobiology, the second from human development and the third from learning theory. First, when children are born, the brain is not fully developed – a social brain has to be built (Gerhardt, 2004). As Gerhardt (2004, p. 38) points out the orbitofrontal cortex's development is dependent on experiences and neuro-researchers call this process 'experience dependent'. The orbitofrontal cortex is that part of the brain which is most responsible for the emotions. If this fails to develop, or if it is damaged, then social life is impaired: 'This means that it (the brain) is built up through experience, probably for good evolutionary reasons: so that each new human can be moulded to the environmental niche in which he finds himself' (Gerhardt, 2004, p. 38 – my parenthesis). The first higher capacities of the brain to develop are experiential and not cognitive, but it is only through adequate love and care that the orbitofrontal cortex develops in the way that it does. Researchers have looked at the significance of cuddling a child, smiling, and so on. These experiences of love and concern help build the social brain and the more powerful the experiences the more the brain incorporates these experiences into its own structures.

Second, we all know that children have to acquire a sense of personal identity, free from that of the social identity that they acquire by virtue of their birth. The process of children learning the concept 'I' has been well documented as children start to acquire language: children start by using their own given name, then they acquire the sense of 'me' and, finally they use 'I'. This linguistic process demonstrates/reflects the mental one in which the child is individualised within the social setting. As children grow during the first years of their lives, so they very gradually develop their own identity and then the self-confidence to act independently. A sense of autonomy is not something with which we are born, but something many of us acquire. Yet we have to recall that Fromm (1942) documented clearly that there is a fear of freedom and scholars like Riesman (1950) have shown how some people are inner-directed, some tradition-directed and others other-directed. Relationship precedes the individual.

But these experiences are not only built into our brains in an empirical sense, they are also learned. It will be recalled that in the opening chapter of this study, and even more so in the first book of this trilogy (Jarvis, 2006) we examined experiential learning as an existential phenomenon. We pointed out that we first learn from experiences that we have through the senses rather than cognitively: that is, we learn by touch, sight, taste, and so on. But we cannot learn cognitively before we have language to conceptualise it, and so, all of our learning is pre-cognitive. In the same way all of our learning is not conscious learning since we are not always fully aware of what is happening to us and neither do we have the cognitive apparatus to conceptualise or to give meaning to our early experiences. These experiences are precognitive and pre-conscious (Jarvis, 1987, 2006). We have the experiences, even in the womb, and they leave sense impressions that we cannot conceptualise and do not conceptualise to a later period, if ever, in our lives. We are all aware of mothers who say that children have particular likes and dislikes that relate to the mother's likes and dislikes during pregnancy. Some primitive peoples have recognised this phenomenon and taught their own pregnant women about it: I recall teaching in Alaska when among the class was a pregnant North American indigenous woman. When we were discussing the significance of pre-conscious learning she said: 'My people teach us to talk to our children in the womb.' She explained that her people recognised the importance of creating this relationship through sound before birth.

Third, psychoanalysis and hypnotism have both, in their different ways, also demonstrated that we learn many things pre-consciously that can be called to mind in certain social situations or specific conditions, although we have to treat much of these data with a degree of scepticism. Some of the work in this field has rightly been frowned upon, even doubted, there is some that has been assumed to be valid and this supports the notion of pre-conscious learning.

This form of pre-conscious learning is not uncommon throughout the whole of our lives[3]: we tend to take for granted many forms of sense experience when we can conceptualise it and so conceptualising and then verbalising removes the object from our primary senses and it becomes a distant and distinct object. In later life, we tend to focus on the cognitive to the exclusion of the sense experience, and in so doing, we undermine those experiences of life that have helped to give us a universal sense of the significance of human love and care. Naturally, this does not always happen and few people are free of their emotions, but the other problem is that as we grow up, the concept of love gets translated from care and concern to friendship and erotic love. But, significantly, without erotic love, there would have been less potential for human reproduction and the perpetuation of agapistic love in the next generation.

There is a sense in which the pre-conscious knowledge which we all gain through our sense experiences is what Polanyi (1967) called tacit knowledge. He (1967, p. 27) concludes his initial exploration into tacit knowing thus:

> Tacit knowledge is shown to account (1) for a valid knowledge of a problem, (2) for the scientist's capacity to pursue it, guided by his sense of approaching a solution, and (3) for a valid anticipation of the yet indeterminate implications of the discovery in the end.
>
> Such indeterminate commitments are necessarily involved in any act of knowing based on indwelling. For such an act relies on interiorising particulars to which we are not attending and which, therefore, we may not be able to specify, and relies further on our attending to a comprehensive entity connecting them in a way we cannot define.

Only when we are forced to bring these experiences to our conscious mind and reflect upon them can we make them meaningful. We learn about many things of which we are not conscious. We learn that love, care and concern are essential to our survival – that it is, therefore, good. In fact this explanation of love as good explains intuitionism. Intuitions do not occur from nowhere: they are the result of preconscious learning.

Levinas has developed this approach in his conception of the Other in relationship and this was cited in the Appendix to volume 2 of this trilogy (Jarvis, 2007b). He is clear that when the person becomes a face and inhibits my spontaneity, i.e. my freedom, this is the beginning of ethics. This is when I recognise my responsibility to the other just because the other exists and this is what we have learned pre-consciously. Honneth (2007, p. 119) wrongly, in my view, says that Levinas' interpretation of responsibility to the face involves need of help, but this is a mis-reading of Levinas. Levinas states quite specifically that it is the existence of the other as a face that generates ethical concern and not the needs of the other, as the following two quotations indicate:

> A relation whose terms do not form a totality can hence be produced within the general economy of being only proceeding from the I to the other, as *face to face*, as delineating a distance in depth – that of conversation, of goodness, of Desire – irreducible to the distance the synthetic activity of the understanding establishes between diverse terms, other with respect to one another, that lend themselves to this synoptic operation.
>
> (Levinas, 1991 [1969], p. 38)

And elsewhere: 'the face speaks to me and thereby invites me to a relation incommensurate with a power exercised, be it enjoyment or knowledge' (Levinas, 1991 [1969], p. 198). Bauman (1993, p. 74) captures Levinas' argument much more clearly than Honneth when he writes:

> I am for the other, means that I give myself to the Other as hostage. I take responsibility for the Other. But I take responsibility not in the way one signs a contract and takes upon himself the obligations that the contract stipulates. It is I who take responsibility and I may take that responsibility or reject it, but as a moral person I am taking this responsibility as if it were not me who has taking it, as if the responsibility was not for taking or rejecting, as if it were 'already' and 'always', as if it were mine without ever being taken by me. My responsibility, which constitutes, simultaneously, the Other as the Face and me as the moral self, is *unconditional*.

We have all experienced this unconditional concern and learned it pre-consciously. It shows itself in the outbursts of generosity when there is tragedy, in the way people band together to care for each other in times of crisis – it is this that unites a people without taking away their independence. It is grounded in our experience of being a face and receiving that care either in the earliest days of life, or at other times in our lives. We have learned the basis of all relationship – and the response to need in the way that Honneth describes is only but a part of the whole. There is also a sense in which analysing society in terms of its social capital (Baron et al., 2000) also captures something of this concern but here relationship is analysed in a less personal manner, but we will return to this in the final chapter of this book.

However, there is a much more telling problem and this is that it is impossible to have universal concern when one exercises love to a particular loved person. However, this objection can be countered by the fact that there are at least two loves operating – agape and either friendship love or erotic love. To exercise the latter does not negate the former but it might involve moral problems for individuals that need to be resolved in their own practice. However, the fact that this does create a problem does not negate the fundamental position here that agape is the sole good and for Levinas, when the relationship is established, there is religion for the 'face to face remains an ultimate solution' (Levinas, 1991 [1969], p. 81): love is now god. Indeed, for Levinas, ethics precedes ontology – relationship precedes being and there is a sense in which the process of development in the womb and the birth relationship do justify this type of conclusion.

Another Utopia?

With the Enlightenment, natural law became the legitimating factor of ethical demand, and then reason, and money and science. Then, in their different ways, each has been seen as the basis for morality but each has been seen to be flawed. Each has removed the legitimating factor of human experience from the argument but here we are suggesting that moral value is legitimated by what is experienced and learned in life, albeit learned first in a preconscious manner and it is this human process that demands a great deal more research. The legitimating basis of morality, according to this argument returns in part to natural law in as much as it bases its argument in one of the unchangeable features of life itself – it is a universal truth that relationship is necessary for the survival of the human species and maybe for a great deal of life itself. Yet this universal relationship that is acknowledged by almost everyone and learned in the most natural manner – pre-consciously – needs no sophisticated conceptualising to understand, but it has rarely intruded into the great debates of morality and politics because it has become a taken-for-granted in everyday life.

Disinterested concern of one for the other, then, is the fundamental ethic of human living: it is the sole ethical good and yet it encapsulates nearly all the moral values of the Enlightenment: it does, however, deny that self-interested individualism (classical liberalism) is good in any way. Indeed, self-interested individualism is nearly always wrong because it does not consider the face and does not let the face intrude into our own spontaneity. In this sense, it is an anti-Enlightenment ethic and yet it captures many of the values of Enlightenment moral philosophy and many of the moral precepts of the Enlightenment period. As we argued in the seventh chapter and again earlier in this chapter, for instance, it is universal in its basis and it is a principle that can/should be universalised in practice, but having made this point we cannot guarantee that any action performed out of disinterested love will automatically have good consequences since human beings are not automata and social living is a complex phenomenon. It also fulfils Kant's moral practical imperative that human beings should always be ends and never means, since it is impossible to act with another in love without making the other's good the objective of the process. While it is a moral responsibility to act in this way, it does not involve the duty of fulfilling a law since it recognises that in this complex society it is impossible to frame laws that are always and in every situation morally correct, and this includes such well-known moral statements as *The Ten Commandments* (Deuteronomy 10 vv.12–22 – The Old Testament). While the morality of disinterested concern is not a crude deontological theory, the face does make a universal demand on the individual.

In precisely the same way, there is a utilitarian dimension to agapism: it does demand that the individual seeks to maximise the other's good and that there is also a sense in which the disinterested concern is extended to the maximum number of people. It is also at this point that this position does have its problems since its present formulation tends to restrict it to two persons in relationship and when there are more than two, a different form of relationship is created – 'two's company, three's a crowd!' Bauman (1993, p. 115) raises this issue:

> When the Other dissolves into the Many, the first thing to dissolve is the Face. The Other(s) is(are) now faceless. They are persons (*persona* means the mask that – like masks do – hides, not reveals the face) I am dealing now with masks (classes of mask, stereotypes to which the masks/uniforms send me) not faces. It is the mask that determines who I am dealing with and what my responses ought to be. I have to learn the meanings of each *kind* of mask and memorise the associated responses. Masks are not as reliable as faces, they may be put on or off, they hide as much (if not more than) they reveal.

It is harder to enter that I–Thou relationship with the many, in which we might meet individuals whom we cannot trust, even though we should still be concerned for them. We all experience something of an ambiguity with people whom we meet and do not know well: we fear the individuals who put themselves first rather than the group. It is here that ethics turns to law and the stranger, whom we would like to treat as a face, is forced to remain a stranger with whom we interact in a more formalised and structured manner: society is about different forms of patterned relationship and that the behaviour of the stranger is regulated by law and yet there is always the possibility that the stranger may become a face. This potentiality is captured by Turner (1969), as Bauman (1993) reminds us, in his distinction between 'communitas' and 'societas' that both co-exist in social living. Bauman (1993, p. 117) characterises the distinction between the two thus:

> If *societas* is characterized by its heterogeneity, inequality, differentiation of statuses, system of nomenclature, *communitas* is marked by homogeneity, equality, absence of status, anonymity.... In other words, *communitas* melts what *societas* tries hard to cast and forge. Alternatively, *societas* moulds and shapes and solidifies what inside *communitas* is liquid and lacks form.

Communitas exists in liminality whereas society is structured and organised: in the first, infinity seems possible since people are free to enter into relationships and strangers become faces, whereas the totality of the latter inhibits and depersonalises. Society is hierarchical and controlled by power (social, economic, persuasive, political), whereas the face has no power and asks only that we freely exercise our freedom to be concerned for the other. *Communitas* is not a utopian state beyond time, it is something that emerges in time – magic moments – when relationships of care and concern are captured and the potential of the I–Thou relationship is rediscovered in a group form. Significantly, this is not an empirical or material phenomenon and yet when it happens there is a sense in which it captures the spirit of humanity. It is no wonder that Ayer (1971) claimed that the word 'good' had no meaning – it is emotive, but not quite in the sense that the emotivists used the term. It is this that is universalisable but it is not practical or possible since society normalises and structurates. This is not a utopia beyond time but, if you like, one within it. There is a strange sense in which it is almost always a potentially present now that can manifest itself in rituals, festivals, special occasions and even without planning – but on occasions it is created. It is this form of relationship that we nearly all experience at some time or another but it is also one that judges society and its structures, norms and mores and shows how dystopian is our society.

Moreover, it takes courage or self-confidence or both, as well as sensitivity, to act morally and to be prepared to try to break down the social structures that exist in society to reach out towards the relationship of *communitas*. Structures inhibit the exercise of morality, since they tend to emphasise the rights of the individual or enable self-interested individuals to pursue their own goals. The moral person has to create *communitas* often in opposition to *societas*.

It is this form of relationship, this manifestation of society that judges global capitalism, dictatorships and even liberal democratic societies. Significantly, its values do not change, even though the society in which we live is changing and the idealistic culture, using Sorokin's phrase, is turning towards a more mixed culture of the ideational and the sensate. *Comunitas* is always *communitas* whatever the form of society that seeks to control it and it is always potentially present in whatever the form of society and social living.

Turner's distinction between *communitas* and *societas* has enabled us to explore the values of relationship and to see how the inter-personal in-depth relationship manifests itself in *communitas* as an ever-present vision of what society could be, and perhaps the best form of society that we can create is one that approaches as closely as it can the state of *communitas* and it has been clear that in many ways democratic society is still seen as the highest form of political organisation for social living and perhaps it captures some of its ideals. As we saw earlier there were three ways of approaching democracy: a liberal or individualistic one, a communitarian one which starts with the solidarity of the whole and the one that stems from deliberative politics: the question needs to be raised as to whether these approaches can be reconciled. Honneth (2007,

p. 254) points out that communitarians and liberals seem to be approaching something of an accord on this matter:

> If we take a look at the current confrontation between liberals and communitarians, we will quickly realize that most of the representatives of both positions appear to have reached agreement on an essential point: without a degree of common attachment to over-arching values, i.e., without what we might call a social community of value or, to take a less freighted term, a form of cultural life, a democratic society's ability to function cannot be guaranteed.

He, therefore, starts his analysis with the concept of community, which is in accord with our own conclusions following Turner's analysis of *communitas*. For Honneth (2007, p. 257) a community is 'patterns of social integration within which individuals are able to recognize one another for their achievements and abilities due to their sharing common notions of value'. Here he tries to combine both the liberal and the communitarian and if the common value in this form of society is the disinterested concern of one for the other in relationship, then it is possible to see that social cohesion can be sustained. At the same time, individuals' needs and contributions to the common good are recognised and the place of the individual is safeguarded. In this sense, justice as fairness can be administered out of concern for the other but only within the context of the good of the community as a whole. The political system can be evaluated by the ethical value of love that manifests itself in its highest form in the I–Thou relationship, which transcends social structures. In many societies, this political system will be democratic but it is possible to conceptualise other forms of society in which this combination of the communitarian and the liberal exist and *communitas* is still hidden just below the surface.

Conclusion

In this chapter we have shown the flaws in Enlightenment thinking but attempts, such as MacIntyre's, to go back to a virtue-based morality also fail. This is in no way to deny that moral virtues are laudable: indeed, in order to treat the stranger as a face and to be prepared to break down the structures of society in order to exercise that concern is a virtue in itself. At the heart of ethics, however, is human relationship manifested in situations where strangers become faces:

> It is therefore to *receive* from the Other beyond the capacity of the I which means exactly: to have the idea of infinity. But this also means: to be taught. The relation with the Other, or Conversation, is a non-allergic relation; but in as much as it is welcomed this conversation is teaching (enseignment). Teaching is not reducible to maieutics; it comes from the

exterior and brings me more than I contain. In it non-violent transitivity the very epiphany of the face is produced.

(Levinas, 1991 [1969], p. 51 – *italics* in original)

In relationship we can break away from the totalisers who would structure our society and control our freedom and reach towards an infinity, which is a sense of perfection, through teaching and learning with the Other. This is utopian but not beyond time but within it, not permanent but in which we live – whether it be liberal democratic or what Rawls (1999) rather condescendingly refers to as 'decent peoples' who have not attained liberal democracy.

Like Habermas, however, Levinas recognises the significance of conversation or a form of deliberation – a teaching and learning – in which we are both teachers and learners in a dialogue of mutual concern – and this reflects Freire's writings about the relationship between teacher and learner. However, this ideal for society calls for a revolution in both conceptions of the learning society and, indeed, for learning itself.

Chapter 12

A revolution in learning

A vision of a better learning society

In the opening chapters of this book we have shown how this globalised world is dominated by a capitalism that demands certain forms of lifelong learning and a certain type of learning society; education has responded to this in its normal manner – as a functionary, a servant of the power elite of society whether it be the church, the state or the economic system. There has, however, always been a critical element in education which led, for instance, to the emergence of critical adult education – but because of this perspective it had never been part of the mainstream and it had to be by-passed when education became an essential contributor to the capitalist system. At the time the mechanism by which it occurred was not really detected: traditional education was extended and continuing education became a part of the educational vocabulary. Having extended schooling, continuing education was like a cuckoo in the nest – it elbowed out critical adult education and made the existence of liberal adult education much more difficult. The changes were hardly noticed because the vocabulary was changed – education became learning, adult education became adult learning and continuing education became lifelong learning. But the institution of learning was still the servant of the supreme master, although it was rarely called vocational education; it also served the second-in-command – the state.

The state, however, still retains political power and political power is still potentially more powerful than economic power – as the cruel dictatorships of Zimbabwe and Burma have shown in recent years. Political power can still be exercised over economic power and so global capitalism could be contained by global political power but at the time of writing this seems unlikely, since the United Nations does not have sufficient unity to act as a world government. But an immanent danger is that if the political re-asserts itself then strong government can become totalitarian in a more repressive sense. Nevertheless, Habermas (2006) has made the point that the politicians might still be trying to play catch-up with the economic forces and so we have to recognise the potential sovereignty of political power. At the present time, however, global industrial capitalism exercises power, not only through traditional manufacture and trade but through the major international financial institutions, such as the World

Bank and the International Monetary Fund. Clearly there has been some opposition to this process but with few exceptions this has come from those nations of the world which are strong enough to oppose the capitalist West, such as China and Russia. Bourdieu (1998, p. 59) commenting on this situation writes:

> If it is true that most of the dominant economic forces operate at world level, transnationally, it is also true that there is an empty space, that of transnational struggles. It is theoretically empty, because it has not been thought through, and it is practically empty, for lack of genuine international organization of the forces capable of countering the new conservative revolution, at least on a European scale.

The United Nations does not provide sufficient unity or force to fill this void and there is no other. The state's role in contemporary society has been varied, from those societies that have sought to cushion their people from the worst ravishes of global capitalism through welfare provision to those which have embraced the modern economic vision and then tried to pick up some of the pieces as the brightness of the vision recedes.

At the same time we have shown that the Enlightenment project has been flawed for a variety of reasons but one of the outsets is that the values that it has been generated are incapable of creating a utopian social reality: yet, we have indicated that there is a nearer vision of a better world and this is to be found in the idea of *communitas*, but the manifestation of this is but a fleeting moment and society always re-establishes boundaries since it is not possible for society to exist in an unstructured manner and, as we know – once this happens there is an iron law of oligarchy. Or, in Levinas' (1991 [1969]) terms, totality is re-established but the potentiality of infinity remains – it is this that we desire but which we cannot reach because of the totality of social structures. Consequently, we look to a society that is always beyond reach, and yet, one which in those fleeting moments of *communitas* we can experience but, there is a sense in which they are antitheses of the reasoned world of modernity and global capitalism. But in this book we have argued for a morality that more widely finds its expression in these fleeting moments and also in the altruism of moral people whose lives manifest agapist: it is a morality that is beyond reason and one that demonstrates the imperfections of the current world. In a sense, one of the major functions of morality is not to try and impose its demands upon the world as if it were a sovereign power so much as to exist, like the Stranger, and remind the people of the world of their responsibility to the planet and to its people; for caring for the Other is the watchword of this form of morality. The religious prophet was the one who demanded that the people should be moral and obeys the dictates of their God. But in this secularised world, the prophet has disappeared and the churches are largely silent or focusing upon an 'other' worldly utopia – or even seeking to avert the apocalypse (see Bull, 1995) through religious devotion rather than social action. Yet, as Freire (1972a) pointed out, denunciation has to precede annunciation and critical adult education was one of the voices of denunciation – as was liberation theology. But what have we to announce? We have seen the problems of utopian thinking – utopia is an unachievable goal – but what of that experience that we all have, of *communitas*?

If we are to look for a just learning society, as Ranson (1994) and Welton (2005) have done, we too have to look for the ideal state at which to aim, but we are confronted with at least three problems: first, we live in a globalised world where a paradox is occurring – as the world gets bigger so the political units get smaller so that each political unit is more exposed to the global power of the sub-structure; second, we do not really know what type of society (political unit) we want, although some form of democratic society seems to be the closest to *communitas* in which people matter and are treated equally as human beings; education has always been the servant of the political unit and since we do not know what type of society we want, it is hard to determine education's aims in political terms that will bring about the end we seek – yet lifelong experiential learning may actually begin to offer something of a solution to this issue since it is not institutionalised education and so it need not perform the servant function but it could help perform a prophetic one. However, the prophetic critical one is easy to perform when all that is required it to criticise, whereas it is much harder to put the ideals into practice, as active citizens, and produce *societas* that satisfies everybody's needs or even the ideals of those who are considered to be the most learned, so that there should always exist a healthy tension between the social criticism and political and economic systems – one in which debate should occur about the way forward. But herein lies the third problem, even if it is possible to produce this forum at local levels it is harder at national and even more difficult at global level. Indeed, it is almost impossible to decide where to begin this process since society is what we make it but we are also the products of the social forces from both within and beyond our life-worlds. This is the supreme paradox of the individual in the group, as we have seen throughout this book. Moreover, in order to be realistic, we have to decide about the group: is it a family or a people, a region, a society or is it global society?

If we are to determine the type of learning society and the forms of lifelong learning that are necessary to create a better world, we have first to try to determine on a 'realistic utopia' in the way that Rawls (1999) did. Like Rawls, we have to recognise the place of morality in that formulation, but unlike him we shall argue that disinterested concern for the Other should lie at the heart of our aims, and this we will do in the first part of this chapter. In the second, we will explore the relationship between politics and morality in both the learning society and lifelong learning and in the final section, we will return to the individual leaders, prophets and teachers who stand outside of society and who through their lifetime learning have acquired the wisdom, expertise and confidence to criticise and to lead.

In a sense, this is a revolutionary agenda but revolutions are about power and while some utopians can call for revolution and others for the eschatological event, neither are realistic, and so we look to social change, which may have to come more quickly than some would like if we are to avert ecological disaster, although this might itself be the immanent danger that calls humankind to curtail the excesses of global capitalism and even to subvert some forms of global economic power. But by so doing, we run the risk of political power assuming sovereign, even dictatorial forms. At the same time, the utopian desire should not be constrained by modernist predispositions or even futuristic ideal structures – only by a morality that puts people first, because at the individual level, strangers become faces and faces become relationships and this is the universal morality.

Communitas, democracy and the learning society

Communitas captures the utopian ideal but does not look to the future since it is something that can occur in social events, festivals, rituals and relationships. It is potentially present in society and there is a sense in which it underlies structured society but is manifest when it breaks through the structures and generates a state of liminality: it is human persons in inter-personal relationship as opposed to people in positions. But Turner (1969, pp. 92–93) shows how it is more than this by suggesting a number of binary opposites that occur in this liminal state – here we extract a few of them to give a feeling for what he is pointing towards:

- transition/state;
- totality/partiality;
- homogeneity/heterogeneity;
- communitas/structure;
- equality/inequality;
- anonymity/systems of nomenclature;
- absence of property/property;
- absence of status/status;
- nakedness or uniform clothing/distinctions in clothing;
- minimalization of sex distinctions/maximalization of sex distinctions;
- absence of rank/distinctions of rank;
- humility/just pride in position;
- unselfishness/selfishness;
- total obedience/obedience only to those of superior rank;
- simplicity/complexity;
- heterogeneity/degrees of autonomy.

His list is incomplete but it is not one which we would totally accept since individualism is lost within this formulation and as we pointed out in the third chapter there are times when individualism is both essential and good. Nevertheless, this list does point to the distinction that we want to draw between the nature of *communitas* and *societas*. Because we experience some aspects of liminality in times of change and at times when we step outside the structures of society, we always feel that this perfect community is always within our grasp, even though we cannot always discover it. Paradoxically, it is also something that can be artificially generated by people who are inebriated or under the influence of other drugs. Indeed, libations of beer and other stimulants were frequently part taken of by primitive peoples in tribal rituals that break down the structures of society. Yet underlying it all, is the sense of relationship, belonging to a people and being concerned for the Other within the group. But existential *communitas* is unstructured, in the same way as we have already suggested that moral acts have to be prepared to break down the inhibiting structures of society to reach the Other, but in enduring social living we cannot get away from structures, as Turner recognised when he talked about normative *communitas*. Normative *communitas* occurs 'where, under the influence of time, the need to mobilize and organize resources, and the necessity for social control among members of the group in pursuance of these goals, the existential *communitas* is organised into a purduring social system' (Turner, 1969, p. 120). Turner's thinking here approximates to Dewey's discussion of social democracy and points us in the direction of a form of democracy that at least embodies some of the elements of *communitas*, although once it becomes a structured community it has become a total system in which infinity, in Levinas' terms, is impossible. The third form of *communitas* is ideological *communitas* and we all have our ideological hopes and aspirations. In a sense, this is precisely the problem that Levinas (1991 [1969]) analysed.

Community, however, is not *communitas* since the former is structured and the latter is not. There is a sense in which Turner's *communitas* and Buber's 'I and Thou' are also similar but not the same – the person relating directly with the other but Levinas points to a fundamental difference – in a normative society, individuals have to be prepared to break down the structures and respond to the Other directly and in this he paints a more realistic picture since he recognises that it is the structural forms of social behaviour that inhibit morality. The questions that this discussion ultimately asks are: How can we build a society that incorporates the value of love as the sole good? How can we build a society in which the politics are based on this morality? The answer, clearly, is that we cannot – for this is but a fleeting glimpse of something beyond but within the everyday. It is a form of morality that has no power to enforce the moral life style: politically disinterested concern is powerless. But if we cannot build the utopian City of Man, then how should we proceed?

There are fundamentally two alternatives: first, that we learn to live together and that we continue to cultivate a life-style that is devoted to person-centred, concerned daily living. But to do this demands a totally different approach to the priorities of life. We need to focus our learning on different knowledge and skills – on those forms of learning that Scheler (1980 [1926]) regarded as more cultural and less artificial. We have systematically pointed out in this study that contemporary society emphasises those academic subjects that have economic and use-value such as the sciences and technology. The key subjects in schools in the UK are Maths, Science and English – they are extremely important for modern society – but they omit so much about morality, philosophy politics, ecology and so on that are as much, or even more, important to the future of our world. Normative *communitas* needs a learning culture and educational policies and schools have to rediscover something of the breadth of learning and incorporate a more human and holistic socialisation process into basic education, even if it means that business and industry has to organise its own education and training. Lifelong learning, if it is to be lifelong, should begin before primary education with families, family festivals and celebrations[1] – early socialisation should instil in children a love of learning not of consuming, and schools should prepare children to be active citizens. It was Dewey (1916, p. 51) who wrote of school education that 'The inclination to learn from life itself, and to make the conditions of life such that all will learn in the process of living is the finest product of schooling'. This will not happen just through the subjects studied but in the ways that the school communities are managed and how the teaching processes are conducted: we learn through the whole of our experiences and not just through our cognitions (see Freire, 1998). The schools should seek to generate *communitas*, should be democratic communities in which learning is treasured and the learner recognised as a whole person who is always the Face for every teacher. Teaching is always a moral process (Jarvis, 1997). In modern jargon, we could say that we are building social capital – but perhaps the language itself becomes a screen which hides the reality of what society should be like, for it is more than democratic – it is a profound moral relationship between persons. While the scientific and the technological still have a place in the curriculum, it is by no means so dominant since the reasons for learning are different and the end product of our learning is the development of persons-in-relationship. This is a totally different form of learning society and it starts with the learning community – the community learning to live together. The emphasis really should be on learning – we need to learn to live together and this must be our primary aim if humankind is to survive. But the community is not the society and the society is not the world – the small community is a totally different social form to the larger society, although we need to capture something of the ethos of community in all aspects of social governance.

It is this for which Rawls (1999) was reaching in his realistic utopian picture of liberal democracy and perhaps Habermas' (1998) deliberative politics is pointing in the same direction. It is the same point that Honneth (2007, p. 254) also recognised when he pointed out that communitarians and liberals seems to be approaching something of an accord in which both agree that the social democratic system must have attachment to agreed values if society's ability to function is to be guaranteed. It was the value of justice as fairness that Rawls (1972) was proposing but we feel that it needs to be pushed even further: that the basis of morality is concern of the one person for the other. This means that 'every case has to be treated on its merits', to cite a frequent excuse made by public authorities for doing precisely the opposite, that is within the dual framework of love and law. Laws need to be framed from within a welfare perspective and their framing and enactment needs to be a matter of public concern. But throughout this book we have faced the situation in which the public both does not know enough technically and is not concerned enough to act – hence the call by the European Community (EC, 1995, 1998, 2000, 2001a, *intern alia*) that one of the aims of lifelong learning should be active citizenship.

If we are to create active citizens we need a learning people whose learning is also practical: a people prepared to seek to understand the complexities of contemporary society and give time and effort to be involved in helping solve the problems: we need people who understand the risks of today's society. In this sense, we need an open democratic society in which the people regard it as their responsibility to learn and to play their role, so that we can all respond to the needs of everybody in social living. The primary aim of the learning society then is to help people learn to love learning – a culture of learning – and regard it as their civic responsibility to continue to learn. In this sense, society has to become reflective as well as reflexive: it has to recognise that by its very existence its structures suppress the moral impulse that can create the form of society which the great majority desire.

It is important for society to recognise those who seek to put their ethics into practice are recognised more often for these are the active citizens for whom the EU calls, and their creation is seen as one of the aims of lifelong learning. Society has to be reflective about the way that it administers law and, therefore, more debate has to be encouraged about moral action and the debate has to be listened to by those who exercise power since their mandate is not one just given at the ballot box but one that has to be earned all the time. This is part of the learning society of the contemporary world. But as Bauman (1999, p. 11) suggests:

> Politicians, people supposed to operate in the public space professionally (they have their offices there, or rather they call 'public' the space where their offices are), are hardly ever well prepared for the invasion of intruders: and inside the public space anyone without the right type of office, and who appears in public space on anything other than that officially scripted, filed and stage-managed occasion and without invitation, is, by definition, an intruder.

There is need to generate public debate about those values that comprise normative *communitas* but which are repressed or neglected by society. Society has to become more publicly reflective – that is an element of the learning society – but calls for lifelong learning and active citizenship are little more than unrealistic dreams unless society's policies and structures encourage this form of reflection. But structures are not the only issues; we need the learned people who will be enabled to fill those public spaces: people who are lifelong learners – people who are modern reflections of the philosopher-rulers of Plato's *Republic*. This means that such topics need to be on their agenda or more precisely these subjects need to be on the educational curriculum.

The policies and practices of learning built into whatever form of democratic society is attainable should be preparing its members to play their part at every level: so that the learning society needs also to comprise learning regions, learning cities and learning organisations – all of which are devoted to similar ends. In fact, the learning regions should be the place where it is most easy to generate moral democratic societies since they are smaller and offer more opportunity of the different sectors of society developing ways of working together to enhance the local community. Indeed, the socio-political nature of learning regions needs to be emphasised not merely as places of work and industry but as places of community, care and concern. Local governments and learning regions should be synonymous and welfare orientated.

The second alternative is to dismiss these ideals as utopian and acknowledge that it is a concept for society that is unrealistic and that we should just abandon it, in precisely the same way that we abandoned society to the individual, even if we do so in a covert manner, and continue to lose ourselves in the luxuries that capitalism provides for us in the West. But the problem about this solution is that since we all have these preconscious learning experiences and all have these moments of *communitas* the ideals do not go away and so we have to learn from our pre-conscious learning that humanity demands of us that we learn to live together.

The public debate – morality and politics

At the conclusion of Honneth's (2007, p. 254) study he suggests that communitarians and liberals are converging on the need for an over-arching set of values: that 'the desired concept of community cannot simply be arbitrary, but possess a normative character'. He goes on to make the point that:

> we could say that from the liberal point of view, the cultural premise for the continuing existence of democratic societies are what make it necessary to form the various circumstances of social life into a *community*, for the communitarians, on the contrary, it is the cultural preconditions of individual self-realization.
>
> (p. 255 – *italics* in original)

And so we see that at the heart of the debate about the nature of society lies the nature of community, but it is clear that there are different starting points from which to achieve this position: these are the continuing paradox of the individual and the group which has been our concern throughout this study, but the fact that the starting points are so far apart illustrates the continuing need for public debate – Rawls' 'public reason' or Habermas' deliberative politics. This is the nature of democracy, but participation in this debate is individual learning and the wider the participation the more we approach the culture of learning. Throughout this study, however, we have harked back to the fact that a great deal of the public debate is unlearned and that many people in society do not enjoin in it, so that those who propound their views in public do so with little fear of refutation since the public forum has almost disappeared. There is a tremendous need for people to learn and engage in the debate – this is the nature of the learning society. Significantly, however, once we bring morality into this framework, it demands not just debate but action. It is not just theory but *praxis* and, as Lyotard (1984) reminded us the legitimation of knowledge in late modern societies is performativity: this has to be practical and so we must not be mislead by the ideas that everything is contained in language – the outcomes of the learning society must be deeds or else learning is incomplete.

We will briefly explore these differing perspectives, starting from a liberal position, as we did at the outset of this study: individuals break away from the group in order to pursue their own ends at the expense of other, or to be creative or even to be the prophet. But in order for individuals to exist, they need the group into which they are born and socialised, but this can also constrain them. But without structure we cannot really grow and develop and so both the freedom and the creativeness of individuals would be lost and yet in order to have them we have to grow beyond the confines of the group so it is perfectly reasonable to accept individualism as a logical position. But without a looseness in the structures, individuals are constrained, over-socialised and conformists (Wrong, 1963). There are many reasons why individualism is necessary, some are selfish and others are altruistic – but there is a sense in which individuals' relationship to the group is always a moral one. Indeed, morality itself tends to be individual and it is the moral impulse that breaks down the group structures. At present these two approaches to social living seem to come together in public protest rather than in public discussion on policy making. Rawls (1999, pp. 140–141), however, maintained that:

> the content of public reason is given by a family of political conceptions of justice, and not by a single one. There are many liberalisms and related views, and therefore many forms of public reason specified by a family of reasonable political conceptions. Of these, justice as fairness, whatever its merits, is but one. The limiting feature of these forms is the criterion of reciprocity, viewed as applied by free and equal citizens, themselves seen as reasonable and rational.

Rawls goes on to specify these conceptions as: rights, liberties and opportunities; assignment of the special priority of these in respect to the claims for the public good and perfectionist values; measures ensuring for all citizens adequate all-purpose means to make effective use of their freedoms.

This then is how Rawls sees a liberal approach to democratic society but, by contrast, if we start from the group, then we can see that the group itself is necessary for the creation of the individual and it has traditionally cared for its own. It needs to respect the personhood of the individuals in the group and provide some forms of recognition for the contribution that individuals make. It has also frequently opposed those who have threatened its existence and one of its greatest punishments has been to excommunicate the disruptive individual – what Agamben (1998) explores under the concept of the ban – although sometimes that opposition and excommunication has wrongly interpreted the motives of the individuals or because they threatened the power of those who claim to act on the group's behalf. But people feel safe in the group and are often happy to accept its protection, even at the cost of their own individuality. Yet people, prophets, teachers and leaders, have also to step outside of the group to instruct, inspire and lead the people: individuals are necessary for the group. Social relations exist and are regulated and such norms and laws can be enacted at local, national and international level. For communitarians, the group comes first and morality is based upon the maintenance of the social whole, almost at whatever cost. Consequently, in the public debate of democratic society, there is bound to be disagreement and so political rulers are necessary – even though they may not be quite so reluctant to assume office as Plato thought the philosopher-kings would be.

Learning each other's view and interpretations of social reality is part of the debate that should occur in democratic society; these are the debates that should occur in a learning society. In this respect we could adjust Rawls' claims slightly to point out that there are many differing views of how society should function and they need to be judged by a morality which, while not far removed from justice as fairness, puts the welfare of persons first, irrespective of their ability to reciprocate in the first instance. In agreement with Rawls (1999, p. 152), however, such a forum would allow both religious and non-religious views to be discussed, and in a multi-cultural society this would mean that many differing religious interpretations could be discussed.

Finally, Rawls (1999, p. 177) makes two other points: reasonable persons recognise the long-term advantages of social cooperation and they accept the consequences of the burden of judgment which should result in further cooperation between persons. Rawls' basis for law was that in the democratic society justice is fairness but we want to take this further and to argue that at the heart of all political consideration and law should be the agapistic principle of disinterested concern for the Other – but, paradoxically, this can become individualistic unless it is put into the context of the community's own existence. Yet, here we reach another supreme paradox: morality by its very nature has no power. The Other remains a stranger until we allow the stranger to become a Face, to inhibit our freedoms and make us act in an apparently non-rational manner, so that we need to explore another form of rationality – value rationality – and this needs to assume a certain dominance in society.

We have widened Rawls' conception of public reason and suggested a new basis for the democratic learning society but we are not painting the picture of a utopian end-product but suggest, with him, that we are engaged in a process – one of learning to live together which, as the Delors Report (1996) suggests, is one of the pillars of learning. Again, however, we return to the same point, we need to create a learning society where children, citizens of the future, learn to play their citizenship roles, just as much as, or even more importantly than they learn to play their occupational ones, they need to learn to play their social ones. This process begins with the family and extends through the whole of life. If it does not happen in schooling, as it might not while schooling is colonised by the dominant sub-structural global forces, we need schooling to reclaim its human place first, and we still need to see a realistic vision of what society can be and learn to protest against what it is, as and when it is appropriate.

In a sense, UNESCO has tried to provide a forum for this public debate through many of its policies in which it has looked at many of the major concerns of global society. It was one of the foremost advocates of lifelong education and it has tried to act as an educative agency in global society: as we argued in the second chapter, it has expressed opinions that have been contrary to those expressed by the dominant global sub-structure and by those organisations which have supported it. The learning society and lifelong learning are quite central to its mission and in the Delors Report we were introduced to four pillars of learning: learning to be, to do, to know and to live together. The concern of this study has been the final one of these but it has not only raised all the inequalities of global capitalism but also the fundamental flaws in modernity itself. In addition, it has pointed us to another pillar essential to the learning society: learning to care for the planet – something that O'Sullivan (1999) has pointed to in his study of *Transformative Learning*. It is essential that we actually transform our understanding of lifelong learning and the learning society and begin to join in the debates that organisations like UNESCO have initiated, so that we can create a learning society in which the debates are not all about wealth-making but about people-caring the world over. Consequently, we can now suggest that the pillars of learning are:

- learning to be/being and becoming – whole persons, body and spirit;
- learning to do – to work and to acquire other skills like engaging in citizenship;
- learning to know – a broad spectrum of knowledge and attaining wisdom;
- learning to live together – responding to the face of the stranger with an ethic of care and concern, and appreciating all the persons with whom we differ;
- learning to care for the planet – because it is more than a resource, it is a home for all of us.

In precisely the same way, the United Nations and the European Community, among others, might begin to extend these debates even further beyond the political to the moral and so help generate a more democratic society where people are even more encouraged to participate in them, both face to face and through the media. But global society is only beginning to embark on this learning journey and learning is not only about all of these, it is also about reflecting – reflecting on the consequences of its actions and discussing them in a reasonable manner. The learning society is a reflective society – one in which people reflect on the processes that occur every day and then contribute to the debate that should necessarily involve those who have taken it upon themselves to lead/govern society.

Prophets, teachers and leaders

Implicit in this study has been the supreme human paradox – how can the individual live as part of the group or how can the group remain a group and allow for the individuality of persons. Basically, we have suggested that the approach of modernity over-emphasised the individual and yet the group can be claustrophobic and deny the individuality of its members. We have sought a middle way and pointed towards the idea of *communitas* but have recognised that this can only exist for fleeting moments that might be the foundations of social democracy and we have pointed to an ethic of love in personal relationships that demands an outworking within the structured framework of society, whatever the consequences. However, throughout history some have stood outside of the group out of self-interest, they have endeavoured to enrich themselves at the expense of the group/community, and so on. They have often been condemned for it, but there are times when the cultural values of society get usurped by the powerful and then those who have enriched themselves at the expense of others have been lauded and given social honours – but such a situation can only depend on the power controlling the information, and so on – just as we have seen in modern society. At the same time, others have stood outside of society for the sake of society as a whole and both condemned the evils of society and pointed to a better world – a utopia, an unrealisable dream. They have often been condemned and sometimes punished for their individuality – their concern for a better society.

Moreover, we have recognised that this utopia, something completely unrealisable within time, finds an expression in the spirit of *communitas* which, in itself, exists as an implicit critique for what actually exists in society – always pointing beyond what is, to what might be, so that we have to keep on learning how to achieve something even better than we have. In this sense, the vision is also a teacher – pointing us beyond ourselves. Such a thought is dangerous to those who exercise power in the present. Indeed, this was well recognised by Plato[2] (Cornford, 1941, p. 331) in his condemnation of poetry – since it calls forth the emotions and undermines reason:

When you meet with admirers of Homer who tell you that he has been an educator of Hellas and that on questions of human conduct and culture he deserves to be constantly studied as a guide by whom to regulate your whole life, it is well to give a friendly hearing to such people, as entirely well meaning according to their lights, and you may acknowledge Homer as the first and greatest of the tragic poets; but you must be quite sure that we can admit into our commonwealth only the poetry which celebrates the praises of the gods and of good men. If you go further and admit the honeyed muse in epic or lyric verse, then pleasure and pain will usurp the sovereignty of law and of the principles always recognized by common consent as the best.

He goes on, on the same page, to write, 'it stands to reason that we could not but banish such an influence from our commonwealth'. Agamben (1999, p. 57), discussing art in general, writes:

it is in the experience of art that man becomes conscious, in the most radical way, of the event in which Hegel has already seen the most essential trait of unhappy consciousness, the event announced by Nietzsche's madman, 'God is dead.'

But there is another picture that we might look at, *Angelus Novus*, by Klee which shows:

an angel looking as though he is about to move away from something he is fixedly contemplating. His eyes are staring, his mouth is open, his wings are spread. This is how one pictures the angel of history. His face is turned towards the past. Where we see a chain of events, he sees one single catastrophe which keeps piling wreckage upon wreckage and hurls it in front of his feet. The angel would like to stay, awaken the dead, and make whole what has been smashed. But a storm is blowing from Paradise: it has got caught in his wing with such violence that the angel can no longer close them. The storm irresistibly propels him into the future to which his back is turned, while the pile of debris before him grows skyward. The storm is what we call progress.

(cited from Agamben, 1999, p. 109)

So wrote Walter Benjamin, in his *Theses on the Philosophy of History* (Agamben, 1999). Depicting what is and suggesting what might have been and pointing beyond what exists to something which does not and cannot exist are the dangers that art presents to the present and so it must be abolished from our commonwealth. But art is not the only thing that has to be abolished from the commonwealth, as we have seen throughout this study – but like the artist, it takes the prophet, teacher and leader to move society on to an unknown but hopefully better future. Our learning society demands the existence of individuals who are our teachers.

Prophets

Early in this study we turned to two prophets, Amos who condemned mercantile capitalism and Jeremiah who called a people back to its traditional ways by introducing us first to the paradoxes of individualism. Prophets today are still here, although not always in religious guise, to condemn, warn and point the way forward – this is both the denunciation and the annunciation that Paulo Freire recognised. Since the establishment of capitalism, as we have seen – long before Marx – there have been those who have condemned the individuals who step outside of the community in the pursuit of self-interest and even condemned the whole group for going in the wrong direction. It is a moral act to do this and politics has always tried to control this process. But it is not just condemning, it is warning of a possible apocalypse: we do not now need to go back to the fanatics or others who have clothed this in religious terms since the ecological message is claiming much more space and a far greater degree of credibility than ever before. We are beginning to learn that the primitive peoples who understood the earth as our home rather than a mine of unlimited resources had a far greater understanding of the world than we gave them credit for. We are constantly being warned (O'Sullivan, 1999; Gaita, 2000, *inter alia*) of this danger. Global warming is a constant concern to scientists and politicians. Those who have stepped outside of the community and pursue unlimited wealth at the expense of the people as a whole and of the earth are destroying a possible future commonwealth.

We have to learn from the prophets rather than condemn them – this becomes part of the agenda of the learning society but it hardly seems like the policy statements that stem from governments concerned about the demands of contemporary global capitalism. But can they announce a future utopia? Of course not, for as we concluded earlier – the concept of utopia is deferred indefinitely. But we can learn to find a better way – one which some people may call utopian in a present sense, and we can point to ways by which we can learn to understand what the natural world and what a common life demands of us; we can begin to learn what it means to try to implement the spirit of *communitas*. We have to learn to listen to the prophets of our day, rather than ridicule them, and understand what it means to create a learning society that responds to the demands that they proclaim.

Teachers

Like the prophet, the teacher stands outside of the community out of love for it: education is about helping people to achieve their humanity and their potential throughout the whole of their lives. Teaching is about having sufficient knowledge and love of learning to help others to learn throughout the whole of their lives and, as we argued earlier teaching is not about indoctrinating nor is it about taking away the freedom of the learners by making them conform: it recognises the different interests and concerns of the learners. Teaching is a highly moral task in which teachers demonstrate their commitment to the wider society: they stand outside of it, like the prophets, for its own good. In this task, there is once again both the denunciation and the annunciation. Freire (1972a, 1972b, *inter alia*) showed us the pedagogy that was demanded by the oppressed – a pedagogy that demanded that we recognise the oppressed and their needs and one that enabled them to achieve freedom. More than this Freire (1998, p. 103) calls for the re-discovery of utopia:

> I have always rejected fatalism. I prefer rebelliousness because it affirms my status as a person who has never given in to the manipulation and strategies designed to reduce the human person to nothing. The recently proclaimed death of history, which symbolizes the death of utopia, of our right to dream, reinforces without doubt the claims that imprison our freedom. This makes the struggle for the restoration of utopia all the more necessary. Educational practice itself, as an experience of humanization, must be impregnated with this ideal.

As individuals, teachers may have to denounce before they announce – to point out what is wrong with society in their opinion and even to teach people to resist the power elite when it is necessary. Newman (2006) captures this in his *Teaching Defiance* for part of our learning must be to defy the immoral and the unjust but also to engage those who wield power in dialogue. This demands a critical approach to society – it demands reflective rather than non-reflective learning – it demands the confidence to be an individual in the face of authority and herein, once again, is the paradox of humanity. Individuality is important for the good of the group but the individual could not exist without the family/community – teachers have to help learners become critical thinkers but also moral ones. This demands not only theories of learning that recognise the humanity of the learners as whole persons but policies of education that encourage critical thought throughout the whole of our lives and a culture that encourages them to practise it. Education needs de-colonising! We need a lifelong learning that can help people gain wisdom as well as knowledge. Aristotle regarded wisdom as something that is gained by age and he suggested that doing mathematics was a young person's pursuit whereas wisdom comes with age, something other peoples in the world accepted and so we must begin to appreciate the wisdom of the elders. Not all elders are sufficiently wise to lead or pronounce or to teach – but some are! We need a learning society where these values are treasured and teachers have the wisdom to teach.

Leaders

Leaders also stand outside of society and work for its good and the term 'leader' is deliberately chosen here, rather than politician, since we are all aware of how many politicians become so embedded in the system that they cannot lead, only administer the system and tweak its laws. Even the European Community documents recognised that European citizens tend to be suspicious of politicians and politics. The message of this study is that society needs leaders that can lead it to a better not necessarily a wealthier society – the good society: those who can point to a better vision of society but not promise an unrealisable utopia. This demands leaders who are willing to keep on learning so that they can encourage others. Increasingly, contemporary research is suggesting that people are not happier with possessions but in relationship with others and so it is in working with people for the common good that happiness might be discovered. Rawls (1999) was careful in his *The Law of the Peoples* that public reason is the discourse of judges, government officials and candidates for public office but it is the discourse of the people's forum. But those who lead need to be knowledgeable, they need to be able to join the public debate about all those aspects of life that concern the people. But people do have different interests and they will not always agree with each other – hence there is a need for public debate. Lifelong learning is an essential tool for those who will lead because they need to join in the public debate and articulate their concerns. But that debate is not just about justice as fairness – it is about the manifestation of those elements of *communitas* that are relevant to the people as a whole and so politics is about making and administering law that is about care, concern and commitment rather than power and self-interest.

The paradox of human living is that the community needs its different individuals, who are committed to the common good, to debate with other active citizens in the spirit of public reason – this is a democratic learning society and like *communitas*, it is so close and yet we cannot seem to reach it. But there are other individuals who stand outside of society for their own self-interest. Wherever we stand is both to expose our individuality and also to take the risk of rejection. Where we stand in society is an important question but perhaps an even more important one is – why are we there? What is clear is that those who stand there for the right reasons need to be lifelong learners so that they can teach others and encourage them to become active citizens as well.

Conclusion

While the new society cannot be utopian in a futuristic sense, we can still hope for a better society – it can become a normative *communitas* in which those elements of the existential *communitas* can find an enduring form. It is not a mystical or mythological future – it is seeking to move society in the direction in which most of us at one time or another have already experienced – this better and more happy inter-personal existence. But it is also calling us back to those early experiences in our own lives when we were in a relationship of love and concern.

This then is a society in which we need the whole spectrum of knowledge, where we need both practice and reflective theory – but this is a society in which we need to have citizens who love the world, love living, love relating and love learning and we need a society in which the love of learning is fostered. Learning for most people never ceases and herein is one of the great lessons of lifelong learning – we all continue to learn for as long as we live – we never arrive at perfection or the end of time. Our successors will keep on learning and so the learning society will keep on changing – it is an existential phenomenon – but the problem, the uncertainty, is we know not where it is going and we have to rely on ourselves – a people who have so far failed to build successfully a City of Man or a New Jerusalem on earth. But, learning is still a process of humanising and hopefully humanising our society, but because human beings are continuing to learn – the project of humanity remains incomplete and unfinished.

Notes

1 Lifelong learning and the learning society

1 This experience is similar to, but not the same as, what the psychologist Csikszentmihaly (1990) calls 'flow' – the way people do things when consciousness is harmoniously ordered – but disjuncture can still occur within the flow experience because 'flow' is about internal consciousness and disjuncture occurs between the internal and the external.

2 I have not included skills here although I have included physical ability because skilled action is a combination of the physical and the mental – knowing how and being able, and the body actually learns as well as the mind. For instance, when we drive a car we acquire such skills that we do not have to think before we act and we know, often feel immediately when we have not performed a procedure correctly.

3 It is significant that when we begin to ask questions about the nature of the human being we can do so in respect to humanity's relationship with the world or with our own animality – it is in transcending the latter that the human learns, grows and develops (see Agamben, 2004) for some aspects of this discussion.

4 While internalisation is used here the process is actually one of construction – but it is rather like that game in which one player tries to build a construction without looking at the original construction by following directions given from an onlooker who can see both the original construction and the one being built by the participant: the finished product is often similar to but very different from the original!

5 Unlearning is, in fact, new learning different things – even contrary ones – to those that had been previously learned.

6 Multi-layered governance is a concept first utilised by Held et al. (1999, pp. 62–77) although I have adopted it in a more simple manner here.

7 In some earlier diagrams, I did not use local but organisational, but I now feel that individual and organisational can be located at any level of the hierarchy.

8 It is really quite significant that at the start of 2007 there were reports in the British media that the trades unions are themselves beginning to globalise – Marx's message to the workers of the world to unite now assumes genuine significance. This is another stage in the development of global civil society.

9 The idea of a reasonably static culture pre-supposes the idea that culture is a unity, but we have already suggested that multiculturalism is now the order of the day – but in the pages that follow, we will also suggest that culture changes in response to the changes and demands that emanate from the sub-structure of the globe.

2 Global and local lifelong learning policies in the knowledge economy

1 A human capital contract is an agreement whereby learners commit a fixed portion of

future earnings for a specified number of years in exchange for a loan to finance an educational programme.

2 The concept was adopted at a World Conference on Adult Education. Since then, there have been a number of other conferences but I have deliberately omitted discussion about these from this study, although I was privileged to take part in the most recent one in Hamburg.

3 It will be recalled that a distinction has already been drawn above between values and ethics: the former relates to the non-moral goods of philosophy whereas ethics is concerned with the moral good.

4 During the time that I was undertaking the final editing of this manuscript I participated in the Sixth National Lifelong Learning Festival in Korea and watched as children and adults joined together in vast numbers to celebrate learning and while I do not know enough about Korea, it was clear that this was a government-sponsored and initiated event, seeking to get people of all ages to enjoy learning and that while employability may be a long-term aim of lifelong learning, it was also one of community. It is clear to me that we, in the West, have a great deal to learn from the East about the way that they have so enthusiastically embraced lifelong learning.

5 Since fundamentalism assumes that the believers are right because they are in a right relationship with God, it is easy to see how this form of certainty is in accord with the certainty that comes from economic success, as Max Weber (1930) demonstrated so clearly.

6 For example, I had reason to write to the Chief Executive Officer of a transnational company in the months before this chapter was written and I complained both about a process of mis-selling and the immorality of the practice; significantly, he rectified the mis-selling without demure but did not respond in any way to the ethical implications which I raised in my letter.

3 The spirit and values of modernity

1 One of the issues that has prevented the churches allowing their knowledge base to evolve has been the concept of revealed knowledge. Had the churches accepted the idea of inspired knowledge they might never have run into many of the epistemological problems that they have faced since the Enlightenment.

2 The place of the young in the whole of this question is crucial and we will keep returning to it since it involves the education of desire, among other things.

3 In an excellent PhD study Paul Kybird (2007) has made an important distinction between Bible as the book and Bible as the scripture – I am using the Bible as the book whenever reference is made to it in this study. Extending this idea, we find the Bible as a rich source in the history of ideas – often older than the Greek literature. The Old Testament is a recorded source of the development of ideas of a people and we can, therefore, ignore claims of revealed knowledge and see it as a historical anthropological document needing considerable interpretation and debate.

4 Further reference is made to this quotation in Chapter 7: prior to this time, families were punished for the wrong-doings of individuals rather than the wrong-doers themselves and in recent years we have seen considerable debate about the need for good parenting etc., but it is not only parenting, it is the loss of community that is part of this discussion.

5 This is an important element in the East–West debate, since in the West with learning being emphasised in the West as an individual process whereas in the East we start from the group: I think that it affects our approach to lifelong learning and the learning society.

6 The whole of this story revolves around the question since Job was both righteous and wealthy and the storyteller suggests that the wealth is God-given and so Job's righteousness has to be tested through all forms of human trials and tribulations.

7 There is very clearly a major difference between the way that wealth was seen as a reward from God for their righteousness and their use of the idea that God rewards the righteous with wealth to legitimate their elitist position. Legitimation must always be seen as a construct of the powerful who influence the social discourse.

8 This chapter was being revised during the period of flooding in UK in July 2007, at which time it became obvious once again that in times of crisis it is not necessarily 'every man for himself' but that people work together for the common good and that this is not a rational social contract.

9 The early books of the Bible are combinations from earlier documents – indeed, the Book of Genesis is itself a fairly late compilation; it is basically drawn from four separate strands, one of which is called J and this was probably written in the ninth century before Christ – the story of Adam and Eve occurs at the start of the J document (von Rad, 1961). Storytelling has always been one way of teaching profound philosophical problems.

10 The concept of prophet in the Bible does not refer to one who seeks to foretell the future but one who speaks out against the present, in the way that Freire discussed the idea of denunciation before annunciation. In this sense Freire was being true to his own Christian convictions and epitomising the prophetic role.

11 In precisely the same way scholars regard witchcraft as a relocation of the deviant outside of the borders of society and then 'normal' society has license to attack the strangers.

4 Capitalism and society

1 In her brilliant study of *Purity and Danger* (1970, p. 40) Mary Douglas writes 'we shall not expect to understand religion if we confine ourselves to considering belief in spiritual beings' and we will return to this insight throughout this book, and to her study in the fourth chapter.

2 Prophecy in the Old Testament was about speaking out and condemning – pointing to a better world but only if the evils of the present one be forsaken. The book of Amos was written in the eighth century before Christ and is, in fact, the very first complete book of the Old Testament – while there are sections of other books written before this, Amos was actually the first complete book written.

3 I am using religion here in a generic sense which incorporates all the major world religions and other faiths although I am writing from a Christian and Western perspective and so my analysis must necessarily be limited. I am also separating religion and morality conceptually throughout this study although specific religions have often been the legitimators of ethical codes. Conceptually neither needs the other.

4 The idea of God being dethroned (the death of God) is nothing new in Hebrew thought: for instance, the story of the Fall (Genesis 3) can actually be interpreted as God having given humankind freewill risked losing his supremacy as a result and when human beings exercise that will, then God is no longer sovereign in their lives unless that is its their choice.

5 The concept of God is itself a problem – but it certainly has nothing to do with a personage located in some mystical heaven like some grand old man/woman in his/her mansion!

6 I think that this is one of the most contentious of all of the discussions; in many of my books I have argued for a form of pre-conscious learning that begins in the womb and which has profound effects in later life. Hence, I will argue that this error needs correcting in both our understanding of the relation of the individual to the group and also in ethics.

7 But since human beings are born in relationship, the social contract is a secondary consideration to the nature of humanity itself and stems from this more significantly than it need come from human reason.

8 The ancient Hebrews regarded themselves as the People of the Covenant.

5 The information society: learning global capitalist culture

1 The celebrities who undertake these assignments have a major moral responsibility which sometimes they may not recognise, such as when well-known sports people advertise products and are paid massive sums for it, but the commodity being advertised is produced by sweated labour who are exploited by capital.

2 There is evidence that transnational corporations persuade governments of poor countries to invest in large prestige projects for which they have to borrow money, so that these governments voluntarily place their countries in debt to Western banks, including the World Bank.

3 While this chapter was being written *The Times Higher Education Supplement* (Sanders, 2006) carried three articles on the universities involvement with business – the first entitled 'Ventures with business present gains and pains' as it analysed the extent to which future university expansion might be based on a false hope. The second one, a week later, also by Sanders, examined the way in which the police force is being professionalised and universities vocationalised.

4 During the time that I was writing this book I spent a considerable amount of time watching children's television with my older grandchild and I was amazed not only with the amount of advertising on children's television chanels but the unrestrained approach to creating the desire to buy and consume in children. It seemed to me that the creation of desire was one of the dominant aims of such advertising.

5 It must be pointed out, however, that value is a social construct or even a personal one but value cannot be equated with what is good. The separation of value and goodness is an important element in this discussion.

6 Note the negative connotations of the word 'whistle blower' – not one who acts in society's interests but one who does not act in the corporation's (or employer's) interests.

7 It is perhaps significant that while this book was being written a *Panorama* programme on BBC1 looked at the effect of television on children's behaviour and to the researchers' surprise, they found that television individuated within the family and that watching less television was associated with enriched family life – *Panorama* BBC1 18 April 2007.

8 Sometimes this misinformation is purveyed by celebrities who are employed and paid vast sums of money to lend their status to the product. It can be argued that celebrities have an important moral role in this process, one which may not be fully considered in exchange for the payment.

9 Governments have introduced many new regulations that infringe human rights, such as DNA databases, photograph and fingerprint records on entering the USA, etc. Many of these actions are introduced by governments as a form of protection of the population against terrorism; be that as it may, these acts still infringe on basic human rights.

10 The fact that we do not internalise the empirical world casts doubt, therefore, on the idea that empiricism can always legitimate knowledge.

11 It is significant that while I was writing this chapter, the Post Office in UK suspended a delivery man from duty because he had advised customers how to stop junk mail being delivered. Despite the rhetoric of many companies of the idea that quality service results in customer satisfaction, this is only true if that satisfaction is not at the expense of profit – since, in this case, the Post Office is paid to deliver the junk mail that the customers do not like.

6 Indoctrination and the learning society

1 The red label in the UK government's Food Standards Agency scheme signifies high, e.g. high salt content, high fat content, high sugar content, high saturates content.

2 During the lobbying process Lawrence (2006, p. 9) illustrates, the power of the large corporation also became apparent, since in an event for British Members of Parliament, the

Kellogg's spokesperson (European President of the Corporation) both reminded the MPs that Kellogg's is a large employer in the UK and that its history is one of selling healthy meals to sick people in a sanatorium.

3 Many years ago, the British Open University summer school in the social science foundation course included a module on advertising and students were asked to analyse adverts that they saw in newspapers. It became a very easy process to analyse many of the techniques being used but what was significant was that by no means all the students were aware of all the techniques and associations being used. It became clear that people were being exposed to many techniques creating desires of which they were not aware.

4 During the period when this book was in preparation, there were many instances where hospitals' activities were curtailed and people's lives and welfare sometimes put at risk for the sake of the finances allocated to the hospitals concerned.

7 Ethics and modernity

1 A great deal of the first part of this chapter relates to the work that I undertook for *Ethics and the Education of Adults in Late Modern Society* (Jarvis 1997) and especially its second and third chapters.

2 This book of Bauman's was published during the time that this study was being written and so I have only made one or two passing references to it, although I feel that he covers many issues with which I am dealing with here.

3 This table has been copied directly from Jarvis (1997, p. 57) although Habermas (1990, pp. 123–135) gives a slightly more elaborated form.

4 The extent to which moral relationships can develop electronically is certainly a growing and significant issue – not just in ethics but in daily living generally.

5 As I argued in the first volume of this trilogy, information processing theories of learning are fundamentally flawed because they assume that human beings process information like computers, but they do not do so. To assume that human beings are like computers is to dehumanise humanity.

6 It is perhaps important to interpret the story of Adam and Eve and original sin in this way: it is a primitive myth trying to explain why humankind does not live in paradise but in dystopian forms of society, and the myth assumes that every phenomenon has a beginning and so the myth claims human beings exercised their freedom and did their own thing although the blame was laid elsewhere – itself a very human attribute!

8 The ethics of lifelong learning and the learning society in global capitalist society

1 I have discussed pre-conscious learning in a number of books (Jarvis, 1987, 1992, 1997) and I intend to return to it, but many societies in the world have recognised the significance of treating the child in the womb as a living being learning through the senses.

2 While this is not the place to argue it, we would certainly be prepared to claim that more education is mis-education than we would want to accept.

3 The happiness, however, may take the form of over-eating, over-drinking, and so on – but three problems are lost if we subsume them within the concept of happiness.

4 Parents are now being punished by law for failing to fulfil their parental duties in this respect which merely reflects a process that was recognised in primitive society – even in the Old Testament of the Bible there was a debate about the guilt of wrongdoers and until Jeremiah taught the Israelites that individuals should be punished it was the whole families which were (see Chapter 2 above).

5 Much of what is spent goes on management, inspections, and so on, but not on the processes of teaching and learning.

6 There are many denials of this from those in authority in the educational and political systems but from nearly 40 years in higher education, I know that the standard of the undergraduate and Masters degrees in many of the universities in which I have examined has fallen by a tremendous amount during my career. At the same time I asked the same type of question to an academic in Korea and she informed me that the standards there are getting higher!

7 It is a great pity that the overlap between the use of the learning society to refer to global capitalism and also to refer to the Europeanisation project has meant that careful analysis of the policy statements from the European Commission has been confused with the aspirations of the Lisbon statement for Europe to be a leading economic power in the world. In a sense, Europeanisation has taken second place to the aspirations of global capitalism in some of the analyses, including my own, but clearly it would also have been unrealistic to try to separate the two too much since Europeanisation is also a global force.

9 Democracy and the learning society

1 Some of Grey's criticisms of liberalism with which we agree should not necessarily include Rawls, who has modified the liberal position quite considerably, especially in this discussion of public reason.

2 The man of understanding.

3 During the time when this book was being revised a scandal occurred in which public broadcasting in the UK was found guilty of fixing the outcomes of a number of apparently participative enterprises, which demonstrate the problems of regarding the media as a potential means of furthering public reason and the democratic debate.

10 Utopia deferred

1 In the Old Testament a myth has no historical validity, it is a philosophical exploration in story form.

2 In the Old Testament of the Bible and written by an unknown writer, commonly referred to as Deutero Isaiah, in about 550 BC.

3 In the New Testament of the Bible, written at the end of the first century when Christians were being persecuted – a message of inspiration in a time of despair.

4 Significantly, because the Christian Church had developed a doctrine of revealed knowledge, it always assumed the primacy of its stories. Had it seen these stories as inspired intellectual attempts to battle an insoluble human problem, it might have joined in the ensuing intellectual debate and allowed its beliefs to evolve with new human questioning.

5 In the sociology of religion, there are major studies of sectarian movements about which many books have been written and the one that I have referenced here is only an introduction to the study.

6 For an anthology of utopian writings, see Carey (1999).

7 It should be made very clear here that when critics of George W. Bush assume that he is a representative of Christianity, that there are many within the churches who are totally opposed both to his fundamentalist belief system and to the actions that he has taken in Iraq and elsewhere in the world. Some Christians even question his Christianity itself, which has been notably silent during this period, when what he has done is a major disfavour to Christianity. Bell Jr (2001) provides an excellent perspective of a contemporary form of Christianity that is foreign to many of those who offer criticisms of it.

8 The same point can be made for some universities, continuously re-structuring and creating insecurity for many previously loyal employees.

9 Many so-called terrorists are fighting in civil conflicts in which they are seeking to establish their own version of the nation state.

10 As I was revising the draft of this chapter I had the privilege to take part in a learning festival in South Korea, in which a city is designated as a learning city and around the international literacy day the whole city celebrated learning. On this occasion there was a
massive festival with thousands of people joining the celebrations with all forms of activities from fun fares and family learning activities to an international academic conference,
a UNESCO workshop and a massive exhibition about learning cities and regions from
around the world. It would not be an over-exaggeration to say that there were many thousands of people participating, especially in the opening and closing ceremonies.

11 Back to the beginning?

1 I am relying heavily on Timisheff's (1957) interpretation of Sorokin's work here.
2 Honneth (2007) surprisingly makes no reference to Buber and little reference to Levinas
and where he makes reference to the latter, I feel that his interpretation is questionable.
3 My own research into experiential learning was unable to isolate pre-conscious learning
although in many workshops participants have affirmed its reality. A major research project
is called for in order to extend our knowledge of this phenomenon.

12 A revolution in learning: a vision of a better learning society

1 In the learning festivals that I witnessed in South Korea, there was – it seemed to me – a
deliberate attempt to instil into very young children both a love of learning and to associate learning with fun and family: there was a sense of *communitas* that is rarely associated
with learning in the Western world.
2 This reference to Plato is well discussed by Agamben (1999).

Bibliography

Abercrombie, N., Hill, S. and Turner, B. (2000) *Dictionary of Sociology* (fourth edition). Harmondsworth: Penguin.

Adorno, T. (1973) *The Jargon of Authenticity*. Evanston: Northwestern University Press.

Agamben, G. (1998) *Homo Sacer*. Stanford, CA: Stanford University Press.

Agamben, G. (1999) *The Man Without Content*. Stanford, CA: Stanford University Press.

Agamben, G. (2004) Trans: K. Attwell, *The Open*. Stanford, CA: Stanford University Press.

Althusser, L. (1972) 'Ideology and Ideological State Apparatuses', in Cosin, B. (ed.) *Education, Structure and Society*. Harmondsworth: Penguin.

Anderson, B. (1958) *The Living World of the Old Testament*. Englewood Cliffs, NJ: Prentice Hall.

Archer, M. (2000) *Being Human: the Problem of Agency*. Cambridge: Cambridge University Press.

Arendt, H. (1958) *The Human Condition*. Chicago, IL: University of Chicago Press.

Arendt, H. (1964) *Eichmann in Jerusalem: A Report on the Banality of Evil*. New York: Viking Press.

Arendt, H. (1968) *Between Past and Future*. Harmondsworth: Penguin.

Arendt, H. (ed.) (1969) *Illuminations*. New York: Schocken.

Arendt, H. (1976) *Totalitarianism*. San Diego, CA: Harvest Book, Harcourt.

Ayer, A. (1971) *Language, Truth and Logic*. Harmondsworth: Penguin.

Barber, B. (2003) *Jihad versus McWorld*. London: Corgi Books.

Baron, S., Field, J. and Schuller, T. (eds) (2000) *Social Capital*. Oxford: Oxford University Press.

Baudrillard, J. (1993) *The Transparency of Evil*. London: Verso.

Baudrillard, J. (1998) *The Consumer Society: Myths and Structures*. London: Sage.

Baudrillard, J. (2006) *Utopia Deferred*. New York: Semiotext(e).

Bauman, Z. (1988) *Freedom*. Milton Keynes: Open University Press.

Bauman, Z. (1992) *Intimations of Post Modernity*. London: Routledge.

Bauman, Z. (1993) *Postmodern Ethics*. Oxford: Blackwell.

Bauman, Z. (1999) *In Search of Politics*. Cambridge: Polity.

Bauman, Z. (2004) *Wasted Lives*. Cambridge: Polity.

Bauman, Z. (2007) *Consuming Life*. Cambridge: Polity.

Bawden, R. (2006) 'Educating for Capability for Inclusive Well-Being', in Campbell, J. *et al.* (eds) *Towards a Global Community*. Dordrecht: Springer.

European Commission (EC) (2006) *Adult Learning: It is Never too Late to Learn*. Brussels: European Commission COM(2006)614 final.

Faure, E. (1972) *Learning to Be*. Paris: UNESCO.

Featherstone, M. (1991) *Consumer Culture and Postmodernism*. London: Sage.

Foucault, M. (1974 [1970]) *The Order of Things*. London: Routledge (1974 – the first paperback edition).

Foucault, M. (1979) *Discipline and Punish*. Harmondsworth: Penguin.

Foucault, M. (1980) *Power/Knowledge: Selected Interviews and Other Writings 1972–1977*. Brighton: Harvester.

Frankena, W. (1963) *Ethics*. Englewood Cliffs, NJ: Prentice Hall.

Freire, P. (1972a) *Cultural Action for Freedom*. Harmondsworth: Penguin.

Freire, P. (1972b) *Pedagogy of the Oppressed*. Harmondsworth: Penguin.

Freire, P. (1998) *Pedagogy of Freedom: Ethics, Democracy and Civic Courage*. Lanham: Rowman and Littlefield.

Fromm, E. (1942) *The Fear of Freedom*. London: ARK paperbacks – published in 1984.

Fryer, R. (Chair) (1997) *Learning for the Twenty-First Century*. London: Department for Education and Employment.

Fukuyama, F. (1992) *The End of History*. New York: The Free Press.

Fukuyama, F. (1995) *Trust*. Harmondsworth: Penguin.

Gaita, R. (2000) *A Common Humanity* (second edition). London: Routledge.

Gehlen, A. (1988) *Man: His Nature and Place in the World*. New York: Columbia University Press.

Gennep, A. van (1908 [1960]) *The Rites of Passage*. London: Routledge and Kegan Paul.

Gerhardt, S. (2004) *Why Love Matters*. London: Routledge.

Gibbons, M., Lomoges, C., Nowotny, H., Schwartzman, S., Scott, P. and Trow, M. (1994) *The New Production of Knowledge*. London: Sage.

Giddens, A. (1998) *The Third Way*. Cambridge: Polity.

Goodchild, P. (2002) *Capitalism and Religion: The Price of Piety*. London: Routledge *Guardian* 15 December 2006.

Gray, J. (1995) *Enlightenment's Wake*. London: Routledge.

Gray, J. (2007) *Black Mass: Apocalyptic Religion and the Death of Utopia*. London: Allen Lane, Penguin Books.

Habermas, J. (1971) *Toward a Rational Society*. London: Heinemann.

Habermas, J. (1972) *Knowledge and Human Interests*. London: Heinemann.

Habermas, J. (1989) *The Structural Transformation of the Public Sphere*. Cambridge: Polity.

Habermas, J. (1990) *Moral Consciousness and Communicative Action*. Cambridge: Polity.

Habermas, J. (1993) *Justification and Application: Remarks on Discourse Ethics*. Cambridge: Polity.

Habermas, J. (1998) *The Inclusion of the Other*. Cambridge: Polity.

Habermas, J. (2001) *The Postnational Constellation* (translated by M. Pensky). Cambridge: Polity.

Habermas, J. (2006) *Time of Transitions* (edited and translated by C. Cronin and M. Pensky). Cambridge: Polity Press.

Hamilton, P. (1992) 'The Enlightenment and the Birth of Social Science', in Hall, S. and Gieben, B. (eds) *Formations of Modernity*. Cambridge: Polity Press in association with the Open University.

Handy, C. (1989) *The Age of Unreason*. London: Arrow Books.

Harvey, D. (1993) 'Class Relations, Social Justice and the Politics of Difference', in Squires, J. (ed.) *Principled Positions*. London: Lawrence and Wishart.

Hayek, F. (1944) *The Road to Serfdom*. London: ARK Paperbacks – published in 1986.

Hayek, F. (1979) *The Political Order of Free People*. London: Routledge and Kegan Paul.

Heater, D. (1999) *What is Citizenship?* Cambridge: Polity Press.

Held, D., McGrew, A., Goldblatt, D. and Perraton, J. (1999) *Global Transformations*. Cambridge: Polity Press.

Heller, A. (1984) *Everyday Life*. London: Routledge and Kegan Paul.

Hobbes, T. (1968 [1651]) *Leviathan*. Harmondsworth: Penguin.

Hoffman, J. (1988) *State, Power and Democracy*. Sussex: Wheatsheaf.

Holy Bible Revised Standard Version.

Honneth, A. (1995) *The Struggle for Recognition: The Moral Grammar of Social Conflicts*. Offord: Polity Press.

Honneth, A. (2007) *Disrespect*. Cambridge: Polity Press.

Hooykaas, R. (1972) *Religion and the Rise of Modern Science*. Edinburgh: Scottish Academic Press.

Hunt, T. (2007) 'Urban Britain is Heading for Victorian Levels of Inequality', *Guardian* 18 July, p. 28. London.

Husen, T. (1974) *The Learning Society*. London: Methuen.

Hutchins, R. (1968) *The Learning Society*. Harmondsworth: Penguin.

Hyslop-Margison, E. and Sears, A. (2006) *Neo-Liberalism, Globalization and Human Capital Learning*. Dordrecht: Springer.

Jackson, M. (2005) *Existential Anthropology*. New York: Berghahn.

James, W. (2000) *Pragmatism and Other Writings*. Harmondsworth: Penguin.

Jarvis, P. (1980) 'Towards a Sociological Understanding of Superstition', *Social Compass* Vol. XXVII: pp. 285–295.

Jarvis, P. (1987) *Adult Learning in the Social Context*. London: Croom Helm.

Jarvis, P. (1992) *Paradoxes of Learning*. San Francisco, CA: Jossey Bass.

Jarvis, P. (1997) *Ethics and the Education of Adults in Late Modern Society*. Leicester: NIACE.

Jarvis, P. (2006) *Towards a Comprehensive Theory of Human Learning*. London: Routledge.

Jarvis, P. (2007a) 'Andragogy versus Pedagogy or from Pedagogy to Andragogy', in *Andragoske studije* October 2006. Belgrade, pp. 5–22.

Jarvis, P. (2007b) *Globalisation, Lifelong Learning and the Learning Society: Sociological Perspectives*. London: Routledge.

Jarvis, P. and Parker, S. (eds) (2005) *Human Learning: A Holistic Perspective*. London: Routledge.

Joll, J. (1977) *Gramsci*. Glasgow: Fontana.

Kant, I. (1997) *Groundwork of the Metaphysics of Morals* (edited by Mary Gregor). Cambridge: Cambridge University Press.

Keddie, N. (1980) 'Adult Education: an Ideology Individualism', in Thompson, I.C. (ed.) *Adult Education for a Change*. London: Heinemann.

Kerr, C., Dunlop, J., Harbison, F. and Myers, C. (1973) *Industrialism and Industrial Man* (second edition). Harmondsworth: Penguin.

Kilpatrick, W. (1972) 'Indoctrination and Respect for Persons', in Snook, I. (ed.) *Concepts of Indoctrination*. London: Routledge and Kegan Paul.

King, R. (ed.) (2004) *The University in the Global Age*. London: Macmillan/Palgrave.

Knowles, M.S. (1970) *The Modern Practice of Adult Education: Andragogy versus Pedagogy.* Chicago, IL: Association Press.

Knowles, M.S. (1980) *The Modern Practice of Adult Education: From Pedagogy to Andragogy* (revised and updated). Chicago, IL: Association Press.

Kohlberg, L. (1976) 'Moral Stages and Moralization. The Cognitive Developmental Approach', in Likona, T. (ed.) *Theory, Research and Social Issues.* New York: Holt, Rinehart and Winston.

Kohlberg, L. (1987) 'The Cognitive Development Approach to Moral Education' in Cathbone Jr, P. (ed.) *Value, Theory and Education.* Malabar, FL: Krieger.

Kolb, D. (1984) *Experiential Learning* Englewood Cliffs, NJ: Prentice Hall.

Korsgaard, C. (1997) 'Introduction', in Kant, I. (1997) *Groundwork of the Metaphysics of Morals* (edited by Mary Gregor). Cambridge: Cambridge University Press.

Korten, D.C. (1995) *When Corporations Rule the World.* London: Earthscan.

Kumar, K. (1987) *Utopia and Anti-Utopia in Modern Times.* Oxford: Blackwell.

Kumar, K. (1991) *Utopianism.* Milton Keynes: Open University Press.

Kybird, P. (2007) 'The Use of the Bible in Adult Christian Education: A Case Study of Britisah Methodism'. Guildford: University of Surrey – Unpublished PhD Thesis.

Laksamba, C. (2005) *Policies and Practices of Lifelong Learning in Nepal.* University of Surrey: Dept of Political, International and Policy Studies – Unpublished PhD.

Lave, J. and Wenger, E. (1991) *Situated Learning.* Cambridge: Cambridge University Press.

Lawrence, F. (2006) 'Why Kellogg's Saw Red Over Labelling Schemes Report', in *The Guardian*, 28 December, pp. 8–9.

Lawton, D. (1973) *Social Change, Educational Theory and Curriculum Planning.* London: Hodder and Stoughton.

Levinas, E. (1985) *Ethics and Infinity.* Pittsburg: Duquesne University Press (trans. R. Cohen).

Levinas, E. (1991 [1969]) *Totality and Infinity.* AH Dordrecht: Kluwer.

Lifton, R. (1961) *Thought Reform and the Psychology of Totalism.* Harmondsworth: Penguin.

Lifton, R.J. (1967) *Thought Reform and the Psychology of Totalism* Harmondswoth: Penguin.

Lively, J. (1975) *Democracy.* Oxford: Basil Blackwell.

Lo Bianco, J. (2006) 'Educating for Citizenship in Global Community: World Kids, World Citizens and Global Education', in Campbell, W., Baikaloff, N. and Power, C. (eds) *Towards a Global Community.* Dordrecht: Springer.

Locke, J. (1690 [1993]) *An Essay Concerning Human Understanding.* Vermont: Everyman.

Longworth, N. (1999) *Making Lifelong Learning Work: Learning Cities for A Learning Century.* London: Kogan Page.

Longworth, N. (2006) *Learning Cities, Learning Regions, Learning Communities.* London: Routledge.

Longworth, N. and Davies, K. (1996) *Lifelong Learning.* London: Kogan Page.

Lucas, C. (1996) *Crisis in the Academy.* London: Macmillan.

Lukes, S. (2005) *Power: A Radical View.* Basingstoke: Palgrave.

Lyotard, J.-F. (1984) *The Postmodern Condition: A Report on Knowledge.* Manchester: Manchester University Press.

MacIntyre, A. (1985) *After Virtue.* London: Duckworth.

MacIntyre, A. (1987) 'The Idea of an Educated Public', in Hayden, G. (ed.) *Education and Values.* London: Institute of Education.

MacIntyre, A. (1988) *Whose Justice? Whose Rationality?* London: Duckworth.

McLaren, P. (2005) *Capitalists and Conquerors: A Critical Pedagogy Against Empire.* Lanham, MD: Rowman and Littlefield.

MacMurray, J. (1979 [1961]) *Persons in Relation.* Atlantic Highlands, NJ: Humanities Press.

Manent, P. (1998) *The City of Man.* Princeton, NJ: Princeton University Press.

Mann, M. (1986) *A History of Power from the Beginning to AD 1760: The Sources of Social Power.* Cambridge: Cambridge University Press.

Marchand, R. (1985) *Advertising the American Dream: Making Way for Modernity 1920–1940.* Berkeley and Los Angeles, CA: University of California Press.

Marin, L. (1984) *Utopics: the Semiotic Play of Textual Space3.* Amherst, NY: Humanity Books.

Marshall, T.H. (1950) *Citizenship and Social Class and Other Essays.* Cambridge: Cambridge University Press.

Meister, J. (2000) *Corporate Universities* (revised edition). New York: McGraw-Hill.

Merquior, J. (1985) *Foucault.* London: Fontana.

Merton, R. (1968) *Social Theory and Social Structure* (second edition). New York: Free Press.

Mill, J. (1910) *Utilitarianism, Liberty and Representative Government.* London: Dent.

Ministry of Education (1999) *Education, Training and Research in an Information Society: A National Strategy for 2000–2004.* Helsinki: Ministry of Education.

Monbiot, G. (2000) *The Captive State.* London: Macmillan.

Monbiot, G. (2007) 'Don't listen to what the rich world's leaders say – look at what they do', *Guardian* 5 June, p. 33.

Moore, G. (1902) *Principia Ethica.* Cambridge: The University Press.

National Statistics (2006) *Social Trends.* Basingstoke: Palgrave/Macmillan.

Newman, M. (2006) *Teaching Resistance.* San Francisco, CA: Jossey Bass.

Nozick, R. (1974) *Anarchy, State and Utopia.* Oxford: Blackwell.

Nozick, R. (1993) *The Nature of Rationality.* Princeton, NJ: Princeton University Press.

O'Neill, J. (1991) 'McTopia: Eating Time', in Kumar, K. and Bann, S. (eds) *Utopias and the Millennium.* London: Reaktion Books.

O'Sullivan, E. (1999) *Transformative Learning.* London: Zed Books.

Oakeshott, M. (1933) *Experience and Its Modes.* Cambridge: Cambridge University Press.

OISE – UNESCO (1973) *Education on the Move.* Paris: UNESCO.

Organisation for Economic Cooperation and Development (OECD) (1973) *Recurrent Education: a Strategy for Lifelong Learning.* Paris: OECD.

Organisation for Economic Cooperation and Development (OECD) (1975) *Recurrent Education: Trends and Issues.* Paris: OECD.

Organisation for Economic Cooperation and Development (OECD) (1977–1981) *Learning Opportunities for Adults* volumes 1–5. Paris: OECD.

Organisation for Economic Cooperation and Development (OECD) (1996) *Lifelong Learning for All:* Paris: OECD.

Outhwaite, W. (1994) *Habermas: A Critical Introduction.* Cambridge: Polity Press.

Paine, T. (1995 [1776]) *Common Sense in Rights of Man, Common Sense and Other Political Writings.* Oxford: Oxford University Press.

Palacios, M. (2003) *Options for Financing Lifelong Learning.* Washington, DC: World Bank Policy Research Working Paper 2994.

Piaget, J. (1929) *The Child's Conception of the World.* London: Routledge and Kegan Paul.

Pilger, J. (2003) *The New Rulers of the World.* London: Verso (Updated).

Polanyi, M. (1967) *The Tacit Dimension*. London: Routledge and Kegan Paul.
Powell, A., Farrar, E. and Cohen, D. (1985) *The Shopping Mall High School*. Boston, MA: Houghton Mifflin.
Putnam, R. (2000) *Bowling Alone*. New York: Simon and Schuster.
Ranson, S. (1994) *Towards the Learning Society*. London: Cassell.
Rasiel, E.M. (1998) *The McKinsey Way*. New York: McGraw-Hill.
Rasmusen, D. 1990) *Reading Habermas*. Oxford: Basil Blackwell.
Rawls, J. (1972) *The Theory of Justice*. Cambridge, MA: The Belknap Press of Harvard University Press.
Rawls, J. (1993) *Political Liberalism*. New York: Columbia University Press.
Rawls, J. (1999) *The Law of Peoples*. Cambridge, MA: Harvard University Press.
Readings, B. (1996) *The University in Ruins*. Cambridge, MA: Harvard University Press.
Reisman, D. (1950) *The Lonely Crowd: A Study of Changing American Culture*. New Haven, CT: Yale University Press.
Robertson, R. (1995) 'Globalization: Time-Space and Homogeneity – Heterogeneity', in Featherstone, M. (ed.) *Undoing Culture: Globalization, Postmodernism and Identity*. London: Sage.
Rose, N. (1999) *Powers of Freedom*. Cambridge: Cambridge University Press.
Rousseau, J.-J. (1973) *The Social Contract and Discourses*. London: Dent.
Sanders, C. (2006) 'A Quiet Revolution for Law and Order', *The Times Higher Education Supplement* 8 September, p. 8. London.
Sanders, C. (2006) 'Ventures with Business Present Pains and Gains', *The Times Higher Education Supplement* 1 September, p. 8. London.
Scheler, M. (1980 [1926]) *Problems of a Sociology of Knowledge*. London: Routledge and Kegan Paul.
Schiller, H. (1992) 'The Context of Our Work', in *Société Française de Sciences d'Information et de la Communication*. Lille: Huitieme Congres National 21 May, pp. 1–6.
Schön, D. (1983) *The Reflective Practitioner*. New York: Basic Books.
Schutz, A. and Luckmann, T. (1974) *The Structures of the Lifeworld*. London: Heinemann.
Scott, P. (1984) *The Crisis of the University*. London: Croom Helm.
Seager, A. (2007) 'Gap Between Rich and Poor Widens', *Guardian* 20 June. London.
Senge, P. (1990) *The Fifth Discipline*. New York: Doubleday.
Sennett, R. (1986) *The Fall of Public Man*. London: Faber and Faber. (First published by: Alfred A. Knorf Inc. in New York in 1977).
Shumar, W. (1997) *College for Sale*. London: Falmer.
Simmel, G. (1971 [1903]) 'The Metropolis and Mental Life', reprinted in Thompson, K. and Tunstall, J. (eds) *Sociological Perspectives*. Harmondsworth: Penguin.
Simmel, G. (1978 [1907]) *The Philosophy of Money*. London: Routledge.
Slaughter, S. and Leslie, L. (1997) *Academic Capitalism*. Baltimore, MD: Johns Hopkins University Press.
Sprigge, T. (1988) *The Rational Foundation of Ethics*. London: Routledge.
Squires, J. (ed.) (1993) *Principled Positions*. London: Lawrence and Wishart.
Stehr, N. (1994) *Knowledge Societies*. London: Sage.
Stevenson, C. (1944) *Ethics and Language*. New Haven, CT: Yale University Press.
Stiglitz, J. (2002) *Globalization and Its Discontents*, New York: WW Norton and Company.
Strauss, A. (ed.) (1964) *George Herbert Mead on Social Psychology*. Chicago, IL: University of Chicago Press.

Tawney, R. (1926 [1938]) *Religion and the Rise of Capitalism*. Harmondsworth: Penguin.

Taylor, C. (1991) *The Ethics of Authenticity*. Cambridge, MA: Harvard University Press.

Taylor, K. (2004) *Brainwashing: The Science of Thought Control*. Oxford: Oxford University Press.

Thompson, E.P. (1977) *William Morris: Romantic Revolutionary*. London: Merlin Press.

Thompson, J. (1995) *The Media and Modernity*. Cambridge: Polity.

Timasheff, N. (1965) *Sociological Theory: Its Nature and Growth* (revised edition). New York: Randon House.

Toennies, F. (1957) *Community and Society*. New York: Harper Row.

Tuckett, A. (2005) 'Enough is Enough', in *Adults Learning*. Leicester: NIACE vol. 17, no 1, pp. 6–7.

Turner, R. (1962) 'Role Taking: Process Versus Conformity', in Rose, A. (ed.) *Human Behavior and Social Processes*. London: Routledge and Kegan Paul.

Turner, V. (1969) *The Ritual Process*. Harmondsworth: Penguin.

UNESCO (2000) *NGO Declaration on Education for All* www.unesco.org/education/efa/wef_2000/cov_ngo_declaration.shtml downloaded 9 January 2006.

UNESCO (2005) *Towards Knowledge Societies*. Paris: UNESCO.

UNESCO (2006) *Education for All Global Monitoring Report*. Paris: UNESCO.

Urmson, J. (1968) *The Emotive Theory of Ethics*. London: Hutchinson.

von Rad, G. (1961) *Genesis*. London: SCM Press.

Waldron, J. (1984) *Theories of Rights*. Oxford: Oxford University Press. Weber, M. (1930) *The Protestant Ethic and the Spirit of Capitalism*. London: Unwin.

Webster, F. (2002) *Theories of the Information Society* (Second edition). London: Routledge.

Weick, K. (2001) *Sense Making in Organizations*. Oxford: Blackwell.

Welton, M. (2005) *Designing the Just Learning Society*. Leicester: NIACE.

Wenger, E. (1998) *Communities of Practice*. Cambridge: Cambridge University Press.

White, J.P. (1972) 'Indoctrination without Doctrines?', in Snook, I. (ed.) *Concepts of Indoctrination*. London: Routledge and Kegan Paul, pp. 190–201.

Wilson, B. (ed.) (1967) *Patterns of Sectarianism*. London: Heinemann.

Wilson, B. (ed.) (1970) *Rationality*. Oxford: Blackwell.

Wilson, J. (1964) 'Education and Indoctrination', in Hollins, T.H.B. (1964) *Aims in Education*. Manchester: Manchester University Press.

Wilson, J. (1972) 'Indoctrination and Freedom', in Snook, I. (ed.) *Concepts of Indoctrination*. London: Routledge and Kegan Paul, pp. 101–105.

Wolfe, A. (1989) *Whose Keeper? Social Science and Moral Obligation*. Berkeley, CA: University of California Press.

World Bank (2003) *Lifelong Learning in the Global Economy*. Washington, DC: World Bank.

Wrong, D. (1963) 'The Over-Socialized Conception of Man in Modern Sociology', in *American Sociological Review* vol. 26, pp. 183–193.

Young-Bruehl, E. (2004) *Hannah Arendt: For Love of the World* (second edition). New Haven, CT: Yale University Press.

Zapf, W. (1983) 'Entwicklungsdilemma und Innovationspotentiale in modernen Geschellschaften', in Matthes, J. (ed.) *Krise der Arbeitsgesellschaft?* Frankfurt.

Index